CFA 2017

Level III CFA® Exam

Welcome

As the VP of Advanced Designations at Kaplan Schweser, I am pleased to have the opportunity to help you prepare for the 2017 CFA® exam. Getting an early start on your study program is important for you to sufficiently **prepare**, **practice**, and **perform** on exam day. Proper planning will allow you to set aside enough time to master the Learning Outcome Statements (LOS) in the Level III curriculum.

Now that you've received your SchweserNotes™, here's how to get started:

Step 1: Access Your Online Tools
Visit www.schweser.com and log in to your online account using the button located in the top navigation bar. After logging in, select the appropriate level and proceed to the dashboard where you can access your online products.

Step 2: Create a Study Plan
Create a study plan with the **Study Calendar** (located on the Schweser dashboard) and familiarize yourself with your financial calculator. Check out our calculator videos in the **Candidate Resource Library** (also found on the dashboard).

Step 3: Prepare and Practice
Read your SchweserNotes™ Volumes 1–5
At the end of each reading, you can answer the Concept Checker questions for better understanding of the curriculum.

Attend a Weekly Class
Attend live classes online or take part in our live classroom courses in select cities around the world. Our expert faculty will guide you through the curriculum with a structured approach to help you prepare for the CFA® exam. The Schweser **On-Demand Video Lectures**, in combination with the **Weekly Class**, offer a blended learning approach that covers every LOS in the CFA curriculum. (See our instruction packages to the right. Visit www.schweser.com/cfa to order.)

Practice with SchweserPro™ QBank
Maximize your retention of important concepts by answering questions in the SchweserPro™ QBank and taking several **Practice Exams**. Use Schweser's **QuickSheet** for continuous review on the go. (Visit www.schweser.com/cfa to order.)

Step 4: Attend a 3-Day, 5-Day, or WindsorWeek™ Review Workshop
Schweser's late-season review workshops are designed to drive home the CFA® material, which is critical for CFA exam success. Review key concepts in every topic, **perform** by working through demonstration problems, and **practice** your exam techniques. (See review options to the right.)

Step 5: Perform
Take a Live or Live Online Schweser Mock Exam to ensure you are ready to **Perform** on the actual CFA® exam. Put your skills and knowledge to the test and gain confidence before the exam. (See exam options to the right.)

Again, thank you for trusting Kaplan Schweser with your CFA exam preparation!

Sincerely,

Tim Smaby, PhD, CFA, FRM
Vice President, Advanced Designations, Kaplan Schweser

The Kaplan Way for Learning

PREPARE
Acquire new knowledge through demonstration and examples.

PRACTICE
Apply new knowledge through simulation and practice.

PERFORM
Evaluate mastery of new knowledge and identify achieved outcomes.

CFA® Instruction Packages:
> Premium Instruction Package
> PremiumPlus™ Package

Final Review Options:
> Live 3-Day Review Workshop
  (held in select cities)
> Live Online 3-Day Review Workshop
> NYC 5-Day Review Workshop
> DFW 5-Day Review Workshop*
> WindsorWeek™*
> Live Schweser Mock Exam
  (offered in select cities worldwide)
> Live Online Schweser Mock Exam

*Only offered for June exam

Contact us for questions about your study package, upgrading your package, purchasing additional study materials, or for additional information:

888.325.5072 (U.S.) | +1 608.779.8327 (Int'l.)

staff@schweser.com | www.schweser.com/cfa

CFA-536505

Book 5 – Trading, Monitoring, and Rebalancing; Performance Evaluation, and Global Investment Performance Standards

SCHWESERNOTES™ 2017 LEVEL III CFA® BOOK 5: TRADING, MONITORING, AND REBALANCING; PERFORMANCE EVALUATION, AND GLOBAL INVESTMENT PERFORMANCE STANDARDS

READINGS AND LEARNING OUTCOME STATEMENTS

READINGS

The following material is a review of the Trading, Monitoring, and Rebalancing; Evaluation and Attribution; and Global Investment Performance Standards (GIPS®) principles designed to address the learning outcome statements set forth by CFA Institute.

STUDY SESSION 16

Reading Assignments
Trading, Monitoring, and Rebalancing, CFA Program 2017 Curriculum, Volume 6, Level III

STUDY SESSION 17

Reading Assignments
Performance Evaluation, CFA Program 2017 Curriculum, Volume 6, Level III

STUDY SESSION 18

Reading Assignments
Global Investment Performance Standards, CFA Program 2017 Curriculum, Volume 6, Level III

LEARNING OUTCOME STATEMENTS (LOS)

The CFA Institute learning outcome statements are listed in the following. These are repeated in each topic review. However, the order may have been changed in order to get a better fit with the flow of the review.

STUDY SESSION 16

The topical coverage corresponds with the following CFA Institute assigned reading:

29. Execution of Portfolio Decisions

The candidate should be able to:

a. compare market orders with limit orders, including the price and execution uncertainty of each. (page 1)

b. calculate and interpret the effective spread of a market order and contrast it to the quoted bid–ask spread as a measure of trading cost. (page 2)

c. compare alternative market structures and their relative advantages. (page 5)

d. compare the roles of brokers and dealers. (page 7)

e. explain the criteria of market quality and evaluate the quality of a market when given a description of its characteristics. (page 7)

f. explain the components of execution costs, including explicit and implicit costs, and evaluate a trade in terms of these costs. (page 8)

g. calculate and discuss implementation shortfall as a measure of transaction costs. (page 9)

h. contrast volume weighted average price (VWAP) and implementation shortfall as measures of transaction costs. (page 13)

i. explain the use of econometric methods in pretrade analysis to estimate implicit transaction costs. (page 14)

j. discuss the major types of traders, based on their motivation to trade, time versus price preferences, and preferred order types. (page 14)

k. describe the suitable uses of major trading tactics, evaluate their relative costs, advantages, and weaknesses, and recommend a trading tactic when given a description of the investor's motivation to trade, the size of the trade, and key market characteristics. (page 15)

l. explain the motivation for algorithmic trading and discuss the basic classes of algorithmic trading strategies. (page 17)

m. discuss the factors that typically determine the selection of a specific algorithmic trading strategy, including order size, average daily trading volume, bid–ask spread, and the urgency of the order. (page 18)

n. explain the meaning and criteria of best execution. (page 20)

o. evaluate a firm's investment and trading procedures, including processes, disclosures, and record keeping, with respect to best execution. (page 20)

p. discuss the role of ethics in trading. (page 21)

The topical coverage corresponds with the following CFA Institute assigned reading:

30. Monitoring and Rebalancing

The candidate should be able to:

a. discuss a fiduciary's responsibilities in monitoring an investment portfolio. (page 34)

b. discuss the monitoring of investor circumstances, market/economic conditions, and portfolio holdings and explain the effects that changes in each of these areas can have on the investor's portfolio. (page 34)

c. recommend and justify revisions to an investor's investment policy statement and strategic asset allocation, given a change in investor circumstances. (page 35)

d. discuss the benefits and costs of rebalancing a portfolio to the investor's strategic asset allocation. (page 35)

e. contrast calendar rebalancing to percentage-of-portfolio rebalancing. (page 36)

f. discuss the key determinants of the optimal corridor width of an asset class in a percentage-of-portfolio rebalancing program. (page 37)

g. compare the benefits of rebalancing an asset class to its target portfolio weight versus rebalancing the asset class to stay within its allowed range. (page 38)

h. explain the performance consequences in up, down, and flat markets of 1) rebalancing to a constant mix of equities and bills, 2) buying and holding equities, and 3) constant proportion portfolio insurance (CPPI). (page 38)

i. distinguish among linear, concave, and convex rebalancing strategies. (page 41)

j. judge the appropriateness of constant mix, buy-and-hold, and CPPI rebalancing strategies when given an investor's risk tolerance and asset return expectations. (page 42)

STUDY SESSION 17

The topical coverage corresponds with the following CFA Institute assigned reading:

31. Evaluating Portfolio Performance

The candidate should be able to:

a. demonstrate the importance of performance evaluation from the perspective of fund sponsors and the perspective of investment managers. (page 55)

b. explain the following components of portfolio evaluation: performance measurement, performance attribution, and performance appraisal. (page 56)

c. calculate, interpret, and contrast time-weighted and money-weighted rates of return and discuss how each is affected by cash contributions and withdrawals. (page 58)

d. identify and explain potential data quality issues as they relate to calculating rates of return. (page 62)

e. demonstrate the decomposition of portfolio returns into components attributable to the market, to style, and to active management. (page 62)

f. discuss the properties of a valid performance benchmark and explain advantages and disadvantages of alternative types of benchmarks. (page 63)

g. explain the steps involved in constructing a custom security-based benchmark. (page 66)

h. discuss the validity of using manager universes as benchmarks. (page 67)

i. evaluate benchmark quality by applying tests of quality to a variety of possible benchmarks. (page 67)

j. discuss issues that arise when assigning benchmarks to hedge funds. (page 69)

k. distinguish between macro and micro performance attribution and discuss the inputs typically required for each. (page 70)

l. demonstrate and contrast the use of macro and micro performance attribution methodologies to identify the sources of investment performance. (page 70)

m. discuss the use of fundamental factor models in micro performance attribution. (page 78)

n. evaluate the effects of the external interest rate environment and active management on fixed-income portfolio returns. (page 79)

o. explain the management factors that contribute to a fixed-income portfolio's total return and interpret the results of a fixed-income performance attribution analysis. (page 79)

p. calculate, interpret, and contrast alternative risk-adjusted performance measures, including (in their *ex post* forms) alpha, information ratio, Treynor measure, Sharpe ratio, and M^2. (page 82)

q. explain how a portfolio's alpha and beta are incorporated into the information ratio, Treynor measure, and Sharpe ratio. (page 87)

r. demonstrate the use of performance quality control charts in performance appraisal. (page 88)

s. discuss the issues involved in manager continuation policy decisions, including the costs of hiring and firing investment managers. (page 89)

t. contrast Type I and Type II errors in manager continuation decisions. (page 90)

STUDY SESSION 18

The topical coverage corresponds with the following CFA Institute assigned reading:

32. Overview of the Global Investment Performance Standards

The candidate should be able to:

a. discuss the objectives, key characteristics, and scope of the GIPS standards and their benefits to prospective clients and investment managers. (page 116)

b. explain the fundamentals of compliance with the GIPS standards, including the definition of the firm and the firm's definition of discretion. (page 118)

c. explain the requirements and recommendations of the GIPS standards with respect to input data, including accounting policies related to valuation and performance measurement. (page 119)

d. discuss the requirements of the GIPS standards with respect to return calculation methodologies, including the treatment of external cash flows, cash and cash equivalents, and expenses and fees. (page 121)

e. explain the requirements and recommendations of the GIPS standards with respect to composite return calculations, including methods for asset-weighting portfolio returns. (page 125)

f. explain the meaning of "discretionary" in the context of composite construction and, given a description of the relevant facts, determine whether a portfolio is likely to be considered discretionary. (page 127)

g. explain the role of investment mandates, objectives, or strategies in the construction of composites. (page 128)

h. explain the requirements and recommendations of the GIPS standards with respect to composite construction, including switching portfolios among composites, the timing of the inclusion of new portfolios in composites, and the timing of the exclusion of terminated portfolios from composites. (page 128)

i. explain the requirements of the GIPS standards for asset class segments carved out of multi-class portfolios. (page 131)

j.   explain the requirements and recommendations of the GIPS standards with respect to disclosure, including fees, the use of leverage and derivatives, conformity with laws and regulations that conflict with the GIPS standards, and noncompliant performance periods. (page 132)

k.   explain the requirements and recommendations of the GIPS standards with respect to presentation and reporting, including the required timeframe of compliant performance periods, annual returns, composite assets, and benchmarks. (page 135)

l.   explain the conditions under which the performance of a past firm or affiliation must be linked to or used to represent the historical performance of a new or acquiring firm. (page 135)

m.   evaluate the relative merits of high/low, range, interquartile range, and equal-weighted or asset-weighted standard deviation as measures of the internal dispersion of portfolio returns within a composite for annual periods. (page 135)

n.   identify the types of investments that are subject to the GIPS standards for real estate and private equity. (page 140)

o.   explain the provisions of the GIPS standards for real estate and private equity. (page 141)

p.   explain the provisions of the GIPS standards for Wrap fee/Separately Managed Accounts. (page 146)

q.   explain the requirements and recommended valuation hierarchy of the GIPS Valuation Principles. (page 148)

r.   determine whether advertisements comply with the GIPS Advertising Guidelines. (page 149)

s.   discuss the purpose, scope, and process of verification. (page 151)

t.   discuss challenges related to the calculation of after-tax returns. (page 152)

u.   identify and explain errors and omissions in given performance presentations and recommend changes that would bring them into compliance with GIPS standards. (page 154)

EXECUTION OF PORTFOLIO DECISIONS[1]

EXAM FOCUS

For the exam, be able to distinguish between limit and market orders and discuss the circumstances under which each is appropriate to use. Be able to calculate midquotes, effective spreads, volume-weighted average price, and implementation shortfall costs. Motivations for trading have always been a CFA Institute favorite, so you should also be able to discuss major trader types, trading tactics, and implementation shortfall strategies.

MARKET AND LIMIT ORDERS

LOS 29.a: Compare market orders with limit orders, including the price and execution uncertainty of each.

Market microstructure refers to the structure and processes of a market that may affect the pricing of securities in relation to intrinsic value and the ability of managers to execute trades. The microstructure of the market and the objectives of the manager should affect the type of order the manager uses.

The two major types of orders are market orders and limit orders. The first offers greater certainty of execution and the second offers greater certainty of price.

A **market order** is an order to execute the trade immediately at the best possible price. If the order cannot be completely filled in one trade, it is filled by other trades at the next best possible prices. The emphasis in a market order is the speed of execution. The disadvantage of a market order is that the price it will be executed at is not known ahead of time, so it has **price uncertainty**.

A **limit order** is an order to trade at the limit price or better. For sell orders, the execution price must be higher than or equal to the limit price. For buy orders, the execution price must be lower than or equal to the limit price. The order could be good for a specified period of time and then expire or could be good until it is canceled. However, if market prices do not move to within the limit, the trade will not be completed, so it has **execution uncertainty**.

---

1. The terminology utilized in this topic review follows industry convention as presented in Reading 29 of the 2017 Level III CFA curriculum.

THE EFFECTIVE SPREAD

LOS 29.b: Calculate and interpret the effective spread of a market order and contrast it to the quoted bid–ask spread as a measure of trading cost.

The bid price is the price a dealer will pay for a security, and the bid quantity is the amount a dealer will buy of a security. The ask or offer price is the price at which a dealer will sell a security and the ask quantity is the amount a dealer will sell of a security. The ask price minus the bid price (the **bid-ask spread**) provides the dealer's compensation. In theory it is the total cost to buy and then sell the security.

An overview of some trading terms will help illustrate some of the concepts involved in trading. The prices a dealer offers are limit orders because they specify the price at which they will transact. A dealer's offering of securities is thus termed the **limit order book**. Several dealers may transact in the same security and compete against each other for the investor's business. The best bid price (the highest bid price from the trader's perspective) is referred to as the **inside bid** or **market bid**. The best ask price (the lowest ask price from the trader's perspective) is referred to as the **inside ask** or **market ask**. The best bid price and the best ask price in the market constitute the inside or market quote. Subtracting the best bid price from the best ask price results in the **inside bid-ask spread** or **market bid-ask spread**. The average of the inside bid and ask is the **midquote**.

The **effective spread** is an actual transaction price versus the midquote of the market bid and ask prices. This difference is then doubled. If the effective spread is less than the market bid-asked spread, it indicates good trade execution or a liquid security. More formally:

effective spread for a buy order = 2 × (execution price – midquote)

effective spread for a sell order = 2 × (midquote – execution price)

Effective spread is a better measure of the effective round trip cost (buy and sell) of a transaction than the quoted bid-asked spread. Effective spread reflects both **price improvement** (some trades are executed at better than the bid-asked quote) and **price impact** (other trades are done outside the bid-asked quote).

> **Example: Effective spread**
>
> Suppose a trader is quoted a market bid price of $11.50 and an ask of $11.56. **Calculate** and **interpret** the effective spread for a buy order, given an executed price of $11.55.

Answer:

The *midquote* of the quoted bid and ask prices is $11.53 [= (11.50 + 11.56) / 2]. The *effective spread* for this buy order is: 2 × ($11.55 − $11.53) = $0.04, which is two cents better than the quoted spread of $0.06 (= $11.56 − $11.50). An effective spread that is less than the bid-asked spread indicates the execution was superior (lower cost) to the quoted spread or a very liquid market.

Effective spread on a single transaction may indicate little but be more meaningful when averaged over all transactions during a period in order to calculate an average effective spread. Lower average effective spreads indicate better liquidity for a security or superior trading.

Example: Average effective spread

Suppose there are three sell orders placed for a stock during a day. Figure A shows bid and ask quotes at various points in the day.

Figure A: Trade Quotes During a Trading Day

Time	Bid Price	Bid Size	Ask Price	Ask Size
10 a.m.	$12.10	300	$12.16	400
1 p.m.	$12.00	300	$12.07	400
2 p.m.	$11.80	300	$11.88	400

Assume the following trades take place:

- At 10 a.m. the trader placed an order to sell 100 shares. The execution price was $12.11.
- At 1 p.m. the trader placed an order to sell 300 shares. The execution price was $12.00.
- At 2 p.m. the trader placed an order to sell 600 shares. The average execution price was $11.75.

Calculate the quoted and effective spreads for these orders. **Calculate** the average quoted and average effective spread. **Analyze** the results.

Answer:

The quoted spread in Figure B for each order is the difference between the ask and bid prices.

Figure B: Calculated Quoted Spreads

Time of Trade	Ask Minus Bid Price	Quoted Spread
10 a.m.	$12.16 − $12.10	$0.06
1 p.m.	$12.07 − $12.00	$0.07
2 p.m.	$11.88 − $11.80	$0.08

The average quoted spread is a simple average of the quoted spreads: ($0.06 + $0.07 + $0.08) / 3 = $0.07.

The effective spread for a sell order is twice the midquote of the market bid and ask prices minus the execution price.

The midquote for each trade is calculated as in Figure C.

Figure C: Calculated Midquotes

Time of Trade	Midquote
10 a.m.	($12.16 + $12.10) / 2 = $12.13
1 p.m.	($12.07 + $12.00) / 2 = $12.035
2 p.m.	($11.88 + $11.80) / 2 = $11.84

The effective spread for each sell order is shown in Figure D.

Figure D: Calculated Effective Spreads

Time of Trade	2 × (Midquote – Execution Price) = Effective Spread
10 a.m.	2 × ($12.13 – $12.11) = $0.04
1 p.m.	2 × ($12.035 – $12.00) = $0.07
2 p.m.	2 × ($11.84 – $11.75) = $0.18

The average effective spread is ($0.04 + $0.07 + $0.18) / 3 = $0.0967.

A weighted-average effective spread can also be calculated using the relative sizes of the orders. The total number of shares transacted over the day is 1,000 shares (100 + 300 + 600). The weighted-average effective spread is then (100 / 1,000)($0.04) + (300 / 1,000)($0.07) + (600 / 1,000)($0.18) = $0.133.

Analysis:

In the first trade, there was price improvement because the sell order was executed at a bid price higher than the quoted price. Hence, the effective spread was lower than the quoted spread. In the second trade, the quoted price and execution price were equal as were the quoted and effective spread. In the last trade, the trade size of 600 was larger than the bid size of 300. The trader had to "walk down" the limit order book to fill the trade at an average execution price that was less favorable than that quoted. Note that the effective spread in this case was higher than that quoted.

Overall, the average effective spreads (both simple and weighted) were higher than the average quoted spread, reflecting the high cost of liquidity in the last trade.

MARKET STRUCTURES

LOS 29.c: Compare alternative market structures and their relative advantages.

Securities markets serve several purposes: **liquidity**—minimal cost and timely trading; **transparency**—correct and up-to-date trade and market information; **assurity of completion**—trouble-free trade settlement (i.e., the trade is completed and ownership is transferred without problems).

There are three main categories of securities markets:

1. Quote-driven: Investors trade with dealers.

2. Order-driven markets: Investors trade with each other without the use of intermediaries.

3. Brokered markets: Investors use brokers to locate the counterparty to a trade.

A fourth market, a hybrid market, is a combination of the other three markets. Additionally, new trading venues have evolved, and the electronic processing of trades has become more common.

Quote-Driven Markets

Quote-driven markets offer liquidity. Traders transact with dealers (a.k.a. *market makers*) who post bid and ask prices, so quote-driven markets are sometimes called **dealer markets**. A dealer maintains an inventory of securities and posts bid and ask prices where he will buy or sell. The dealer is providing liquidity by being willing to buy or sell and seeking to earn a profit from the spread.

Many markets that trade illiquid securities (e.g., bond markets) are organized as dealer markets because the level of natural liquidity (trading volume) is low. In such markets, dealers can provide immediate liquidity when none would otherwise exist because they are willing to maintain an inventory of securities. Dealers also provide liquidity for securities whose terms are negotiated (e.g., swap and forward markets). Note that the dealer that offers the best price is not always the one to get a trader's business because credit risk is more important in some markets (e.g., currency markets) than price.

In some dealer markets, the limit order book is closed to the average investor. In these **closed-book** markets, an investor must hire a broker to locate the best quote.

Order-Driven Markets

Order-driven markets may have more competition resulting in better prices. Traders transact with other traders. There are no intermediary dealers as there are in quote-driven markets. Dealers may trade in these markets but as a trader, prices are set by supply and demand. The disadvantage is that because there may not be a dealer willing to maintain an inventory of a security, liquidity may be poor. In an order-driven market, orders drive the market and the activity of traders determines the liquidity for a security. Execution of a trade is determined by a mechanical rule, such as matching prices between a willing buyer and seller.

There are three main types of order-driven markets: electronic crossing networks, auction markets, and automated auctions. In an **electronic crossing network**, the typical trader is an institution. Orders are batched together and crossed (matched) at fixed points in time during the day at the average of the bid and ask quotes. The costs of trading are low because commissions are low and traders do not pay a dealer's bid-ask spread. A trade may not be filled or may be only partially filled if there is insufficient trading activity.

The trader usually does not know the identity of the counterparty or the counterparty's trade size in an electronic crossing network. Because of this, there is no price discovery (i.e., prices do not adjust to supply and demand conditions). This also results in trades unfilled or only partially filled because prices do not respond to fill the traders' orders.

In an **auction market**, traders put forth their orders to compete against other orders for execution. An auction market can be a periodic (a.k.a. batch) market, where trading occurs at a single price at a single point during the day, or a continuous auction market, where trading takes place throughout the day. An example of the former is the open and close of some equity markets. Auction markets provide price discovery, which results in less frequent partial filling of orders than in electronic crossing networks.

Automated auctions are also known as electronic limit-order markets. Examples include the electronic communication networks (ECNs) of the NYSE Arca Exchange in the United States and the Paris Bourse in France. These markets trade throughout the day and trades are executed based on a set of rules. They are similar to electronic crossing networks in that they are computerized and the identity of the counterparty is not known. Unlike electronic crossing networks, they are auction markets and thus provide price discovery.

Brokered Markets

In brokered markets, brokers act as traders' agents to find counterparties for the traders.

Hybrid Markets

Hybrid markets combine features of quote-driven, order-driven, and broker markets. The New York Stock Exchange, for example, has features of both quote-driven and order-driven markets. It has specialist dealers so it trades as a quote-driven market. It also trades throughout the day as in a continuous auction market and trades as a batch auction market at the opening of the exchange.

BROKERS AND DEALERS

LOS 29.d: Compare the roles of brokers and dealers.

Dealers are just other traders in the market seeking to earn a profit by offering a service. When taking the other side of a transaction, the dealer is an adversary in the sense that any buyer and seller are adversaries seeking to earn profit. The dealer, as discussed earlier, offers liquidity.

A **broker** also seeks to earn a profit in exchange for service but the broker has a **principal and agent relationship with the trader**. The broker acts as the trader's agent, which imposes a legal obligation to act in the best interests of the trader (the principal). As the trader's agent the broker can:

- **Represent the order** and advise the trader on likely prices and volume that could be executed.
- **Find counterparties to the trade.** The broker will frequently have contacts and knowledge of others who may be interested in taking the other side of the trade. The broker could even step into the role of the dealer and take the other side of the trade. It would be important to know if this is occurring because the broker now becomes a dealer and reverts to the typical adversarial buyer versus seller role.
- **Provide secrecy.** A trader may not want others to know their identity. Perhaps their ultimate goal is to acquire the company. As an agent, the broker keeps the trader anonymous.
- **Provide other services** such as record keeping, safe keeping of securities, cash management, and so forth; but not liquidity, which is the role of a dealer.
- **Support the market.** While not a direct benefit to any single client, brokers help markets function.

MARKET QUALITY

LOS 29.e: Explain the criteria of market quality and evaluate the quality of a market when given a description of its characteristics.

A security market should provide *liquidity, transparency,* and *assurity of completion.* Accordingly, the markets should be judged to the extent that they succeed in providing these to traders.

A **liquid** market has small bid-ask spreads, market depth, and resilience. If a market has small spreads, traders are apt to trade more often. Market *depth* allows larger orders to trade without affecting security prices much. A market is *resilient* if asset prices stay close to their intrinsic values, and any deviations from intrinsic value are minimized quickly.

In a liquid market, traders with information trade more frequently and security prices are more efficient. Corporations can raise capital more cheaply and quickly, as more liquidity lowers the liquidity risk premium for securities. Investors, corporations, and securities increase in wealth or value in liquid markets.

There are several factors necessary for a market to be liquid, including:

- An abundance of buyers and sellers, so traders know they can quickly reverse their trade if necessary.
- Investor characteristics are diverse. If every investor had the same information, valuations, and liquidity needs, there would be little trading.
- A convenient location or trading platform which lends itself to increased investor activity and liquidity.
- Integrity as reflected in its participants and regulation, so that all investors receive fair treatment.

In a **transparent** market, investors can, without significant expense or delay, obtain both pre-trade information (regarding quotes and spreads) and post-trade information (regarding completed trades). If a market does not have transparency, investors lose faith in the market and decrease their trading activities.

When markets have **assurity of completion**, investors can be confident that the counterparty will uphold its side of the trade agreement. To facilitate this, brokers and clearing bodies may provide guarantees to both sides of the trade.

To evaluate the quality of a market, one should examine its liquidity, transparency, and assurity of completion. While transparency and assurity of completion require a qualitative assessment, liquidity can be measured by the quoted spread, effective spread, and ask and bid sizes. Lower quoted and effective spreads indicate greater liquidity and market quality. Higher bid and ask sizes indicate greater market depth, greater liquidity, and higher market quality.

EXECUTION COSTS

LOS 29.f: Explain the components of execution costs, including explicit and implicit costs, and evaluate a trade in terms of these costs.

The **explicit costs** of trade execution are directly observable and include commissions, taxes, stamp duties, and fees. **Implicit costs** are harder to measure, but they are real. They include the bid-ask spread, market or price impact costs, opportunity costs, and delay costs (i.e., slippage costs). They must be inferred by measuring the results of the trade versus a reference point.

Volume-Weighted Average Price (VWAP)

Implicit costs are measured using some benchmark, such as the midquote used to calculate the effective spread. An alternative is the VWAP. VWAP is a weighted average of execution prices during a day, where the weight applied is the proportion of the day's trading volume.

For example, assume the only trades for a security during the day are:

- At 10 a.m. 100 shares trade at $12.11.
- At 1 p.m. 300 shares trade at $12.00.
- At 2 p.m. 600 shares trade at $11.75.

The total number of shares traded is 1,000, so the VWAP is:

$$\text{VWAP} = \left(\frac{100}{1,000}\right)\$12.11 + \left(\frac{300}{1,000}\right)\$12.00 + \left(\frac{600}{1,000}\right)\$11.75 = \$11.86$$

VWAP has shortcomings.

- It is not useful if a trader is a significant part of the trading volume. Because her trading activity will significantly affect the VWAP, a comparison to VWAP is essentially comparing her trades to herself. It does not provide useful information.
- A more general problem is the potential to "game" the comparison. An unethical trader knowing he will be compared to VWAP could simply wait until late in the day and then decide which trades to execute. For example, if the price has been moving down, only execute buy transactions which will be at prices below VWAP. If prices are moving up for the day, only execute sales.
- This is related to the more general problem that VWAP does not consider missed trades.

IMPLEMENTATION SHORTFALL

LOS 29.g: Calculate and discuss implementation shortfall as a measure of transaction costs.

Implementation shortfall (IS) is more complex but can address the shortfalls of VWAP. It is a conceptual approach that measures transaction costs as the difference in performance of a hypothetical portfolio in which the trade is fully executed with no cost and the performance of the actual portfolio.

IS can be reported in several ways. Total IS can be calculated as an amount (dollars or other currency). For a per share amount, this total amount is divided by the number of shares in the initial order. For a percentage or basis point (bp) result, the total amount can be divided by the market value of the initial order. Total IS can also be subdivided into component costs, which will sum up to the total IS if additional reference prices are assumed.

Total IS is based on an initial trade decision and subsequent execution price. In some cases, a trade may not be completed in a manner defined as timely by the user or the entire trade may not be completed. For all of the IS components to be computed, revisions to the initial price when the order was originated and/or a cancelation price for the order will be needed. Key terms include:

- Decision price (DP): The market price of the security when the order is initiated. Often orders are initiated when the market is closed and the previous trading day's closing price is used as the DP.

- Execution price (EP): The price or prices at which the order is executed.
- Revised benchmark price (BP*): This is the market price of the security if the order is not completed in a timely manner as defined by the user. A manager who requires rapid execution might define this as within an hour. If not otherwise stated, it is assumed to be within the trading day.
- Cancelation price (CP): The market price of the security if the order is not fully executed and the remaining portion of the order is canceled.

> For the Exam: The CFA text does not use consistent terminology or formulas in this section. Instead, you are expected to understand and be able to apply the concepts to the case specifics and questions. We do apply standardized terminology and formulas in our Notes to assist in learning the concepts, but you will need to work practice questions to develop the skills to apply the IS approach.

Basic Concepts of Calculation

IS calculations must be computed in amount and also interpreted:

- For a purchase:
  - An increase in price is a cost.
  - A decrease in price is an account benefit (a negative cost).
- For a sale:
  - An increase in price is an account benefit (a negative cost).
  - A decrease in price is a cost.

Total IS can be computed as the difference in the value of the hypothetical portfolio if the trade was fully executed at the DP (with no costs) and the value of the actual portfolio.

Missed trade (also called opportunity, or unrealized profit/loss) is the difference in the initial DP and CP applied to the number of shares in the order not filled. It can generally be calculated as

$$|CP - DP| \times \text{\# of shares canceled}$$

Explicit costs (sometimes just referred to as commissions or fees) can be computed as:

$$\text{cost per share} \times \text{\# of shares executed}$$

Delay (also called slippage) is the difference in the initial DP and revised benchmark price (BP*) if the order is not filled in a timely manner, applied to the number of shares in the order subsequently filled. It can generally be calculated as:

$$|BP^* - DP| \times \text{\# of shares later executed}$$

Market impact (also called price impact or realized profit/loss) is the difference in EP (or EPs if there are multiple partial executions) and the initial DP (or BP* if there is delay) and the number of shares filled at the EP. It can generally be calculated as:

$$|EP - DP \text{ or } BP^*| \times \# \text{ of shares executed at that EP}$$

Example: Of implementation shortfall and decomposition
- On Wednesday, the stock price for Megabites closes at $20 a share.
- On Thursday morning before market open, the portfolio manager decides to buy Megabites and submits a limit order for 1,000 shares at $19.95. The price never falls to $19.95 during the day, so the order expires unfilled. The stock closes at $20.05.
- On Friday, the order is revised to a limit of $20.06. The order is partially filled that day as 800 shares are bought at $20.06. The commission is $18. The stock closes at $20.09 and the order for the remaining 200 shares is cancelled.

Answer:

The DP is $20.00. There was a delay, in this case due to the use of a limit order to buy below the market price. The BP* is $20.05. The increase of $0.05 is a cost in a buy order. The order is partially filled at an EP of $20.06 and there is missed trade cost. 200 shares were not filled and the CP is 20.09. Commissions were $18.00.

The **gain or loss on the paper portfolio** versus the actual portfolio gain or loss is the total implementation shortfall. The paper portfolio would have purchased all the shares at the decision price with no costs.

- The investment made by the paper portfolio is 1,000 × $20.00 = $20,000.
- The terminal value of the paper portfolio is 1,000 × $20.09 = $20,090. This is based on the price when the trade is completed, which in this case is when it is canceled.
- The gain on the paper portfolio is $20,090 – $20,000 = $90.

The **gain or loss on the real portfolio** is the actual ending value of the portfolio versus the actual expenditures, including costs.

- The investment made by the real portfolio is (800 × $20.06) + $18 = $16,066.
- The terminal value of the real portfolio is 800 × $20.09 = $16,072.
- The gain on the real portfolio is $16,072 – $16,066 = $6.

Total implementation shortfall is the difference in results of the hypothetical and actual portfolio of $84.00. The smaller actual gain is a cost.

On a per share basis, this is allocated to the full order of 1,000 shares:

$84 / 1,000 = $0.084 per share

As percentage and bp, this is allocated to the hypothetical portfolio cost of $20,000 (= 1,000 × $20.00):

$84 / $20,000 = 0.42% = 42 bp

The IS components are:

Missed trade is the CP versus DP on 200 shares. The price increased, which is a cost on a purchase:

$$|\$20.09 - 20.00| \times 200 = \$18.00$$

$$\$18 / 1,000 = \$0.018 \text{ per share}$$

$$\$18 / \$20,000 = 0.09\% = 9 \text{ bp}$$

Explicit costs are $18 and are a cost:

$$\$18 / 1,000 = \$0.018 \text{ per share}$$

$$\$18 / \$20,000 = 0.09\% = 9 \text{ bp}$$

Delay is BP* versus DP on 800 shares. The price increased, which is a cost on a purchase:

$$|\$20.05 - 20.00| \times 800 = \$40.00$$

$$\$40 / 1,000 = \$0.04 \text{ per share}$$

$$\$40 / \$20,000 = 0.20\% = 20 \text{ bp}$$

Price impact is EP versus DP or in this case versus BP* because there was a delay on 800 shares. The price increased, which is a cost on a purchase:

$$|\$20.06 - 20.05| \times 800 = \$8.00$$

$$\$8 / 1,000 = \$0.008 \text{ per share}$$

$$\$8 / \$20,000 = 0.04\% = 4 \text{ bp}$$

Verification of total versus components:

$$\$84 = \$18 + 18 + 40 + 8$$

$$\$0.084 = \$0.018 + 0.018 + 0.040 + 0.008$$

$$0.42\% = 0.09\% + 0.09 + 0.20 + 0.04$$

$$42 \text{bp} = 9 \text{bp} + 9 + 20 + 4$$

Adjusting for Market Movements

We can use the market model to adjust for market movements, where the expected return on a stock is its alpha, α_i, plus its beta, β_i, multiplied by the expected return on the market, $E(R_M)$:

$$E(R_i) = \alpha_i + \beta_i E(R_M)$$

Alpha is assumed to be zero. If the market return was 0.8% over the time period of this trading and the beta was 1.2 for Megabites, the expected return for it would be 0.8% × 1.2 = 0.96%. Subtracting this from the 0.42% results in a *market-adjusted implementation shortfall* of 0.42% – 0.96% = –0.54%. With this adjustment, the trading costs are actually negative.

Negative cost means a benefit to the portfolio. The purchase was executed above the original benchmark price (DP) but, when the general increase in market prices is considered, the execution was more favorable than expected.

VWAP vs. Implementation Shortfall

LOS 29.h: Contrast volume weighted average price (VWAP) and implementation shortfall as measures of transaction costs.

As mentioned previously, VWAP has its shortcomings. Its advantages and disadvantages, as well as those for implementation shortfall, are summarized as follows:

Advantages of VWAP:

- Easily understood.
- Computationally simple.
- Can be applied quickly to enhance trading decisions.
- Most appropriate for comparing small trades in nontrending markets (where a market adjustment is not needed).

Disadvantages of VWAP:

- Not informative for trades that dominate trading volume (as described earlier).
- Can be gamed by traders (as described earlier).
- Does not evaluate delayed or unfilled orders.
- Does not account for market movements or trade volume.

Advantages of Implementation Shortfall:

- Portfolio managers can see the cost of implementing their ideas.
- Demonstrates the tradeoff between quick execution and market impact.
- Decomposes and identifies costs.
- Can be used in an optimizer to minimize trading costs and maximize performance.
- Not subject to gaming.

Disadvantages of Implementation Shortfall:

- May be unfamiliar to traders.
- Requires considerable data and analysis.

ECONOMETRIC MODELS

LOS 29.i: Explain the use of econometric methods in pretrade analysis to estimate implicit transaction costs.

Econometric models can be used to forecast transaction costs. Using market microstructure theory, it has been shown that trading costs are nonlinearly related to:

- Security liquidity: trading volume, market cap, spread, price.
- Size of the trade relative to liquidity.
- Trading style: more aggressive trading results in higher costs.
- Momentum: trades that require liquidity (e.g., buying stock costs more when the market is trending upward).
- Risk.

The analyst would use these variables and a regression equation to determine the estimated cost of a trade.

The usefulness of econometric models is twofold. First, trading effectiveness can be assessed by comparing actual trading costs to forecasted trading costs from the model. Second, it can assist portfolio managers in determining the size of the trade. For example, if a trade of 100,000 shares is projected to result in round-trip trading costs of 4% and the strategy is projected to return 3%, then the trade size should be decreased to where trading costs are lower and the strategy is profitable.

MAJOR TRADER TYPES

LOS 29.j: Discuss the major types of traders, based on their motivation to trade, time versus price preferences, and preferred order types.

The first type of traders we examine are **information-motivated traders**. These traders have information that is time sensitive, and if they do not trade quickly, the value of the information will expire. They therefore prefer quick trades that demand liquidity, trading in large blocks. Information traders may trade with a dealer to guarantee an execution price. They are willing to bear higher trading costs as long as the value of their information is higher than the trading costs. Information traders will often want to disguise themselves because other traders will avoid trading with them. They use market orders to execute quickly because these commonly used orders are less noticeable.

Value-motivated traders use investment research to uncover misvalued securities. They do not trade often and are patient, waiting for the market to come to them with security prices that accommodate their valuations. As such, they will use limit orders because price, not speed, is their main objective.

Liquidity-motivated traders transact to convert their securities to cash or reallocate their portfolio from cash. They are often the counterparts to information-motivated and value-motivated traders who have superior information. Liquidity-motivated traders should be cognizant of the value they provide other traders. They freely reveal their benign motivations because they believe it to be to their advantage. They utilize market orders and trades on crossing networks and electronic communication networks (ECNs). Liquidity-motivated traders prefer to execute their order within a day.

Passive traders trade for index funds and other passive investors, trading to allocate cash or convert to cash. They are similar to liquidity-motivated traders but are more focused on reducing costs. They can afford to be very patient. Their trades are like those of dealers in that they let other traders come to them so as to extract a favorable trade price. They favor limit orders and trades on crossing networks. This allows for low commissions, low market impact, price certainty, and possible elimination of the bid-ask spread.

A summary of the major trader types, including their motivations and order preferences, is presented in Figure 1.

Figure 1: Summary of Trader Types and Their Motivations and Preferences

Trader Types	Motivation	Time or Price Preference	Primary Preferred Order Types
Information-motivated	Time-sensitive information	Time	Market
Value-motivated	Security misvaluations	Price	Limit
Liquidity-motivated	Reallocation & liquidity	Time	Market
Passive	Reallocation & liquidity	Price	Limit

Other trader types include **day traders** and **dealers**. Dealers were discussed earlier and seek to earn the bid-asked spread and short-term profits. Day traders are similar in that they seek short-term profits from price movements.

TRADING TACTICS

LOS 29.k: Describe the suitable uses of major trading tactics, evaluate their relative costs, advantages, and weaknesses, and recommend a trading tactic when given a description of the investor's motivation to trade, the size of the trade, and key market characteristics.

Most portfolio managers have different trading needs at different times. Few can pursue the same trading strategy all the time. In the material to follow, we discuss various trading tactics.

In a **liquidity-at-any-cost** trading focus, the trader must transact a large block of shares quickly. The typical trader in this case is an information trader but can also be a mutual fund that must liquidate its shares quickly to satisfy redemptions in its fund. Most counterparties shy away from taking the other side of an information trader's position. The liquidity-at-any-cost trader may be able to find a broker to represent him though because of the information the broker gains in the process. In any event, this trader must be ready to pay a high price for trading in the form of either market impact, commissions, or both.

In a **costs-are-not-important** trading focus, the trader believes that exchange markets will operate fairly and efficiently such that the execution price they transact at is at best execution. These orders are appropriate for a variety of trade motivations. Trading costs are not given consideration, and the trader pays average trading costs for quick execution. The trader thus uses market orders, which are also useful for disguising the trader's intentions because they are so common. The weakness of a market order is that the trader loses control over the trade's execution.

In a **need-trustworthy-agent** trading focus, the trader employs a broker to skillfully execute a large trade in a security, which may be thinly traded. The broker may need to trade over a period of time, so these orders are not appropriate for information traders. The trader cedes control to the broker and is often unaware of trade details until after the order has executed. The weakness of this strategy is that commissions may be high and the trader may reveal his trade intentions to the broker, which may not be in the trader's best interests.

In an **advertise-to-draw-liquidity** trading focus, the trade is publicized in advance to draw counterparties to the trade. An initial public offering is an example of this trade type. The weakness of this strategy is that another trader may front run the trade, buying in advance of a buy order, for example, to then sell at a higher price.

In a **low-cost-whatever-the-liquidity** trading focus, the trader places a limit order outside of the current bid-ask quotes in order to minimize trading costs. For example, a trader may place a limit buy order at a price below the current market bid. The strength of this strategy is that commissions, spreads, and market impact costs tend to be low. Passive and value-motivated traders will often pursue this strategy. Patience is required for this strategy, and indeed its weakness is that it may not be executed at all. Additionally, if it is executed, the reason may be that negative information has been released. For example, a buy order of this type may only be executed when bad news is released about the firm.

A summary of trading tactics is presented in Figure 2. Note that the motivations for need-trustworthy-agent and advertise-to-draw-liquidity tactics are nonspecific but would exclude information-based motivations.

Figure 2: Summary of Trading Tactics

Trading Tactic	Strengths	Weaknesses	Usual Trade Motivation
Liquidity-at-any-cost	Quick, certain execution	High costs & leakage of information	Information
Costs-are-not-important	Quick, certain execution at market price	Loss of control of trade costs	Variety of motivations
Need-trustworthy-agent	Broker uses skill & time to obtain lower price	Higher commission & potential leakage of trade intention	Not information
Advertise-to-draw-liquidity	Market-determined price	Higher administrative costs & possible front running	Not information
Low-cost-whatever-the-liquidity	Low trading costs	Uncertain timing of trade & possibly trading into weakness	Passive and value

ALGORITHMIC TRADING

LOS 29.l: Explain the motivation for algorithmic trading and discuss the basic classes of algorithmic trading strategies.

Algorithmic trading is the use of automated, quantitative systems that utilize trading rules, benchmarks, and constraints. Algorithmic trading is a form of automated trading, which refers to trading not conducted manually. Automated trading accounts for about one-quarter of all trades, and algorithmic trading is projected to grow.

The **motivation for algorithmic trading** is to execute orders with minimal risk and costs. The use of algorithmic trading often involves breaking a large trade into smaller pieces to accommodate normal market flow and minimize market impact. This automated process must be monitored, however, so that the portfolio does not become over-concentrated in sectors. This might happen if certain sectors are more liquid than others.

Algorithmic trading strategies are classified into *logical participation strategies*, *opportunistic strategies*, and *specialized strategies*. Of logical participation strategies, there are two subtypes: simple logical participation strategies and implementation shortfall strategies. We examine these subtypes first.

Simple logical participation strategies break larger orders up into smaller pieces to minimize market impact. There are several subsets to this strategy.

A **VWAP strategy** seeks to match or do better than the day's volume weighted average price. The historical daily volume pattern is used as the base to determine how to allocate the trade over the day; however, any given day's actual daily volume pattern can be substantially different.

A **time-weighted average price strategy** (TWAP) spreads the trade out evenly over the whole day so as to equal a TWAP benchmark. This strategy is often used for a thinly traded stock that has volatile, unpredictable intraday trading volume. Total trading volume can be forecasted using historical data or predictive models.

A **percent-of-volume strategy** trades a set percentage of normal trading volume until the order is filled.

Implementation shortfall strategies, or arrival price strategies, seek to jointly minimize market impact and opportunity (missed trade) cost. Logically and empirically, it has been demonstrated that the volatility of trading cost increases with delay in execution. The market price can move against the trade, driving up opportunity and therefore total trade cost. This variability tends to rise exponentially with the length of the time taken to execute, which has two implications. To minimize implementation shortfall (IS), the trade should general be front-loaded and favor immediate execution. However, the decision also depends on risk aversion. Higher risk aversion will seek immediate execution for certainty of cost. It accepts greater market impact to minimize potential opportunity cost. Lower risk aversion will allow patient trading in an effort to lower market impact while risking higher opportunity cost and making total cost more variable. This trade-off decision is analogous to mean variance optimization and an efficient frontier. In this case, the two axes are expected trading cost and variability of trading cost.

Specialized algorithmic trading strategies include hunter strategies, where the size of the order or portion seeking execution is adjusted to take advantage of changing market liquidity; market-on-close, which targets the closing price as execution price; and smart routing, which monitors multiple markets and routes the order to the most liquid market.

CHOOSING AN ALGORITHMIC TRADING STRATEGY

LOS 29.m: Discuss the factors that typically determine the selection of a specific algorithmic trading strategy, including order size, average daily trading volume, bid–ask spread, and the urgency of the order.

Consider the following:

- Size of the order as a percentage of average daily trading volume.
- Bid-asked spread.
- Urgency of the trade.

Algorithmic strategies are best suited when all three are low, possibly VWAP. It is a conservative strategy in that it seeks more immediate execution. The smaller size of the order and spread suggest more complex strategies are not needed.

©2016 Kaplan, Inc.

Low size and spread with high urgency may favor an implementation shortfall strategy as it seeks to minimize impact and opportunity cost. The high urgency makes the trade strategy decision more difficult.

A broker or a crossing network can be appropriate if size and spread are high, but the trader can be patient and take the time to try and minimize market impact by seeking out a counterparty to the trade.

 Professor's Note: Hopefully it is occurring to you this entire section is advanced trading strategies for generally larger orders. If you want to buy 100 shares, use a market or limit order.

Example: Choosing the appropriate algorithmic strategy

Figure A: Order Management System

Stock Ticker	Trade Size	Average Daily Volume	Price	Spread	Urgency
ABCD	20,000	250,000	$24.67	0.06%	Low
LMNO	50,000	125,000	$12.18	0.45%	Low
WXYZ	150,000	2,500,000	$37.88	0.05%	High

Discuss the appropriate trading strategy that should be used to place each order.

Answer:

First calculate each trade size as a percentage of average daily volume, as in Figure B.

Figure B: Trade Sizes as a Percentage of Average Daily Volume

Stock Ticker	Trade Size as a Percentage of Average Daily Volume
ABCD	20,000 / 250,000 = 8%
LMNO	50,000 / 125,000 = 40%
WXYZ	150,000 / 2,500,000 = 6%

Although the trade for stock WXYZ is the largest in absolute size, it is the smallest in relative terms. The trade for stock ABCD is also relatively small, and in both cases the spreads are fairly low. The ABCD trade is of low urgency and can be traded over time. It is thus suitable for a simple participation strategy based on VWAP or another benchmark. The WXYZ trade is of high urgency, however, and should be traded more quickly using an implementation shortfall strategy.

The LMNO trade is of relatively large size and has a large spread. Because of these characteristics, it should be traded through a skilled broker or through a crossing system to minimize the spread.

BEST EXECUTION

LOS 29.n: Explain the meaning and criteria of best execution.

Best execution is an important concept because it impacts the client's portfolio performance. The CFA Institute has published Trade Management Guidelines for pursuing best execution.[2] The Institute compares best execution to prudence. Prudence refers to selecting the securities most appropriate for an investor, whereas best execution refers to the best means to buy or sell those securities. They are similar in that they both attempt to improve portfolio performance and meet fiduciary responsibilities.

The Institute report specifies four characteristics of best execution:

1. Best execution cannot be judged independently of the investment decision. A strategy might have high trading costs, but that alone does not mean the strategy should not be pursued as long as it generates the intended value.

2. Best execution cannot be known with certainty ex ante (before the fact); it depends on the particular circumstances of the trade. Each party to a trade determines what best execution is.

3. Best execution can only be assessed ex post (after the fact). While cost can be measured for any single trade, quality of execution is assessed over time. The cost of a single trade execution is very dependent on the reference or decision price used in its calculation. There can always be distortions. But over time and multiple trades, those costs can be used to indicate the quality of execution.

4. Relationships and practices are integral to best execution. Best execution is ongoing and requires diligence and dedication to the process.

EVALUATING TRADING PROCEDURES

LOS 29.o: Evaluate a firm's investment and trading procedures, including processes, disclosures, and record keeping, with respect to best execution.

The CFA Institute's Trade Management Guidelines are split into three parts: processes, disclosures, and record keeping. These guidelines are meant to assist investment management firms in achieving best execution and maximum portfolio value for their clients.

In regard to processes, firms should have policies and procedures that have the intent of maximizing portfolio value using best execution. These policies and procedures should also help firms measure and manage best execution.

---

2. Available at *http://www.cfapubs.org/doi/pdf/10.2469/ccb.v2004.n3.4007*, accessed May 2016.

Investment management firms should also provide disclosure to their clients and potential clients regarding (1) general information on their trading techniques, markets, and brokers and (2) their conflicts of interest related to trading. This information should be provided periodically to clients to help them assess the firm's ability to provide best execution.

In regard to record keeping, investment management firms should maintain the documentation supporting (1) the firm's compliance with its policies and procedures and (2) disclosures made to its clients. In doing so, the firm also provides evidence to regulators as to how the firm pursues best execution for its clients.

LOS 29.p: Discuss the role of ethics in trading.

Trading is based on word of honor. Buy-side and sell-side traders must honor their verbal agreements or they will quickly find that no one wants to take the opposite side of their trade. The development of complex trading techniques and the decline in explicit commissions have increased the opportunity and temptation to act unethically.

Regardless of these developments, buy-side traders should always act in the best interests of their clients. Buy-side traders and portfolio managers have a fiduciary duty to maximize the value of their client's portfolio. The buy-side trader's relationships with sell-side traders must never come before the interests of the trader's clients.

KEY CONCEPTS

LOS 29.a

A **market order** is an order to execute the trade immediately at the best possible price. If the order cannot be completely filled in one trade which offers the best price, it is filled by other trades at the next best possible prices. The emphasis in a market order is the speed of execution. The disadvantage of a market order is that the price it will be executed at is not known ahead of time, so it has **price uncertainty**.

A **limit order** is an order to trade at the limit price or better. For sell orders, the execution price must be higher than or equal to the limit price. For buy orders, the execution price must be lower than or equal to the limit price. If not filled on or before the specified date, limit orders expire. A limit order emphasizes the price of execution. It however may not be filled immediately and may even go unfilled or partially unfilled. A limit order thus has **execution uncertainty**.

LOS 29.b

The effective spread is compared against the quoted spread to evaluate the cost of trading. It captures both price improvements and the costs of market impact:

$$\text{effective spread}_{\text{buy order}} = 2 \times (\text{execution price} - \text{midquote})$$
$$\text{effective spread}_{\text{sell order}} = 2 \times (\text{midquote} - \text{execution price})$$

LOS 29.c

- Quote-driven markets: Investors trade with dealers.
- Order-driven markets: Investors trade with each other without the use of intermediaries. There are three main types:
  1. In an *electronic crossing network*, orders are batched together and crossed (matched) at fixed points in time during the day at the average of the bid and ask quotes.

  2. In *auction markets*, trader orders compete for execution.

  3. *Automated auctions* are computerized auction markets and provide price discovery.

- Brokered markets: Investors use brokers to locate the counterparty to a trade. This service is valuable when the trader has a large block to sell, when the trader wants to remain anonymous, and/or when the market for the security is small or illiquid.
- A hybrid market is a combination of the other three markets. For example, the New York Stock Exchange has features of both quote-driven and order-driven markets.

LOS 29.d

The relationship between a **trader and the broker** is one of a *principal and agent*. The broker acts as the trader's agent and locates the necessary liquidity at the best price. The broker may even take a position in the security to facilitate the trade. Many buy-side traders prefer their anonymity so as not to tip off other traders to their actions. At the same time, the trader may be able to extract information from the broker on the depth of the market for a security and the identity of other traders. The broker may also provide record keeping, financing, cash management, and other services to the trader.

In contrast, the **trader and the dealer** often have *opposing interests*. For example, dealers want to maximize the trade spread while traders want to minimize it. In addition, when a trader has information that the dealer does not have, the trader profits at the dealer's expense. When a trader enters the market with information others do not have, the result is adverse selection risk for the dealer. It is in the trader's interest to conceal her intent, while it is in the dealer's interest to find out who the informed traders are.

LOS 29.e

A security market should provide liquidity, transparency, and assurity of completion. A liquid market has small bid-ask spreads, market depth, and resilience. Market depth allows larger orders to trade without affecting security prices much. A market is resilient if asset prices stay close to their intrinsic values.

In a transparent market, investors can, without significant expense or delay, obtain both pre-trade information and post-trade information. If a market does not have transparency, investors lose faith in the market and decrease their trading activities. When markets have assurity of completion, investors can be confident that the counter-party will uphold their side of the trade agreement. To facilitate this, brokers and clearing bodies may provide guarantees to both sides of the trade.

LOS 29.f

The **explicit costs** in a trade are readily discernible and include commissions, taxes, stamp duties, and fees. **Implicit costs** are harder to measure, but they are real. They include the bid-ask spread, market or price impact costs, opportunity costs, and delay costs (i.e., slippage costs).

LOS 29.g

Implementation shortfall is the difference between the actual portfolio's return and a paper portfolio's return.
- For a purchase:
  - An increase in price is a cost.
  - A decrease in price is an account benefit (a negative cost).
- For a sale:
  - An increase in price is an account benefit (a negative cost).
  - A decrease in price is a cost.

Total IS can be computed as the difference in the value of the hypothetical portfolio if the trade was fully executed at the DP (with no costs) and the value of the actual portfolio.

Missed trade (also called opportunity, or unrealized profit/loss) is the difference in the initial DP and CP applied to the number of shares in the order not filled. It can generally be calculated as

$$|CP - DP| \times \text{\# of shares canceled}$$

Explicit costs (sometimes just referred to as commissions or fees) can be computed as:

$$\text{cost per share} \times \text{\# of shares executed}$$

Delay (also called slippage) is the difference in the initial DP and revised benchmark price (BP*) if the order is not filled in a timely manner applied to the number of shares in the order subsequently filled. It can generally be calculated as:

$$|BP^* - DP| \times \text{\# of shares later executed}$$

Market impact (also called price impact or realized profit/loss) is the difference in EP (or EPs if there are multiple partial executions) and the initial DP (or BP* if there is delay) and the number of shares filled at the EP. It can generally be calculated as:

$$|EP - DP \text{ or } BP^*| \times \text{\# of shares executed}$$

LOS 29.h

Advantages of VWAP:
- Easily understood.
- Computationally simple.
- Can be applied quickly to enhance trading decisions.
- Most appropriate for comparing small trades in nontrending markets (where a market adjustment is not needed).

Disadvantages of VWAP:
- Not informative for trades that dominate trading volume.
- Can be gamed by traders.
- Does not evaluate delayed or unfilled orders.
- Does not account for market movements or trade volume.

Advantages of Implementation Shortfall:
- Portfolio managers can see the cost of implementing their ideas.
- Demonstrates the tradeoff between quick execution and market impact.
- Decomposes and identifies costs.
- Can be used in an optimizer to minimize trading costs and maximize performance.
- Not subject to gaming.

Disadvantages of Implementation Shortfall:
- May be unfamiliar to traders.
- Requires considerable data and analysis.

LOS 29.i

Econometric models can be used to forecast transaction costs. Using market microstructure theory, it has been shown that trading costs are nonlinearly related to:

- Security liquidity: trading volume, market cap, spread, price.
- Size of the trade relative to liquidity.
- Trading style: more aggressive trading results in higher costs.
- Momentum: trades that require liquidity [e.g., buying (selling) when the market is trending upward (downward)].
- Risk.

The analyst uses these variables and a regression equation to forecast the estimated cost of a trade.

The usefulness of econometric models is twofold. First, trading effectiveness can be assessed by comparing actual trading costs to forecasted trading costs from the model. Second, it can assist portfolio managers in determining the size of the trade.

LOS 29.j

Information-motivated traders trade based on time-sensitive information; thus, they prefer market orders because their trades must take place quickly. Their trades demand liquidity, and they are willing to bear higher trading costs.

Value-motivated traders use investment research to uncover misvalued securities. They will use limit orders because price, not speed, is their main objective.

Liquidity-motivated traders transact to convert their securities to cash or reallocate their portfolio from cash. They utilize market orders and trades on crossing networks and electronic communication networks (ECNs). Liquidity-motivated traders prefer to execute their order within a day.

Passive traders trade for index funds and other passive investors. They favor limit orders and trades on crossing networks. This allows for low commissions, low market impact, price certainty, and possible elimination of the bid-ask spread.

LOS 29.k

In a liquidity-at-any-cost trading focus, the trader must transact a large block of shares quickly. The typical trader in this case is an information trader but can also be a mutual fund that must liquidate its shares quickly to satisfy redemptions in its fund. This trader must be ready to pay a high price for trading in the form of market impact, commissions, or both.

In a costs-are-not-important trading focus, the trader believes that exchange markets will operate fairly and efficiently such that the execution price they transact at is at best execution. The trader thus uses market orders.

In a need-trustworthy-agent trading focus, the trader employs a broker to skillfully execute a large trade in a security, which may be thinly traded. The weakness of this strategy is that commissions may be high and the trader may reveal his trade intentions to the broker.

In an advertise-to-draw-liquidity trading focus, the trade is publicized in advance to draw counterparties to the trade. The weakness of this strategy is that another trader may front run the trade, buying in advance of a buy order.

In a low-cost-whatever-the-liquidity trading focus, the trader places a limit order outside of the current bid-ask quotes in order to minimize trading costs. Passive and value-motivated traders will often pursue this strategy.

LOS 29.l

Algorithmic trading is the use of automated, quantitative systems that utilize trading rules, benchmarks, and constraints to execute orders with minimal risk and costs. Algorithmic trading strategies are classified into logical participation strategies (simple logical and implementation shortfall strategies), opportunistic strategies, and specialized strategies.

Simple logical participation strategies seek to trade with market flow so as to not become overly noticeable to the market and to minimize market impact.

Implementation shortfall strategies, or arrival price strategies, minimize trading costs as defined by the implementation shortfall measure or total execution costs.

Opportunistic participation strategies trade passively over time but increase trading when liquidity is present.

Specialized strategies include passive strategies and other miscellaneous strategies.

LOS 29.m

Consider the order size as a percentage of daily trading volume, size of spread, and urgency of the trade:
- Algorithmic strategies when all three are low (e.g., VWAP strategy).
- Implementation shortfall for low size and spread but with high urgency.
- A broker or crossing network when size and spread are high but urgency is low.

LOS 29.n

CFA Institute compares best execution to prudence. Prudence refers to selecting the securities most appropriate for an investor, whereas best execution refers to the best means to buy or sell those securities. They are similar in that they both attempt to improve portfolio performance and meet fiduciary responsibilities.

Four characteristics of best execution:
1. It depends on the value added of the trade versus cost.

2. Best execution and value added cannot be known ex ante.

3. Best execution and cost can only be calculated ex post. Assessing value added may take even longer to evaluate if the idea works out.

4. Relationships and practices are integral to best execution. Best execution is ongoing and requires diligence and dedication to the process.

LOS 29.o

The CFA Institute's Trade Management Guidelines are split into three parts:

1. **Processes:** Firms should have policies/procedures that have the intent of maximizing portfolio value using best execution. These should help firms determine and manage best execution.

2. **Disclosures:** Investment management firms should provide disclosure to their clients and potential clients regarding (1) general information on their trading techniques, markets, and brokers and (2) their conflicts of interest related to trading. This information should be provided periodically to clients.

3. **Record Keeping:** Investment management firms should maintain the documentation supporting (1) the firm's compliance and (2) disclosures made to its clients. In doing so, the firm also provides evidence to regulators as to how the firm pursues best execution for its clients.

LOS 29.p

Trading is based on word of honor. Buy-side and sell-side traders must honor their verbal agreements or they will quickly find that no one wants to take the opposite side of their trade. The development of complex trading techniques and the decline in explicit commissions have increased the opportunity and temptation to act unethically.

Regardless of these developments, buy-side traders should always act in the best interests of their clients. Buy-side traders and portfolio managers have a fiduciary duty to maximize the value of their client's portfolio. The buy-side trader's relationships with sell-side traders must never come before the interests of the trader's clients.

CONCEPT CHECKERS

1. **Discuss** why a limit order has execution uncertainty.

2. There were three sell orders placed for a stock during a day. The following are the quoted bid and ask quotes at various points in the day.

Time of Trade	Bid Price	Bid Size	Ask Price	Ask Size
11 a.m.	$20.00	400	$20.08	500
12 p.m.	$20.08	400	$20.18	500
2 p.m.	$20.12	400	$20.24	500

- At 11 a.m. the trader placed an order to sell 200 shares. The execution price was $20.02.
- At 12 p.m. the trader placed an order to sell 300 shares. The execution price was $20.11.
- At 2 p.m. the trader placed an order to sell 500 shares. The average execution price was $20.09.

    Calculate the quoted and effective spreads for these orders and the spread averages. **Comment** on any possible price improvement in each trade.

3. Suppose a trader has a large block of an emerging market stock to sell and would like to do so surreptitiously. In which type of market would be best for him to trade?

4. **Discuss** the adverse selection risk faced by a dealer.

5. An analyst is comparing two markets. Market A has higher average bid and ask sizes than Market B. **Discuss** which market has the higher quality and why.

6. Suppose there is an illiquid stock that has a limited market of buyers and sellers. In fact, the majority of trading in this firm's stock is dominated by one trader. **Discuss** the use of the volume-weighted average price (VWAP) to compare this trader to another trader.

7. Use the following information to **calculate** the implementation shortfall and its components as a percentage.
   - On Wednesday, the stock price closes at $50 a share.
   - On Thursday morning before market open, the portfolio manager decides to buy Megawidgets and transfers a limit order for 1,000 shares at $49.95. The order expires unfilled. The stock closes at $50.05.
   - On Friday, the order is revised to a limit of $50.07. The order is partially filled that day as 700 shares are bought at $50.07. The commission is $23. The stock closes at $50.09 and the order is cancelled.

8. Suppose a firm was concerned that its traders were gaming its trading costs analysis. **Suggest** a measurement of trading costs that is less susceptible to gaming.

9. Are econometric models used as ex ante (before the fact) or ex post (after the fact) investment tools?

10.   Why do value-motivated and passive traders prefer limit orders?

11.   **Explain** why momentum markets would be problematic for a low-cost-whatever-the-liquidity trading focus.

12.   A market observer notices that a particular trading firm tends to execute its trades early in the day, with volume falling off later in the day. What type of algorithmic trading system is the firm likely using?

13.   What is the primary indication that a trader should not utilize algorithmic trading and instead use a broker or a crossing network?

14.   John Booker is a manager at a trading firm. He is quite upset because yesterday a junior trader had excessive trading costs. **Critique** Booker's perspective.

15.   **Discuss** two recent developments that could make the relationship between buy-side and sell-side traders more problematic.

For more questions related to this topic review, log in to your Schweser online account and launch SchweserPro™ QBank; and for video instruction covering each LOS in this topic review, log in to your Schweser online account and launch the OnDemand video lectures, if you have purchased these products.

©2016 Kaplan, Inc.

ANSWERS – CONCEPT CHECKERS

1. A limit order has execution uncertainty because it is not known when the order will be filled, if at all. If the limit price cannot be satisfied in the current market, the order will go unfilled. Because limit orders have an expiration date, the limit may go unfilled or partially unfilled if it cannot be satisfied prior to expiration.

2. The quoted spread for each order is the difference between the ask and bid prices:

Time of Trade	Ask Minus Bid Price	Quoted Spread
11 a.m.	$20.08 – $20.00	$0.08
12 p.m.	$20.18 – $20.08	$0.10
2 p.m.	$20.24 – $20.12	$0.12

The average quoted spread is a simple average of the quoted spreads: ($0.08 + $0.10 + $0.12) / 3 = $0.10.

The effective spread for a sell order is twice the midquote of the market bid and ask prices minus the execution price.

The midquote for each trade is calculated as:

Time of Trade	Midquote
11 a.m.	($20.08 + $20.00) / 2 = $20.04
12 p.m.	($20.08 + $20.18) / 2 = $20.13
2 p.m.	($20.24 + $20.12) / 2 = $20.18

The effective spread for each sell order is:

Time of Trade	2 × (Midquote – Execution Price) = Effective Spread
11 a.m.	2 × ($20.04 – $20.02) = $0.04
12 p.m.	2 × ($20.13 – $20.11) = $0.04
2 p.m.	2 × ($20.18 – $20.09) = $0.18

The average effective spread is ($0.04 + $0.04 + $0.18) / 3 = $0.0867.

The weighted-average effective spread is (200 / 1,000)$0.04 + (300 / 1,000)$0.04 + (500 / 1,000)$0.18 = $0.11.

In the first and second trade, there was price improvement because the sell orders were executed at bid prices higher than the quoted prices. Hence, the effective spread was lower than the quoted spread. In the last trade, the trade size was larger than the bid size. The effective spread in this case was higher than that quoted due to the market impact of the large order.

Overall, the simple average effective spread was lower than the average quoted spread, reflecting the price improvement in the first two trades. The weighted-average effective spread was higher than the average quoted spread, reflecting the market impact of the last trade, which was larger than either of the first two trades.

3. The market probably most suitable is a brokered market. A broker can place the order without revealing his client's identity. He can discreetly shop the stock and find the necessary liquidity. He may even take a position in the stock with his own capital.

   An electronic crossing network might be another possibility because traders usually do not know the identity of their counterparty or their trade size. The question states, however, that the stock is an emerging market stock for which brokered markets are particularly suited. Brokered markets are important in countries where public capital markets are not well developed.

4. When a trader has information that the dealer does not, the trader profits at the dealer's expense. Traders are more likely to trade when they have information that others do not. This results in adverse selection risk for the dealer. The trader's profit is the dealer's loss once the information is revealed to the market.

5. Market A is of higher quality. The larger the bid and ask sizes (the number of shares offered by a dealer or trader at a specified price), the greater the market depth and the greater the liquidity.

6. It is difficult to use VWAP to compare two traders, one of which does not dominate the markets for the securities he trades in and the other does. If a trader dominates trading in a security, VWAP will be close to the trade price. The trader will have appeared to minimize costs, even if he traded at unfavorable prices. This trader will appear better than another trader who does not dominate the trading.

7. First, organize the information. The trade decision was made while the market was closed, making DP the previous close of 50.00. There was a one day delay in execution making BP* 50.05. There was an unexecuted trade portion and a CP of 50.09. EP was 50.07. Total explicit costs are given as $23. (Note that a limit price is not a direct part of IS calculations, though it may affect EP and create delays.)
   - Explicit cost—the commission as a percentage of the paper portfolio investment is $23 / $50,000 = 0.05%.
   - Realized profit and loss is EP – DP (or BP*). This is divided by the DP and weighted by proportion of the order filled. It is (700 / 1,000) × ($50.07 – $50.05) / $50.00 = 0.03%.
   - Delay cost is BP* – DP and then divided by the DP. It is weighted by the portion of the order filled. It is (700 / 1,000) × ($50.05 – $50.00) / $50.00 = 0.07%.
   - Missed trade opportunity cost is CP – DP and then divided by the DP. It is weighted by the portion of the order that is not filled. It equals (300 / 1,000) × ($50.09 – $50.00) / $50.00 = 0.05%.

   The sum of the components is the total implementation cost: 0.05% + 0.03% + 0.07% + 0.05% = 0.20%.

8. The best measurement would be the implementation shortfall measure. VWAP can be gamed by traders, who might time their trades until the VWAP makes their trading costs appear favorable. The effective spread can also be gamed. A trader can trade at favorable bids and asks by waiting for orders to be brought to the trader. In both cases, a trader might forgo profits through delay.

9. Actually, they can be used as both. Before the fact, econometric models can assist portfolio managers in determining the size of the trade. After the fact, trading effectiveness can be assessed by comparing actual trading costs to forecasted trading costs from the models.

10. Value-motivated and passive traders prefer limit orders because their primary motivation is to minimize trading costs and transact at favorable prices. They do not need the immediate execution of market orders and can afford to be patient.

11. In a low-cost-whatever-the-liquidity trading focus, the trader places a limit order outside of the current bid-ask quotes in order to minimize trading costs. Momentum markets can make their execution problematic though. If, for example, a trader has placed a buy order and the market trends upward, the order may never be filled. If the market trends downward, the trader's order may be filled, but the stock price may keep trending downward.

12. The firm is likely using an implementation shortfall strategy. These strategies trade heavier early in the day to ensure order completion, reduce opportunity costs, and minimize the volatility of trading costs.

13. When a trade is of relatively large size and has a large spread, it should be traded through a broker or a crossing system in order to minimize the spread.

14. Booker is perhaps overreacting. It is difficult to judge a trader's performance over just one day. The market conditions may have been so severe that measurement of trading costs would be flawed. Although best execution can be measured ex post over time, it cannot be legitimately measured over a short time period.

15. First, the popularity of electronic trading venues has provided more anonymity for traders. A trader who gains information from another trader can use this information against the other trader discreetly. Second, brokerage commissions have fallen dramatically. The temptation is for a trader to shift costs to those that are implicit, rather than explicit.

The following is a review of the Trading, Monitoring, and Rebalancing principles designed to address the learning outcome statements set forth by CFA Institute. Cross-Reference to CFA Institute Assigned Reading #30.

Monitoring and Rebalancing

Exam Focus

From earlier sessions, you know that the passage of time plus changes in market and client circumstances require review and possible updating of the IPS. That may also trigger a need to rebalance the portfolio assets. We will look at different rules to trigger rebalancing plus the consequences of following a buy and hold, constant mix, or CPPI strategy. These three strategies are presented in terms of a risky and risk-free asset. This makes the outcomes neat and clean. But, if you generalize the discussion to riskier equity and less risky fixed income, you will have a better appreciation of why the topic is important.

LOS 30.a: Discuss a fiduciary's responsibilities in monitoring an investment portfolio.

A portfolio manager who is in a position of trust has a fiduciary duty to monitor the portfolio to be sure it continues to meet the client's needs as client circumstances, capital markets conditions and expectations, and portfolio percentage allocations may all change over time. Changes in client circumstances may require an update of the IPS, changes in capital market conditions may lead to a change in strategic allocation, and changes in portfolio percentage allocations may require rebalancing.

LOS 30.b: Discuss the monitoring of investor circumstances, market/economic conditions, and portfolio holdings and explain the effects that changes in each of these areas can have on the investor's portfolio.

Over time, investor circumstances may change and portfolio managers must take account of these changes. Advisors may need to update the IPS for the investor whenever there are significant changes in the investor's risk and return objectives, time horizon, tax circumstances, liquidity needs, legal and regulatory environment, or unique circumstances. Changes in an investor's IPS will reflect changes in these objectives and constraints. Essentially, this involves constructing a new IPS that reflects these changes and perhaps the strategic asset allocation for the portfolio as well.

Even in the absence of significant changes in an investor's circumstances, changing capital market conditions may require altering the investor's asset allocation. Changes in asset class returns or returns volatility will most likely lead to revised expected returns and risk attributes requiring updating the strategic asset allocation. Changes in the phase of a market cycle, central bank policy, or the yield curve and inflation may suggest changes in tactical asset allocation to exploit opportunities for increased returns.

Finally, as asset values change within the portfolio this may require rebalancing the portfolio to a different asset allocation. We discuss rebalancing costs, benefits, and strategies later in this topic review.

LOS 30.c: Recommend and justify revisions to an investor's investment policy statement and strategic asset allocation, given a change in investor circumstances.

The principles underlying the recommendation of changes to an investor's IPS or strategic asset allocation are exactly the same ones we covered in Study Session 4. We illustrate this with some examples.

- Marriage is a change in circumstances that could affect multiple constraints, as well as risk and return objectives, depending on the age, wealth, children, and risk tolerance of the spouse.
- Birth of a child could add an investment horizon and change the investor's liquidity needs as plans are made for the child's education.
- A desire for funds to be left as a bequest could lead to changes in the IPS as well.
- Receiving an inheritance or a new desire to make significant charitable contributions may change several elements of an investor's IPS.

 Professor's Note: Recognize this is another, and light, review of IPS issues. If in doubt about anything, follow the material in the earlier primary study sessions.

LOS 30.d: Discuss the benefits and costs of rebalancing a portfolio to the investor's strategic asset allocation.

Over time as market valuations change, the percentage of a portfolio's value in each asset class will change from the initial asset allocation. If we assume that the initial asset allocation was optimal in terms of exposure to systematic risk factors and expected return, deviations from the initial asset allocation percentages will reduce the expected utility of the portfolio to the investor. Thus, we can view the benefits of portfolio rebalancing in theory as being equal to the loss in expected utility that is avoided by rebalancing.

Consider, for simplicity, an optimal portfolio allocation of 60% to equities and 40% to fixed income securities. If equities are the riskier asset and have the greater mean return, the allocation to equities will tend to increase over time. The result is a portfolio that becomes more risky and has higher expected returns over time and no longer satisfies the investors risk and return objectives. In the absence of changes in asset class returns distributions and correlations, rebalancing the portfolio to the 60%/40% mix will restore the portfolio risk/return characteristics to their optimal levels for the investor.

From a practical view, if asset classes are sometimes overvalued and sometimes undervalued, rebalancing can increase returns as allocations to overvalued assets are reduced and allocations to undervalued assets increased. The discipline of rebalancing can help investors avoid a tendency to hold increased weights in assets that have had high returns over a period, only to see returns for those assets perform relatively poorly in subsequent periods. While rebalancing will not necessarily improve returns and reduce risk over all periods, it has had those effects on average over longer periods.

The primary costs of rebalancing are the transactions costs incurred and the tax liability generated by selling assets that have appreciated in value. Transactions costs include the commissions paid for a trade the bid-ask spread and the market impact of the trade. The market impact of a trade is the change in price as a result of entering a trade and can be expected to be greater for larger positions. We cannot observe the price that would have prevailed had the trade not been entered, so estimating the additional transaction costs due to market impact is difficult.

While it may be difficult to estimate the true transaction cost, it is certain that costs will be incurred over time as the portfolio is rebalanced. In contrast, the benefits of rebalancing are less certain and, as we will see, depend on the subsequent market environment.

LOS 30.e: Contrast calendar rebalancing to percentage-of-portfolio rebalancing.

As its name implies, **calendar rebalancing** refers to rebalancing a portfolio to its strategic allocation on a predetermined, regular basis (e.g., monthly, quarterly, or annually). The primary *benefit* to calendar rebalancing is that it provides discipline without any requirement to monitor the portfolio allocation between rebalancing dates. A *drawback* of calendar rebalancing is that the portfolio allocation could differ significantly from its optimal weights between rebalancing dates. With calendar rebalancing, asset class returns do not enter into the rebalancing decisions. We might find that deviations from optimal weights are relatively small at the rebalancing date so that the costs of rebalancing are greater than the benefit. On the other hand, if there are significant deviations from optimal weights at the rebalancing date, the market impact of the rebalancing trades may be large, which will also reduce returns.

With **percentage-of-portfolio rebalancing** (PPR), also referred to as *percent range rebalancing* or *interval rebalancing*, rebalancing is triggered by changes in relative asset values rather than simply by the passage of time. For an asset class with an optimal target allocation, *T*, and a specified maximum percentage change in that allocation, *P*, a portfolio manager can set what are called *tolerance bands* or *corridors* for that asset class:

$$\text{corridor} = T \pm (P \times T)$$

©2016 Kaplan, Inc.

For example, assume the manager sets a 40% target allocation (T) for domestic equity and a 10% maximum percentage change (P). The resulting corridor for domestic equity is 40% ± 0.10(40%) = 40% ± 4%; that is, a corridor of 36% to 44% for the allocation to domestic equity. With corridor rebalancing, the portfolio allocation must be monitored over time and ideally this would be done daily. The value of P in the corridor calculation of 10% is an ad hoc value—we could just have easily used 5% to establish the corridor values.

LOS 30.f: Discuss the key determinants of the optimal corridor width of an asset class in a percentage-of-portfolio rebalancing program.

Using the same maximum percentage change for all asset classes ignores differences in transactions costs and other relevant factors. A value of 10%, for example, may be too high for very liquid assets and too low for illiquid assets.

In establishing the band for an asset class under a percentage-of-portfolio rebalancing program, evidence suggests that a manager should consider five factors.

1. Transactions costs.

   The higher the transactions costs (the lower the liquidity) for an asset class, the greater the deviation from its target allocation must be for the benefits to outweigh the costs; therefore, higher transactions costs will increase the optimal width of the corridor for that asset class.

2. Risk tolerance.

   The higher an investor's risk tolerance, the lower the impact on the investor of deviations from target allocation weights. This implies that greater risk tolerance leads to wider optimal corridors.

3. Correlation of returns with other asset classes.

   When asset class returns tend to move together, the impact of deviations from target allocations on portfolio risk are less. Higher correlations, therefore, suggest wider optimal corridors.

4. Volatility of asset class returns.

   Greater volatility of asset class returns make deviations from target weights potentially more costly and suggest narrower optimal corridor widths.

5. Volatility of the returns on the other assets in the portfolio.

   Greater volatility of the returns on the other assets in a portfolio (viewed as a single asset for simplicity) also suggests narrower optimal corridor widths because deviations from optimal weights can lead to even greater deviations when asset returns are highly volatile.

LOS 30.g: Compare the benefits of rebalancing an asset class to its target portfolio weight versus rebalancing the asset class to stay within its allowed range.

So far we have only considered the alternative of returning the portfolio asset allocations to their target values when rebalancing is indicated. Another alternative is to only rebalance to the extent necessary to move asset class weights back within their corridor values. One rule that would accomplish this is to move the asset class weights halfway back to their target values. Under this rule, an asset class with a target allocation of 30% and a corridor of +/– 3% that has reached a weight of 35% in the portfolio would be reduced to 32.5% of the portfolio. Clearly, if asset prices were trending higher, this smaller adjustment would improve portfolio returns compared to reducing the allocation to the target weight of 30%. If asset prices were volatile but not trending, reducing the asset class weight to its target of 30% could result in higher portfolio returns compared to a smaller reduction.

Studies that have compared these two rebalancing schemes are mixed in their results so that there is no clear answer to the question of which one produces better results. As we would expect, the relative performance of different rebalancing strategies depends on whether asset values are trending upward or downward or are volatile but do not exhibit longer term trends. We will compare rebalancing strategies under different market conditions in the next section.

LOS 30.h: Explain the performance consequences in up, down, and flat markets of 1) rebalancing to a constant mix of equities and bills, 2) buying and holding equities, and 3) constant proportion portfolio insurance (CPPI).

We can compare rebalancing strategies by their effects on portfolio performance in various market return scenarios. For simplicity we will consider a portfolio that contains only two assets, equities and cash (or bills with a 0% return), with target weights of 60% for equities and 40% for cash.

The three strategies we consider are:

Buy-and-hold: Once the initial allocation is made, no rebalancing is done. If equities increase in value the weight in equities increases, and if equities decrease in value the weight in equities decreases.

Constant mix: This is the strategy of rebalancing the portfolio to its target weights, either on a periodic basis or when asset class weights move from the selected weights.

Constant proportion portfolio insurance (CPPI): Under this strategy, target weight in equities varies directly with the difference between the portfolio value and some minimum value. The difference is called the cushion. As equities increase in value, the cushion increases, and the weight of equities in the portfolio is increased as a result.

©2016 Kaplan, Inc.

A decrease in equities values decreases the cushion, and the target weight in equities decreases as a result.

Under this strategy the amount invested in equities is given as:

target equities investment = M(portfolio value − floor value) = M(cushion)

Where M is the constant proportion of the cushion invested in equities. The M selected must be greater than 1.0 and does not change once selected, in order to produce CPPI strategy.

If M is set equal to 1.0 and the initial percentage allocation to cash (or bills) and equity is set in place so that the target equities investment = portfolio value − cash value, the result will be the buy-and-hold strategy.

If M is set less than 1.0 with a floor value at zero, so that target equities investment = M(portfolio value), the result will be the constant mix strategy and M is the target proportion for equities in the portfolio.

The relative performance results of these three strategies or rules will depend on the subsequent market environment.

Up or Down Trending Market:

- The CPPI will outperform. If the equity market increases in value, the weight in equities and the cushion increases. The increase in cushion under CPPI results in an additional purchase of equity so that subsequent increases in equity values have a greater positive impact on portfolio value. In a downward trending market the weight in equities and cushion decrease. The decrease in cushion requires selling equities so that subsequent decreases in equity values have a smaller negative impact on portfolio values. Notice that this produces a buy winners sell losers result.
- The buy and hold strategy will underperform CPPI because no purchases or sales of equity are made and there is no amplification of subsequent gain or reduction of subsequent loss as the market continues to trend.
- The constant mix strategy will have the worst performance in a trending market. An increase in equity values will increase the percentage allocation to equity and require selling equity to restore the initial percentage allocation. This lowers the exposure to subsequent equity increases in a trending market. In a downward equity market the percentage allocation to equity will fall and constant mix will dictate purchasing equity which will increase exposure to any further decline. Notice this produces a sell winners buy losers result.

Nontrending, Mean-Reverting Markets

- CPPI will have the worst performance. A rise in equity values will dictate buying more equity, which increases exposure to the subsequent reversal and downturn in equity prices. A fall in equity values will dictate a sale of equities, which will limit the recovery to the subsequent reversal and upturn in equity prices. Notice CPPI now produces a buy high sell low result.
- Buy and hold will produce a better result than CPPI because no purchases or sales are made.

- The constant mix strategy will have the best performance in a volatile, non-trending market. An increase in equity values will increase the percentage allocation to equity and require selling equity to restore the initial percentage allocation. This lowers the exposure to subsequent equity decline when the market mean reverts. In a downward equity market, the percentage allocation to equity will fall and constant mix will dictate purchasing equity which will increase exposure to the subsequent reversal when the market mean reverts and rises. Notice constant mix now produces a sell high buy low result.

Here, we consider the math and performance of the three strategies in various scenarios to support these conclusions. In all cases the initial portfolio value is 100 and the initial percentage in equity is 60%. The constant mix (CM) and buy-and hold (BH) portfolio strategies initially both allocate 60% to equities, and for the CPPI strategy the floor value is 50 and the multiplier is 1.2.

The initial allocations to equities are all equal with BH equity value = 60, CM equity value = $0.6 \times 100 = 60$, and the CPPI equity value = $1.2 (100 - 50) = 60$.

If in the first period equity value decreases to 50 all three portfolios have a value of $40 + 50 = 90$ and the portfolio values after rebalancing are:

BH = 50 equities, 40 cash = 90
CM = $0.6 \times 90 = 54$ equities, 36 cash = 90
CPPI = $1.2 (90 - 50) = 48$ equities, 42 cash = 90

If in the second period equity values decline further by 10% the portfolio values are as follows:

BH = $40 + 50(0.9) = 85$
CM = $36 + 54(0.9) = 84.6$
CPPI = $42 + 48(0.9) = 85.2$

When equities values are trending down, CPPI performs best, and BH outperforms CM.

If, instead, equity values increase by 20% in the second period the portfolio values are as follows:

BH = $40 + 1.2(50) = 100$
CM = $36 + 1.2(54) = 100.8$
CPPI = $42 + 1.2(48) = 99.6$

When equity value is oscillating with no trend, CM performs the best, and BH outperforms CPPI.

Finally, consider an increase in equity value from 60 to 70 in the first period so that all portfolio values increase to 110. After rebalancing, portfolio allocations are:

BH = 70 equity, 40 cash = 110
CM = $(0.6)110 = 66$ equity, 44 cash = 110
CPPI = $(1.2) (110 - 50) = 72$ equity, 38 cash = 110

If equity values increase again in the second period by 10%, portfolio values are:

BH = $40 + 1.1(70) = 117$
CM = $44 + 1.1 (66) = 116.6$
CPPI = $38 + 1.1(72) = 117.2$

©2016 Kaplan, Inc.

When equity values are trending up, CPPI performs best, and BH outperforms CM; overall, we can say that CPPI performs best (and CM worst) in trending markets and CM performs best (and CPPI worst) in oscillating (non-trending) markets.

LOS 30.i: Distinguish among linear, concave, and convex rebalancing strategies.

Here the terms *linear, concave,* and *convex* refer to the relationship between portfolio returns and equity returns. Recalling our simplifying assumption that the cash portion of the portfolio has a zero return, the buy-and-hold strategy results in portfolio returns that are linearly related to equity returns with a slope equal to the initial target equities allocation. With an equities allocation of 60%, a 5% increase in the value of equities will increase the portfolio value by $0.6 \times 5\% = 3\%$ and a 10% increase in the value of equities will increase the portfolio value by $0.6 \times 10\% = 6\%$. This is a linear relationship between equities value and portfolio value with a slope of 0.6 as shown in Figure 1.

Figure 1: Buy-and-Hold Strategy

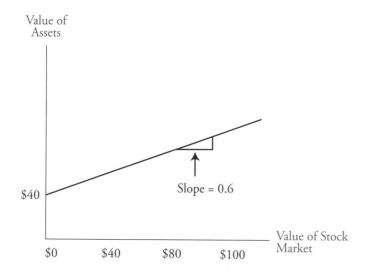

With a constant mix strategy, the reduction in the equity allocation as equity values increase reduces the increase in portfolio value compared to a buy-and-hold strategy and produces the concave relationship shown in Figure 2.

Figure 2: Constant-Mix Strategy

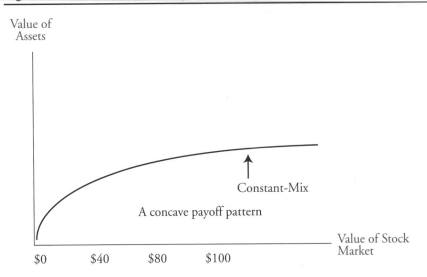

With a CPPI strategy, the equity allocation increases as equity values increase, magnifying the impact of further increases in equities values. This strategy produces the convex relationship shown in Figure 3.

Figure 3: CPPI Strategy

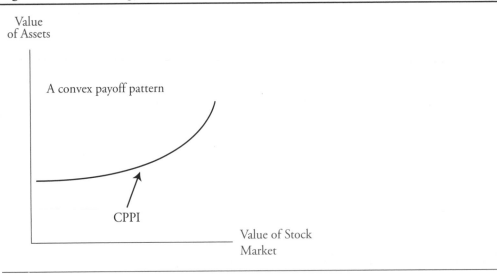

LOS 30.j: Judge the appropriateness of constant mix, buy-and-hold, and CPPI rebalancing strategies when given an investor's risk tolerance and asset return expectations.

With buy and hold, the percentage and monetary allocation to the risky asset increases with a rising market and wealth. It decreases with a falling market and wealth. The strategy is therefore appropriate for an investor whose risk tolerance increases and decreases with wealth. The risk tolerance is zero if the value of the market reaches zero as the investor is left with the initial amount allocated to the risk-free asset.

With constant mix, the percentage allocation to the risky asset is maintained at a fixed initial percentage through dynamic rebalancing. This is consistent with an investor whose risk tolerance is independent of the investor's level of wealth. However, the amount of money in the risky asset increases with a rising market and wealth but decreases with a falling market and wealth, so it can also be said the risk tolerance is proportionate with wealth.

 Professor's Note: Even though I understand what this is saying, I find the terminology awkward. Think of it as percentage allocation to risky is fixed and independent of wealth, but monetary allocation increases and decreases proportionate with wealth.

Constant portion strategies are so named because a constant portion (> 100%) of the cushion (portfolio value – floor value) is held in the risk asset. Both the percentage and monetary allocation to the risky asset increase and decrease more rapidly than for buy and hold (or CM). Because the cushion multiplier exceeds the 100% used for the buy-and-hold strategy, CPPI is considered suited to investors with higher risk tolerance. However, risk tolerance drops to zero if the cushion is lost.

The following paragraphs summarize the key characteristics of each of the three allocation strategies.

Buy-and-hold

A buy and hold strategy is static, with a floor value equaling the initial allocation to the risk-free asset. It fits investors whose risk tolerance increases and decreases with their level of wealth (but less rapidly than for CPPI). It is the most tax and transaction efficient. M is equal to one and produces a linear payoff pattern.

Constant mix

A constant mix strategy has no floor value. Portfolio value can reach 0 as the risky asset is continually purchased as it declines. It fits investors whose risk aversion increases and decreases proportionate with wealth (but maintains a constant percentage exposure to the risky asset). It performs best in volatile mean reverting markets and worst in trending markets. M is less than one and produces a concave payoff pattern.

CPPI

A constant proportion portfolio insurance strategy has a floor value that is reached dynamically and is higher than the initial allocation to risk-free. It fits investors who require a floor value and whose risk tolerance increases and decreases rapidly with their level of wealth. It performs best in trending markets and worst in volatile mean reverting markets. M is greater than one and produces a convex payoff pattern.

KEY CONCEPTS

LOS 30.a

The portfolio manager who is in a position of trust has a fiduciary duty to construct the portfolio to meet the needs of the client as specified in the IPS and the duty to monitor the portfolio to be sure it continues to meet the client's needs.

The initial construction of the portfolio is based on the client's circumstances and long-term capital market expectations at the time. The manager's duty is to continually monitor both the client's circumstances (objectives and constraints) and the market to identify changes in factors that could possibly require a change in the strategic allocation.

LOS 30.b

Monitoring investor circumstances: As the investor ages, objectives and constraints are subject to change. The investor's risk tolerance declines over time as liquidity needs increase. The implications are that the portfolio manager must monitor the client's circumstances and determine when to start shifting out of equities and real estate and into bonds and other less risky assets. Remember that changes in any one of the investor's objectives and/or constraints can potentially affect all of them.

Monitoring market/economic conditions: Because the performance of all assets is tied to the health of the overall economy, the portfolio manager must regularly monitor and reevaluate economic forecasts. Remember that long-term capital market expectations are incorporated into asset prices as well as the client's IPS and original asset allocation.

Monitoring the portfolio: The manager must regularly monitor the performance of the portfolio. The different asset allocations may grow at different rates, for example, and the allocation could change significantly. Also, the returns on the various classes might not be as expected, or the client's constraints could change such that the class is no longer appropriate for the portfolio.

LOS 30.c

- **Changes in wealth:** With an increase in wealth, the investor may become more or less tolerant of risk or experience absolutely no change in risk tolerance. The portfolio will experience an increased *ability* to tolerate risk.
- **Time horizon:** As the investor ages, financial capital increases while human capital decreases. As the investor's human capital dwindles, she may become less tolerant of risk.
- **Liquidity requirements:** As liquidity requirements increase, the ability of the portfolio to tolerate risk generally declines. If spending needs increase, the portfolio should be shifted into fixed-income securities, from both a cash flow and risk perspective.
- **Tax concerns:** The manager must always consider the tax implications of any investment and should always seek ways to minimize the tax liability.
- **Legal and regulatory:** An individual's portfolio is not subject to the legal and regulatory scrutiny of an institutional investor's portfolio. The primary concern for institutional investors is changes in laws and regulations.

LOS 30.d

Benefits of rebalancing: The primary benefit is maintaining the investor's desired exposure to systematic risk factors. If the portfolio is allowed to simply drift as it will, the riskier assets in the portfolio tend to take over. Rebalancing also provides discipline. Successful performance can make the client want to react to temporary market conditions rather than follow a long-term, disciplined approach.

Costs of rebalancing: When equities become too large a portion of the portfolio and we sell them to rebalance, there is an associated tax liability. Of course, these transactions are not costless, so the investor faces transactions costs. Primarily for institutional investors, the costs of rebalancing also include the market conditions under which the trade is made. If the manager is selling when other managers are selling (e.g., CPPI strategy), the trade *requires liquidity* and the transaction cost can be substantial. If the trade *provides liquidity* (e.g., constant-mix strategy), the transaction costs may be minimal.

LOS 30.e

Calendar rebalancing: As its name implies, calendar rebalancing is rebalancing the portfolio to its strategic allocation on a predetermined, regular basis. Generally, the frequency of rebalancing depends on the volatility of the portfolio, but sometimes rebalancing is scheduled to coincide with review dates. The primary benefit to calendar rebalancing is that it provides discipline without the requirement for constant monitoring. The drawback is that the portfolio could stray considerably between rebalancing dates.

Percentage-of-portfolio rebalancing (PPR): With PPR, rebalancing is triggered by changes in value rather than calendar dates. The manager sets what are called *tolerance bands* or *corridors* that are considered optimal for each asset class. By not waiting for specified rebalancing dates, PPR provides the benefit of minimizing the degree to which asset classes can violate their allocation corridors. The primary cost to PPR is associated with the need to constantly monitor the portfolio. This requires the time and expense of continually assessing the values of the asset classes and making necessary trades.

LOS 30.f

1. Transactions costs.

The higher the transactions costs (the lower the liquidity) for an asset class, the greater the deviation from its target allocation must be for the benefits to outweigh the costs; therefore, higher transactions costs will increase the optimal width of the corridor for that asset class.

2. Risk tolerance.

The higher an investor's risk tolerance, the lower the impact on the investor of deviations from target allocation weights. This implies that greater risk tolerance leads to wider optimal corridors.

3. Correlation of returns with other asset classes.

When asset class returns tend to move together, the impact of deviations from target allocations on portfolio risk are less. Higher correlations, therefore, suggest wider optimal corridors.

4. Volatility of asset class returns.

Greater volatility of asset class returns make deviations from target weights potentially more costly and suggest narrower optimal corridor widths.

5. Volatility of the returns on the other assets in the portfolio.

Greater volatility of the returns on the other assets in a portfolio (viewed as a single asset for simplicity) also suggests narrower optimal corridor widths because deviations from optimal weights can lead to even greater deviations when asset returns are highly volatile.

LOS 30.g

Rebalancing an allocation to its precise target weights requires more or less constant trading. With constant analysis and trading come the associated transactions costs and the inability to time trades. (Timing here refers to the ability to provide rather than require liquidity.)

Rather than set strict target allocations, managers will set allowable ranges that they consider optimal for the asset classes. Then, to provide discipline to portfolio rebalancing, managers can adopt either calendar rebalancing or percentage-of-portfolio balancing.

LOS 30.h

The buy-and-hold strategy is a do-nothing strategy. The constant-mix strategy requires constant rebalancing of the portfolio to the specified allocations, using corridors or calendar dates. In a constant-proportion portfolio insurance (CPPI) strategy, the allocation to equities is by formula.

Impact of Strategies on Risk and Return

	Buy-and-Hold	Constant-Mix	CPPI
Return	Outperforms a constant-mix strategy in a trending market; outperforms CPPI in a *flat* but *oscillating* market.	Outperforms a comparable buy-and-hold strategy, which, in turn, outperforms a CPPI strategy in a *flat* but *oscillating* market.	Outperforms a comparable buy-and-hold strategy, which, in turn, outperforms a constant-mix strategy in trending markets.
Risk	Passively assumes that risk tolerance is directly related to wealth.	Assumes that relative risk tolerance is constant because the proportion of equity in the portfolio is held constant regardless of the level of wealth. Constant-mix assumes increasing absolute risk tolerance because more equity is held as wealth increases.	Actively assumes that risk tolerance is directly related to wealth.

LOS 30.i
Buy-and-Hold (BH)
- Exposure diagram's slope is equal to one.
- Does not rebalance regardless of the portfolio wealth level.

Convex (CPPI) represents the purchase of portfolio insurance.
- Exposure diagram's slope is greater than one.
- Any procedure that buys when stocks rise or sells when stocks fall is a convex strategy.
- The more investors follow convex strategies, the more volatile the markets will become.

Concave (CM) represents the sale of portfolio insurance.
- Exposure diagram's slope is less than one.
- Any procedure that buys when stocks fall or sells when stocks rise is a concave strategy.
- If more investors follow concave strategies, the markets will become too stable.

LOS 30.j
Constant-Mix (CM)
- *Absolute* risk tolerance varies directly with wealth.
- *Relative* risk tolerance remains constant regardless of wealth level.
- Investors using this strategy will hold stocks at all levels of wealth.

Buy-and-Hold (BH)
- The investor's tolerance for risk is zero if the value of the investor's assets falls below the floor value.
- Otherwise, passively, risk tolerance increases proportionately with wealth.

Constant-Proportion Portfolio Insurance (CPPI)
- Investor risk tolerance is similar to that of the BH methodology.
- Investor risk tolerance drops to zero when total assets drop below the floor value.
- However, CPPI assumes that investor risk tolerance is more dramatically affected by changes in wealth levels than BH (e.g., as stocks increase, CPPI aggressively pursues more stocks; as stocks decrease, CPPI aggressively rids the portfolio of stocks).

CONCEPT CHECKERS

1. Suppose at time 0 you initially have $100 in stock and $35 in T-bills so that total assets are $135. Suppose also that the stock market index at time 0 was 124, and at time 1, it rose to 135. At time 2, the stock market had fallen back to 130. Assume that at time 0, you are at your optimal stock-to-total-assets ratio (S/TA). **Calculate** the following:

    i. Your optimal allocation to stock.

    ii. Your stock holdings at time 1 (under a buy-and-hold strategy).

    iii. Your stock holdings at time 2 (under a buy-and-hold strategy).

    iv. The amount of stock you should buy or sell at t = 1 (under a constant-mix strategy).

    v. The amount of stock you should buy or sell at t = 2 (under a constant-mix strategy).

2. **Identify** the relative investor risk tolerance characteristics of each of the following investing strategies:

    (1) Buy-and-hold.

    (2) Constant-mix.

    (3) Constant-proportion portfolio insurance (CPPI).

3. You expect the stock market to be relatively volatile over the next year. You also expect that the annual holding period return will be roughly zero. **Recommend** and **justify** a portfolio investment strategy given your forecast.

4. Jamie Gardner, CFA, makes the following statement at a conference of portfolio managers: "I believe that many managers rebalance before they should. If they were aware of the mathematics of rebalancing, they would rebalance less frequently." Assess the validity of Gardner's statement. Is she correct or incorrect? If correct, **provide** an example that supports her statement. If incorrect, **explain** why.

5.   For each of the following, **state** whether the optimal corridor width should be wide or narrow and **justify** your response with one reason.

High aversion to risk:

Illiquid assets:

High volatility:

6.   **List** and **describe** four factors that would result in a portfolio manager for an individual investor to reassess their client's portfolio.

7.   Based upon a recent analysis of his objectives and constraints in conjunction with capital market expectations, Brian Amallater's portfolio has the following strategic allocation:

Class	Currently
Cash and equivalents	5%
LT Treasury bonds	5%
Domestic corporate bonds	5%
Domestic equities	50%
International equities	20%
Real estate (raw land)	15%

Using only the current allocation, **estimate** Brian's age, wealth, and tolerance for risk and **discuss** factors that you considered.

8. While employed as a factory worker for 30 years, Millie D'Marco, who has never been married and has no dependents, accumulated a retirement portfolio that has grown to $55,000 and is currently invested in cash ($10,000 savings and checking) and bank CDs. Since retiring ten years ago, Millie has been receiving a $24,000 per year retirement annuity from her employer's defined benefit pension plan. She lives with her two dogs, Gregory and Douglas, and her cat, Timothy.

With no hobbies, few expenses, and no real cares in the world, Millie buys a $1 lottery ticket each week and has just won $1,000,000 (lump sum after taxes). Immediately upon hearing the news, Millie called her half-sister (Molly), who implored Millie to set aside funds to provide college educations for Molly's three grandchildren (currently 8, 9, and 11 years old). Millie states that she has no real need for the money and her pension meets all her current living expenses, so she plans to "travel until they plant me in the ground." She's not sure whether she will provide any money for Molly's grandchildren but states that "they can have what's left when I die."

Discuss each of the usual objectives and constraints associated with Millie's IPS.

For more questions related to this topic review, log in to your Schweser online account and launch SchweserPro™ QBank; and for video instruction covering each LOS in this topic review, log in to your Schweser online account and launch the OnDemand video lectures, if you have purchased these products.

ANSWERS – CONCEPT CHECKERS

1. i.   Time 0 is stated as the optimal allocation: 100 / 135 = 0.7407, or 74.1%

    ii. percent increase in market = (135 − 124) / 124 = 0.0887 or 8.87%

         s = $100 × 1.088 = $108.87

    iii. percent decrease in market = (130 − 135) / 135 = −0.037, or −3.7%

         s = $108.87 × (1 − 0.037) = $104.84

    iv. At time 1, the value of the portfolio has increased to 108.87 + 35 = 143.87. The stock is now worth 108.87 and is 108.87 / 143.87 = 75.67% of the portfolio.

         Under constant mix, the allocation should be 74.1%. This is a stock sale of (75.67% − 74.1%)(143.87) = 2.26.

    v.   Under constant mix the portfolio began period 2 with:

         stock = 108.87 − 2.26 = 106.61

         T-bill = 35 + 2.26 = 37.26

         During period 2, the stock decreased to 106.61(1 − 0.037) = 102.67 and the portfolio is worth 102.67 + 37.26 = 139.93. The stock is 102.67 / 139.93 = 73.37% of the portfolio. Under constant mix, it should be 74.1%. (74.1% − 73.37%)(139.93) = 1.02 stock to buy.

2. 1) *Buy-and-hold.* The investor's tolerance for risk is zero if the value of the investor's assets falls below the floor value (zero equity allocation) but increases as stocks increase in value.

    2) *Constant-mix.* Investors' relative risk tolerance remains constant regardless of their wealth level. They will hold stocks at all levels of wealth.

    3) *CPPI.* Investor risk tolerance is similar to that of the buy-and-hold methodology. Investor risk tolerance drops to zero when total assets drop below the floor value.

3. The constant-mix strategy will perform the best. Although the constant-mix strategy will underperform in steady bull or bear markets, constant-mix outperforms in an oscillating environment because you are always buying more shares whenever the market falls. Hence, each up movement will have a slightly higher level of capital gains.

4. Gardner is correct. An increase in the value of an individual asset class will result in an increase in the value of the total portfolio. For example, consider a $1,000 portfolio that consists of 50% equity and 50% debt, and the manager wants a 10% corridor. A 10% corridor would imply that equity and debt must stay within 50 ± 5%. If either debt or equity increased $30 (a 6% increase), its new allocation would be $530 / 1,030 = 51.5%, not 56%, so no rebalancing would be required. If assets are positively correlated, rebalancing is even less frequent, as stocks and bonds will grow together and proportions will be relatively stable.

    You might have argued that Gardner is incorrect if you assumed that the debt and equity portions of the portfolio are highly negatively correlated. In that case, the asset values would move opposite each other, increasing the need to rebalance.

5. High aversion to risk: narrow corridor width—investors have a high level of risk aversion meaning they have below-average risk tolerance and are averse to changes in the portfolio allocation and thus require more frequent rebalancing.

    Illiquid assets: wide corridor width—illiquid assets imply high transactions costs to buy and sell the assets; therefore, to minimize transaction costs, the corridor should be set wider, resulting in less rebalancing and reducing transaction costs.

    High volatility: narrow corridor width—assets that exhibit a lot of volatility should have a narrow corridor width to be able to detect when the asset is out of range and to quickly rebalance before the asset allocation gets farther out of the desired range.

6. Client circumstances may change for any one or more of the following reasons and force the client to rebalance her portfolio:
    *   *Change in wealth.* A change in wealth may cause an increase, decrease, or no change in the investor's willingness to tolerate risk. The manager must reevaluate the portfolio allocation, incorporating any changes in the investor's objectives or constraints. The manager must also be prepared for irrational behavior associated with newfound wealth.
    *   *Changing time horizons.* Usually, as the time horizon shortens, the investment mix becomes more conservative.
    *   *Changing liquidity requirements.* An increase in liquidity needs means higher allocations to cash and safer investments.
    *   *Tax circumstances.* An increase in wealth brings an increasing need for tax planning. Tax-exempt and tax-sheltered investments become relatively more attractive. Generally, during high-income years, the investor's portfolio should be allocated to low-income-generating investments, and in low-income years, to high-income-generating investments.
    *   *Laws and regulations.* Changes in laws and regulations are more of a concern for institutional investors than for individuals. Regulatory concerns become an issue if the individual wants to establish a trust, for example.
    *   *Unique circumstances/preferences.* A client's unique needs must be assessed on a continual basis, and appropriate changes must be made whenever these preferences change over time.

7. 70% is allocated to equities, including 20% to international equities.
    *   15% is allocated to raw land, which is considered both risky and illiquid.
    *   Only 5% is held in cash and 10% in LT bonds.

    Interpretation: The allocation of 85% of the portfolio to risky *financial capital* would imply the investor's *human capital* is rather high and the investor doesn't need liquidity in the portfolio. Remember that human capital can be thought of as *bond-like*, so the portfolio can be heavily (nearly 100%) allocated to equities and other risky assets with returns coming mostly in the form of capital gains.

    Brian is probably a young professional with a high-income potential, little need for current income, a long time horizon, the need to avoid taxable gains, and fairly low current wealth. Assuming Brian is a young professional, his tolerance for risk (both willingness and ability) is above average.

8. The facts of the mini-case are deliberately vague. For example, Millie has stated nothing about her willingness to tolerate risk, and we have no idea how much money she will spend annually on traveling. There are probably several scenarios you can think of that would require different portfolio allocations.

Before discussing the objectives and constraints, we should mention a few things about this case. First, the financial adviser must be prepared for just about anything (i.e., the concept of investing a lot of money is new to Millie, so the financial adviser must be prepared for irrational statements or spending desires). Millie doesn't seem to have any investing experience other than with the local bank.

Millie seems very "casual" and doesn't seem to plan for the future with regard to accumulating wealth (i.e., Millie seems to live for the day). This would probably indicate the need to educate Millie in all aspects of disciplined, rational investing with well-defined objectives and constraints.

Liquidity

A specific spending requirement is (the possibility of) providing for the children's educations, which will start in about ten years. In addition, because Millie has a modest retirement income, she will probably have to meet her travel expenses from the portfolio.

Legal and Regulatory

Millie might decide to establish trust funds for Molly's grandchildren. If she does, she should seek legal counsel. As compared to institutional investors, individuals don't typically have many legal or regulatory concerns.

Taxes

Millie, as a typical individual investor, is subject to taxes. We don't know the relevant tax rates, but the financial manager should always strive to optimize the tax treatment of portfolio income with respect to the client's needs.

Time Horizon

Because Millie retired ten years ago, she probably has a single-stage time horizon of about 10 to 15 years, which could be considered fairly long term. When she dies, her portfolio will continue, but that is more or less irrelevant for Millie's IPS, especially because she has no stated amount she wishes to leave to Molly's grandchildren.

Unique Circumstances

Unique needs are spending requirements outside the ordinary (e.g., large donations) or factors that affect the way the portfolio is to be allocated. Unique needs can be a problem for financial advisers because they frequently pertain to disallowed investments, without regard for the potential portfolio benefits. For example, the individual may prohibit investments in companies doing business with certain countries or instruct the manager to avoid certain classes of investments. Millie has stated nothing out of the ordinary, so we wouldn't list any unique circumstances. However, the portfolio manager must always honor the client's unique needs.

Risk

Willingness: Because all her money is in bank deposits and CDs, one interpretation is that Millie has no idea of the risks associated with investing in capital markets. Alternatively, she may have made a conscious decision to stay out of securities markets because she perceives them as too risky. We really don't know which. If she had made specific statements regarding risk, we would have been able to asses her willingness to tolerate risk.

Relevant statements might be obvious, such as, "I can't stand the thought of losing money." They might also be vague: "I'm not real sure about investing in the stock market." In either case, however, the investor would probably be perceived as having below-average willingness to tolerate risk.

In Millie's case, we will assume below-average willingness due to her highly concentrated investments in cash. Playing the lottery, due to the very small amount gambled, does not by itself imply she has above-average or even average willingness.

Ability: Because her pension meets her living expenses and the travel expenses might be construed as a desired rather than required spending need, the portfolio can probably tolerate above-average risk.

Overall: You should never indicate an overall tolerance for risk that exceeds the investor's willingness. You can sometimes recommend more risk than desired if the investor has well-above-average ability to tolerate risk due to significant wealth and low spending needs.

Recommendation: Below-average risk tolerance.

Return

Once we determine the future, after-tax amount necessary to provide for the grandchildren's educations in "today's" dollars and the after-tax nominal annual travel expenses, we can solve for the after-tax required return using a financial calculator:

FV	= – college expenses (fixed, after-tax amount in "today's" dollars)
PMT	= – travel expenses (assumed constant nominal, after-tax)
PV	= \$1,000,000
N	= 10
CPT → I/Y	= after-tax real return in "today's" dollars

We then add inflation to arrive at the after-tax, nominal required return. Expenses are already expressed in nominal terms, so we do not have to adjust them for inflation. The inflation adjustment is necessary to protect the real value of the portfolio.

EVALUATING PORTFOLIO PERFORMANCE[1]

Study Session 17

EXAM FOCUS

Performance evaluation is important to both managers and clients. Both want to understand the sources of value added and lost. The calculations can be long, repetitive, and use extensive subscript notation; begin by understanding the intent of the calculations and then practice making them. There is an equal chance the questions will focus on understanding the output of performance evaluation as on making calculations. Also be aware there are differences of opinion on the best way to perform such analysis. The CFA material is presenting possible approaches. For the exam, do it the way it is presented in the material.

PERFORMANCE EVALUATION

LOS 31.a: Demonstrate the importance of performance evaluation from the perspective of fund sponsors and the perspective of investment managers.

Professor's Note: In a large portfolio with multiple managers there are typically decisions made by the fund sponsor as well as decisions made by the individual managers within the fund that affect portfolio performance. Performance evaluation can deconstruct return to show which decisions made by whom add or subtract value in the fund. The fund sponsor perspective will capture all value added or lost while the manager perspective will focus only on what a particular manager did to add or lose value for the fund. This material presupposes a fund sponsor is an entity like a pension fund, endowment, or foundations using several investment managers.

Fund sponsor's perspective. Performance evaluation improves the effectiveness of a fund's investment policy by acting as a feedback and control mechanism. It does the following:

1. Shows where the policy and allocation is effective and where it isn't.

2. Directs management to areas of value added and lost.

3. Quantifies the results of active management and other policy decisions.

---

1. The terminology utilized in this topic review follows industry convention as presented in Reading 31 of the 2017 Level III CFA curriculum.

4. Indicates where other, additional strategies can be successfully applied.

5. Provides feedback on the consistent application of the policies set forth in the IPS.

The increased complexity of institutional investment management has led to a greater need for sophisticated performance evaluation from the fund sponsor's perspective.

Investment manager's perspective. As with the fund sponsor's perspective, performance evaluation can serve as a feedback and control mechanism. Some investment managers may simply compare their reported investment returns to a designated benchmark. Others will want to investigate the effectiveness of each component of their investment process.

Components of Performance Evaluation

LOS 31.b: Explain the following components of portfolio evaluation: performance measurement, performance attribution, and performance appraisal.

Performance evaluation will involve:

1. *Performance measurement* to calculate rates of return based on changes in the account's value over specified time periods.

2. *Performance attribution* to determine the sources of the account's performance.

3. *Performance appraisal* to draw conclusions regarding whether the performance was affected primarily by investment decisions, by the overall market, or by chance.

Return Calculations With External Cash Flows

Professor's Note: External cash flows are funds the client adds or withdraws from the portfolio. They must be removed from the change in market value of the portfolio to determine the remaining change in value that is due to investment performance. They must also be considered to determine how much money was available for use. Conceptually, the percentage return is the investment gain or loss divided by the weighted average of the funds available to use.

The rate of return on an account is the percentage change in the account's market value over a defined time period (known as the measurement or evaluation period). An account's rate of return needs to factor in external cash flows. External cash flows refer to contributions and withdrawals made to and/or from an account, as opposed to internal cash flows, such as interest or dividends.

If there is an external cash flow at the *beginning* of the evaluation period, the account's return is calculated as follows:

$$r_t = \frac{MV_1 - (MV_0 + CF)}{MV_0 + CF}$$

If there is an external cash flow at the *end* of the evaluation period, it should be subtracted from (if a withdrawal, added to) the account's ending value, as it has no impact on the investment-related value of the account:

$$r_t = \frac{(MV_1 - CF) - MV_0}{MV_0}$$

Example: Rate of return calculation

The Keane account was valued at $12,000,000 at start of the month (before any contributions). At the month end, its value was $12,260,000. During the month, the account received a contribution of $40,000.

Calculate the rate of return if the contribution was received (1) on the first day of the month and (2) on the last day of the month.

Answer:

If the contribution was received on the *first day of the month*, the rate of return for the month would be:

$$r_t = \frac{\$12,260,000 - (\$12,000,000 + \$40,000)}{(\$12,000,000 + \$40,000)} = 0.018272 = 1.8272\%$$

If the $40,000 contribution was received on the *last day of the month*, the rate of return would be:

$$r_t = \frac{(\$12,260,000 - \$40,000) - \$12,000,000}{\$12,000,000} = 0.018333 = 1.8333\%$$

Note: A contribution on the last day of the month has no impact on the investment-related value of the account. This is because the contribution is deducted before calculating the return.

When the external cash flows do not occur at the beginning or end of the period, other approaches are required.

CALCULATING TIME- AND MONEY-WEIGHTED RETURNS

LOS 31.c: Calculate, interpret, and contrast time-weighted and money-weighted rates of return and discuss how each is affected by cash contributions and withdrawals.

For the Exam: These calculations are also covered in GIPS.

Time-Weighted Rate of Return

The **time-weighted rate of return** (TWRR) calculates the compounded rate of growth over a stated evaluation period of one unit of money initially invested in the account. It requires a set of subperiod returns to be calculated covering each period that has an external cash flow. This approach requires a fund market value on the date of each external cash flow. The subperiod results are then compounded together. The resulting TWRR is unaffected by the external cash flows.

Example: Time-weighted rate of return

The Rooney account was $2,500,000 at the start of the month and $2,700,000 at the end. During the month, there was a cash inflow of $45,000 on day 7 and $25,000 on day 19. The values of the Rooney account are $2,555,000 and $2,575,000 (inclusive of the cash flows for the day) on day 7 and day 19, respectively. **Calculate** the time-weighted rate of return (assuming 30 days in the month).

Answer:

First, calculate three subperiod returns using the rate of return calculation when external cash flows occur at the end of the evaluation period:

Subperiod 1 (days 1–7)

$$r_{t,1} = \frac{\left[(\$2,555,000 - \$45,000) - \$2,500,000\right]}{\$2,500,000} = 0.004 = 0.4\%$$

Subperiod 2 (days 8–19)

$$r_{t,2} = \frac{\left[(\$2,575,000 - \$25,000) - \$2,555,000\right]}{\$2,555,000} = -0.002 = -0.2\%$$

Subperiod 3 (days 20–30)

$$r_{t,3} = \frac{(\$2,700,000 - \$2,575,000)}{\$2,575,000} = 0.049 = 4.9\%$$

Second, compound the returns together (chain-link) to calculate an overall time-weighted rate of return:

$$TWRR = (1 + 0.004)(1 - 0.002)(1 + 0.049) - 1 = 0.051 = 5.1\%$$

Money-Weighted Rate of Return

The **money-weighted rate of return** (MWRR) is an internal rate of return (IRR) on all funds invested during the evaluation period, including the beginning value of the portfolio. In equation form, the periodic MWRR is the rate, R, that solves:

$$MV_1 = MV_0(1 + R)^m + \sum_{i=1}^{n} CF_i(1 + R)^{L(i)}$$

where:
MV_1 = ending value of the portfolio
MV_0 = beginning value of the portfolio
m = number of time units in the evaluation period (e.g., number of days in the month)
CF_i = cash flow i
$L(i)$ = number of time units (days, etc.) cash inflow i is in the portfolio or cash outflow i is absent from the portfolio

For the Exam: Solving any IRR equation (including MWRR) is a trial and error process of guessing a return and solving for ending value until a return is guessed that produces a result equal to the actual ending value of the portfolio. The CFA text states that solving MWRR is better suited to spreadsheet software.

You may recall from other levels that if the subperiods are of equal length, your calculator can perform the trial and error analysis. This will not work in the example that follows shortly or in the example in the CFA text because the subperiods vary in length. There is a trick that will allow the calculator to solve the problem, but it is cumbersome and easy to get wrong. Enter a cash flow for every single day in the total analysis period. Most of those days will be 0 cash flow, and each day must be entered. The solution will be a daily IRR that is compounded for the requested solution. For example, if the daily IRR is 0.2%, the monthly IRR is $(1.002)^{30} - 1$, assuming the month is 30 days. This is a lot of work, and you are off track from the primary issues being discussed.

TWRR vs. MWRR

MWRR is an average growth rate of all funds in the account. It is affected by both the returns generated on the assets and the timing of external cash flows. For example, if the assets first appreciate significantly and then depreciate significantly and a large external cash flow is made, the timing of the external cash flow will significantly affect the MWRR. If a large external cash flow is received at the very beginning of the period it is exposed to the increase and decrease in asset values. If it occurs after the appreciation period but before the decline, the MWRR will be lower because relatively more funds were exposed to the decline than to the increase. In contrast, TWRR is only a linking of subperiod returns and is not affected by external cash flows.

- Generally, TWRR is used for manager evaluation and GIPS® reporting because it reflects only the return of the assets and not client decisions to add or subtract funds.
- A special case can exist if the manager controls the timing of fund additions and withdrawals. This can happen with some portfolios, such as hedge funds and other limited partnership investments. If the manager controls the timing of cash flows, MWRR is appropriate for performance reporting and GIPS®.
- TWRR reflects what would have happened to the beginning value if no external cash flows had occurred.
- TWRR calculations can be data intensive and expensive to perform because they require a portfolio market value on the date of all external cash flows.
- MWRR only requires a beginning and end of period market value.

A Bank Administration Institute (BAI)[2] study recommends that TWRR can be approximated by calculating the MWRR over frequent time intervals and then chain-linking those returns over the evaluation period. The BAI study concluded that only if there are large (> 10% of the account's value) external cash flows or volatile performance swings will this linked internal rate of return (LIRR) fail to provide a close approximation to the true TWRR.

The Effect of External Contributions and Withdrawals

If the external cash flows are large relative to the account's value, and the account's performance is quite volatile, there can be a significant difference between the TWRR and MWRR.

---

2. See *http://www.bai.org/research/* for more on BAI research. Accessed May 2016.

Example: TWRR vs. MWRR

The Neville account is valued at $400,000 at the beginning of the month. On day 8, it is valued at $1,300,000 after receiving a $900,000 contribution on that day. At the end of the month, the account is valued at $2,695,398. The TWRR is:

Subperiod 1 (days 1–8)

$$r_{t,1} = \frac{\left[(\$1,300,000 - \$900,000) - \$400,000\right]}{\$400,000} = 0.0 = 0\%$$

Subperiod 2 (days 9–30)

$$r_{t,2} = \frac{\left[\$2,695,398 - \$1,300,000\right]}{\$1,300,000} = 1.0734 = 107.34\%$$

Compounding the returns produces a time-weighted rate of return:

$$\text{TWRR} = (1 + 0)(1 + 1.0734) - 1 = 2.0734 - 1 = 1.0734 = 107.34\%$$

The MWR is:

$$\$2,695,398 = \$400,000(1 + R)^{30} + \$900,000(1 + R)^{22}$$

By trial and error, R = 0.03. Converting to a monthly basis:

$$\text{MWRR} = 1.030^{30} - 1 = 1.427 = 142.7\%$$

Explain why based on the specific circumstances in the Neville account, the MWRR is much higher than the TWRR.

Answer:

The first subperiod had a 0.0% return and the second subperiod had a 107.34% return. The client added funds right before the second subperiod so more funds where in the account during the subperiod of high return. MWRR weights returns by the amount of funds invested; more funds in the high return subperiod produce a higher MWRR than TWRR. TWRR is unaffected by external cash flows.

DATA QUALITY

LOS 31.d: Identify and explain potential data quality issues as they relate to calculating rates of return.

The phrase "garbage in, garbage out" is quite appropriate for return calculations. That is, the calculated return is only as accurate as the inputs. The following are potential problems relating to data quality:

- When accounts contain illiquid (infrequently priced) assets, estimates or educated guesses must sometimes be used to calculate returns.
- For many thinly-traded fixed-income securities, current market prices may not be available. Estimated prices may be derived from dealer quoted prices on securities with similar attributes. This is known as **matrix pricing**.
- Highly illiquid securities may be carried at cost or the price of the last trade, thus, not reflecting the current price.
- Account valuations should include trade date accounting, including accrued interest and dividends.

PORTFOLIO RETURN COMPONENTS

LOS 31.e: Demonstrate the decomposition of portfolio returns into components attributable to the market, to style, and to active management.

 Professor's Note: The three components of return (market, style, and active management) are the foundation for portfolio performance attribution. This approach decomposes portfolio return into overall market return, the style of the manager, and active management decisions the manager makes.

A portfolio return can be broken up into three components: market, style, and active management.

$$P = M + S + A$$

where:
P = investment manager's portfolio return
M = return on the market index
S = B – M = excess return to style; difference between the manager's style index (benchmark) return and the market return. S can be positive or negative.
A = P – B = active return; difference between the manager's overall portfolio return and the style benchmark return.

This relationship recognizes first that the manager's style benchmark can earn more or less than the market. Had the manager taken a passive position in a broad market index, the return on that index, *M*, would be an appropriate benchmark, and S = 0. Because the manager might specialize in a particular style, however, we add (if B > M, S > 0) or subtract (if B < M, S < 0) the difference between the benchmark and market returns. Finally, the return to active management, A, is the difference between the manager's portfolio return and the benchmark return and is attributed to active management.

Example: Portfolio return components

The Pallister account has a total monthly return of 5.04%. During the same period, the portfolio benchmark returned 5.32% and the market index returned 3.92%. **Calculate the amount of the portfolio return attributable to the manager's active management and style.**

Answer:

The return to active management is the difference between the portfolio return, P, and the manager's style benchmark, B:

$$A = P - B = 5.04\% - 5.32\% = -0.28\%$$

The return to style is the difference between the manager's style benchmark, B, and the market, M:

$$S = B - M = 5.32\% - 3.92\% = 1.4\%$$

BENCHMARK PROPERTIES

LOS 31.f: Discuss the properties of a valid performance benchmark and explain advantages and disadvantages of alternative types of benchmarks.

To effectively evaluate performance, a valid benchmark should possess the following seven characteristics, which should align the benchmark's style and risk with that of the manager and provide the manager with an appropriate management objective:

1. *Specified in advance.* The benchmark is known to both the investment manager and the fund sponsor. It is specified at the start of an evaluation period.

2. *Appropriate.* The benchmark is consistent with the manager's investment approach and style.

3. *Measurable.* Its value and return can be determined on a reasonably frequent basis.

4. *Unambiguous.* Clearly defined identities and weights of securities constituting the benchmark.

5. *Reflective of the manager's current investment opinions.* The manager has current knowledge and expertise of the securities within the benchmark.

6. *Accountable.* The manager(s) should accept the applicability of the benchmark and agree to accept differences in performance between the portfolio and benchmark as caused only by his active management.

7. *Investable.* It is possible to replicate the benchmark and forgo active management.

Advantages and Disadvantages of Benchmarks

The seven primary types of benchmarks in use are:

1. **Absolute.** An absolute benchmark is a return objective (i.e., aims to exceed a minimum target return).

   Advantage:

   - Simple and straightforward benchmark.

   Disadvantage:

   - An absolute return objective is not an investable alternative.

2. **Manager universes.** The median manager or fund from a broad universe of managers or funds is used as the benchmark. The *median manager* is the fund that falls at the middle when funds are ranked from highest to lowest by performance.

   Advantage:

   - It is measurable.

   Disadvantages:

   - Manager universes are subject to "survivor bias," as underperforming managers often go out of business and their performance results are then removed from the universe history.
   - Fund sponsors who choose to employ manager universes have to rely on the compiler's representations that the universe has been accurately compiled.
   - Cannot be identified or specified in advance so it is not investable.

3. **Broad market indices.** There are several well-known broad market indices that are used as benchmarks [e.g., the S&P 500 for U.S. common stocks, the Morgan Stanley Capital International (MSCI) and Europe, Australasia and Far East (EAFE) for non-U.S. developed market common stocks, and so on.].

   Advantages:

   - Well recognized, easy to understand, and widely available.
   - Unambiguous, generally investable, measurable, and may be specified in advance.
   - It is appropriate to use if it reflects the approach of the manager.

   Disadvantage:

   - The manager's style may deviate from the style reflected in the index. For example, it is not appropriate to use the S&P 500 for a small-capitalization U.S. growth stock manager.

©2016 Kaplan, Inc.

4. **Style indices.** Investment style indices represent specific portions of an asset category. Four well-known U.S. common stock style indices are (1) large-capitalization growth, (2) large-capitalization value, (3) small-capitalization growth, and (4) small-capitalization value.

    Advantage:

    - Widely available, widely understood, and widely accepted.
    - If the index reflects the manager's style and it is investable, it is an appropriate benchmark.

    Disadvantages:

    - Some style indices can contain weightings in certain securities and sectors that may be larger than considered prudent.
    - Differing definitions of investment style can produce quite different benchmark returns.
    - In these cases they are not appropriate benchmarks.

5. **Factor-model-based.** Factor models involve relating a specified set of factor exposures to the returns on an account. A well-known 1-factor model is the market model where the return on a portfolio is expressed as a linear function of the return on a market index. A generalized factor model equation would be:

    $$R_P = a_p + b_1 F_1 + b_2 F_2 + \ldots + b_K F_K + \varepsilon$$

    where:
    R_P = periodic return on an account
    a_p = "zero factor" term, representing the expected value of R_p if all factor values were zero
    F_i = factors that have a systematic effect on the portfolio's performance, i = 1 to K
    b_i = sensitivity of the returns on the account to the returns generated from factor *i*
    ε = error term; portfolio return not explained by the factor model

    Some examples of factors are the market index, industry, growth characteristics, a company's size, and financial strength.

    The benchmark portfolio (i.e., the *normal portfolio*) is the portfolio with exposures to the systematic risk factors that are typical for the investment manager. The manager's past portfolios are used as a guide.

    Advantage:

    - Useful in performance evaluation.
    - Provides managers and sponsors with insight into the manager's style by capturing factor exposures that affect an account's performance.

    Disadvantages:

    - Focusing on factor exposures is not intuitive to all managers or sponsors.
    - The data and modeling are not always available and may be expensive.
    - It may be ambiguous because different factor models can produce different output.

6. **Returns-based.** Returns-based benchmarks are constructed using (1) the managed account returns over specified periods and (2) corresponding returns on several *style indices* for the same periods.

   These return series are submitted to an allocation algorithm that solves for the combination of investment style indices that most closely tracks the account's returns.

   Advantages:

   - Generally easy to use and intuitive.
   - Meets the criteria of a valid benchmark.
   - Useful where the only information available is account returns.

   Disadvantages:

   - The style indices may not reflect what the manager owns or what the manager or client would be willing to own.
   - A sufficient number of monthly returns would be needed to establish a statistically reliable pattern of style exposures.
   - Will not work when applied to managers who change style.

7. **Custom security-based.** Custom security-based benchmarks are designed to reflect the manager's security allocations and investment process. (See the following LOS for further discussion.)

   Advantages:

   - Meets all of the required benchmark properties and all of the benchmark validity criteria.
   - Allows continual monitoring of investment processes.
   - Allows fund sponsors to effectively allocate risk across investment management teams.

   Disadvantages:

   - Can be expensive to construct and maintain.
   - A lack of transparency by the manager (e.g., hedge funds) can make it impossible to construct such a benchmark.

CONSTRUCTING CUSTOM SECURITY-BASED BENCHMARKS

LOS 31.g: Explain the steps involved in constructing a custom security-based benchmark.

The construction of a custom security-based benchmark entails the following steps:

Step 1: Identify the important elements of the manager's investment process.
Step 2: Select securities that are consistent with that process.
Step 3: Weight the securities (including cash) to reflect the manager's process.
Step 4: Review and adjust as needed to replicate the manager's process and results.
Step 5: Rebalance the custom benchmark on a predetermined schedule.

VALIDITY OF USING MANAGER UNIVERSES AS BENCHMARKS

LOS 31.h: Discuss the validity of using manager universes as benchmarks.

Fund sponsors often use the median account in a particular "universe" of account returns as a benchmark. However, even though finishing in the top half of all managers with the same style might be a good performance objective, this form of benchmark has a number of drawbacks:

1. Apart from being measurable, it fails the other properties of a valid benchmark:
   - It is not possible to identify the median manager in *advance*.
   - Because the median manager cannot be determined ahead of time, the measure also fails the *unambiguous* property.
   - The benchmark is not *investable*, as the median account will differ from one evaluation period to another.
   - It is impossible to verify the benchmark's *appropriateness* due to the ambiguity of the median manager.

2. Fund sponsors who choose to employ manager universes have to rely on the compiler's representations that the accounts within the universe have been appropriately screened, input data validated, and calculation methodology approved.

3. As fund sponsors will terminate underperforming managers, universes will be subject to "survivor bias." As consistently underperforming accounts will not survive, the median will be biased upwards. Without a valid reference point, evaluating manager performance using this benchmark becomes suspect.

TESTS OF BENCHMARK QUALITY

LOS 31.i: Evaluate benchmark quality by applying tests of quality to a variety of possible benchmarks.

An important part of performance evaluation and risk management, it is essential to distinguish good benchmarks from bad ones. Some issues to consider in benchmark evaluation are:

- **Systematic bias.** There should be minimal systematic bias in the benchmark relative to the account. To assess the relationship between returns on the benchmark and the account, the manager can calculate the *historical beta* of the account relative to the benchmark (i.e., regress the portfolio returns on the benchmark returns). A beta near 1.0 would indicate that the benchmark and portfolio tend to move together (i.e., they are sensitive to the same systematic factors). If the beta differs significantly from 1.0, the benchmark may be responding to different factors and thus have a different set of risk factor exposures.

Another method to identify systematic bias is looking at *correlations*. Consider the relationships seen earlier:

$$A = P - B$$

$$S = B - M$$

where:
A = excess return attributable to the management's active management decisions
P = investment manager's portfolio return
B = benchmark return
S = excess return attributable to the manager's investment style

Returns to the manager's active decision making (*A*) should be *uncorrelated* with the manager's investment style (*S*). That is, whether the style benchmark performs well should have no effect on the manager's ability to generate active return, *A*.

An interesting multiple correlation is that between the style benchmark return (*B*), the return on the market (*M*), and the return on the portfolio (*P*). Specifically, if the style benchmark outperforms the market (i.e., B > M), we would expect to see the manager's portfolio outperform the market (i.e., P > M). Accordingly, there should be a strong positive relationship between (B – M) and (P – M).

- **Tracking error.** Tracking error is defined as the volatility (standard deviation) of *A*, the excess return earned due to active management (i.e., P – B). If the appropriate benchmark has been selected, the standard deviation of the difference between the returns on the portfolio and the benchmark (the tracking error) will be smaller than that of the difference between the portfolio and a market index. This would indicate that the benchmark is capturing important elements of the manager's investment style. Further differences between the portfolio and benchmark returns can be attributed primarily to active management.
- **Risk characteristics.** An account's exposure to systematic sources of risk should be very similar to those of the benchmark; that is, the systematic risk may be higher or lower during individual periods but should average that of the benchmark over time. If the account tends to consistently exhibit more or less risk than the benchmark, this would indicate a systematic bias.
- **Coverage.** Benchmark coverage is defined as the percentage of a portfolio that is made up of securities that are also in the benchmark. The *coverage ratio* is the market value of the securities that are in both the portfolio and the benchmark as a percentage of the total market value of the portfolio. The higher the coverage ratio, the more closely the manager is replicating the benchmark (i.e., the more the benchmark reflects the manager's universe).
- **Turnover.** Benchmark turnover is the proportion of the benchmark's total market value that is bought or sold (i.e., turned over) during periodic rebalancing. Passively managed portfolios should utilize benchmarks with low turnover.
- **Positive active positions.** An active position is the difference between the weight of a security or sector in the managed portfolio versus the benchmark. For example, if the account has 5% in Vodafone and the benchmark has 3%, the active position is 5% – 3% = 2%.

If the benchmark includes many securities for which the manager has no opinions and does not own, the number of negative active positions will be large. If the portion of negative positions is large, it may indicate the benchmark does not reflect the manager's process and is not appropriate for the manager.

HEDGE FUND BENCHMARKS

LOS 31.j: Discuss issues that arise when assigning benchmarks to hedge funds.

 Professor's Note: This section is qualitative in nature even when presenting formulas. No calculations are shown or covered. The issue is the difficulty of identifying suitable benchmarks.

The diversity and lack of transparency of hedge funds makes benchmark identification difficult or impossible.

1. The difficulties start with calculating the return of a hedge fund. Most hedge funds hold long and short positions and some hedge funds have minimal or theoretically zero capital in relation to the total of long and short positions. Trying to apply the basic accounting rate of return calculation when V_0 is very small or theoretically zero can produce results that are difficult to interpret.

$$r = \frac{V_1 - V_0}{V_0}$$

2. One approach is to evaluate performance in terms of value-added return:

$$R_V = R_P - R_B$$

   where:
   R_V = value-added return
   R_P = portfolio return
   R_B = benchmark return

To replicate a zero net asset hedge fund, R_V is the value-added return on a long-short portfolio. Although the weights can sum to zero, a return can be calculated by summing up the returns on all the individual security positions, long and short. Even this seemingly simple process is complicated, however, as active managers trade frequently, resulting in changing asset positions.

The calculations associated with determining the manager's value-added return (not required by the LOS) must distinguish between the return earned by simply holding an asset and the value-added return due to over- (under-) weighting the asset relative to the benchmark. Recall that, for a long-only manager, overweighting a security relative to the benchmark results in a positive *active weight*. For hedge fund managers, determining a value-added return is, of course, complicated by the manager's ability to sell short. In addition, the extremely wide range of funds that fall under the hedge fund classification makes it difficult, if not impossible, to define a benchmark that is applicable to all hedge funds.

3. Some hedge funds target an absolute return target and argue comparison benchmarks are irrelevant.

4. Other funds may have clearly defined styles (such as long-short equity) and it may be possible to compare results of the manager to other managers of the same style. But other funds have no definable style on which to base a comparison.

5. The difficulty of defining benchmarks has led others to use the Sharpe ratio as the basis of comparing hedge fund managers. The same difficulties in identifying comparable managers with which to compare still arise. In addition, the use of standard deviation is questionable when many hedge funds show skewed returns.

MACRO AND MICRO PERFORMANCE ATTRIBUTION

LOS 31.k: Distinguish between macro and micro performance attribution and discuss the inputs typically required for each.

LOS 31.l: Demonstrate and contrast the use of macro and micro performance attribution methodologies to identify the sources of investment performance.

The second phase of performance evaluation is performance attribution. The basic concept is to identify and quantify the sources of returns that are different from the designated benchmark. There are two basic forms of performance attribution: micro and macro attribution. **Macro performance attribution** is done at the fund sponsor level. The approach can be carried out in percentage terms (i.e., rate-of-return) and/or in monetary terms (i.e., dollar values). **Micro performance attribution** is done at the investment manager level.

Professor's Note: Essentially, the goal of macro attribution is to gain insight into the decisions made by the sponsor and measure the effect of those decisions on the portfolio. One of those sponsor decisions is which managers to hire and how those managers perform. The goal of micro attribution is to analyze an individual manager's decisions and determine how that manager added or lost value for the sponsor. The CFA text focuses on the concept and use of macro analysis. For micro attribution the attention is more evenly divided between concept, use, and calculations. All of this is prime test material.

Macro Performance Attribution

There are three main inputs into the **macro attribution** approach: (1) policy allocations; (2) benchmark portfolio returns; and (3) fund returns, valuations, and external cash flows.

1. **Policy allocations.** It is up to the sponsor to determine asset categories and weights as well as allocate the total fund among asset managers. As in any IPS development, allocations will be determined by the sponsor's risk tolerance, long-term expectations, and the liabilities (spending needs) the fund must meet.

2. **Benchmark portfolio returns.** A fund sponsor may use broad market indices as the benchmarks for asset categories and use narrowly focused indices for managers' investment styles.

3. **Fund returns, valuations, and external cash flows.** When using percentage terms, returns are calculated at the individual manager level. This enables the fund sponsor to make decisions regarding manager selection.

   If also using monetary terms, account valuation and external cash flow data are needed to compute the value impacts of the fund sponsor's investment policy decision making.

Conducting a Macro Attribution Analysis

Macro attribution starts with the fund's beginning market value and ends with its ending market value. In between are six levels of analysis that attribute the change in market value to sources of increase or decrease in market value. The levels are:

1. Net contributions.

2. Risk-free asset.

3. Asset categories.

4. Benchmarks.

5. Investment managers.

6. Allocation effects.

Level 1, **net contributions,** is the net sum of external cash flows made by the client into or withdrawn from the portfolio. Net contributions increase or decrease ending market value but are not investment value added or lost.

Level 2, **risk-free investment,** simulates what the fund's ending value would have been if the beginning value and external cash flows had earned the risk-free return.

Level 3, **asset categories,** recognizes that most sponsors will consider risk-free investments as too conservative. It simulates the ending value of beginning value and external cash flows if funds had been invested in asset category benchmarks weighted in accord with the fund's strategic policy (in other words, passively replicating the strategic asset allocation with index funds).

The incremental return to the asset category level is the weighted average of the categories' returns over the risk-free asset. Level 3's incremental return could be calculated as:

$$R_{AC} = \sum_{i=1}^{A}(w_i)(R_i - R_F)$$

where:

R_{AC} = incremental return (above the risk-free rate) for the asset category strategy

$(R_i - R_F)$ = excess return (above the risk-free rate) for asset category i

w_i = weight of asset category i

A = number of asset categories

Up to this point, all results could have been achieved by passively implementing the fund's strategic asset allocation.

Level 4, the **benchmark level**, allows the sponsor to select and assign managers a benchmark different from the policy benchmark. This is tactical asset allocation by the sponsor. For example, 60% in the S&P 500 might fit the fund's strategic objective but the sponsor may expect value stocks to outperform the S&P. The sponsor could direct the manager to use the S&P value index as that manager's target or *manager benchmark*. Level 4 simulates the return of the beginning market value and external cash flows if invested in manager benchmarks. The Level 4 result can also be passively achieved but reflects active decision making by the sponsor to deviate from strategic benchmarks. The level 4 incremental return could be calculated as:

$$R_B = \sum_{i=1}^{A}\sum_{j=1}^{M}(w_i)(w_{i,j})(R_{B,i,j} - R_i)$$

where:

R_B = incremental return for the benchmark strategy

w_i = policy weight of asset category i

$w_{i,j}$ = weight assigned to manager j in asset category i

$R_{B,i,j}$ = return for manager j's benchmark in category i

R_i = return on asset category i

A = number of asset categories

M = number of managers in asset category i

The formula allows for more than one portfolio manager in each asset category. If we assumed only one manager per category, the formula would simplify to:

$$R_B = \sum_{i=1}^{A}(w_i)(R_{B,i} - R_i)$$

Level 5, **investment managers** or **active management**, simulates the results of investing the fund's beginning value and external cash flows and earning the returns actually produced by the managers. The simulation assumes the sponsor has actually allocated funds in accord with the policy allocations, an assumption that is usually not perfectly implemented. The level 5 incremental return could be calculated as:

$$R_{IM} = \sum_{i=1}^{A} \sum_{j=1}^{M} \left(w_i\right)\left(w_{i,j}\right)\left(R_{A,i,j} - R_{B,i,j}\right)$$

where:
R_{IM} = incremental return for the investment manager level
w_i = policy weight of asset category i
$w_{i,}$ = weight assigned to manager j in asset category i
$R_{A,i,j}$ = return for manager j's portfolio in category i
$R_{B,i,j}$ = return for jth manager's benchmark for asset category i
A = number of asset categories
M = number of managers in asset category i

Level 6, **allocation effects**, is simply a residual plug to sum to the portfolio ending value. If all policies were perfectly implemented, the allocation effect would be zero.

> *Professor's Note: You will find many attribution models include a residual "plug." It should not be surprising that complex calculations designed to analyze events will not always add up perfectly. As a rough analogy you could think of residual error in quantitative modeling. You will find that one of the reasons that multiple approaches to attribution are discussed is that a given approach may be more suited to a given situation. In general, if an approach to a specific situation has a large residual plug, it would be wise to consider if another approach yields better results or if the calculations are just wrong.*

Figure 1: Macro Attribution Analysis, Brice Pension Fund, September 2014

Decision-Making Level	Fund Value	Incremental % Return Contribution	Incremental Value Contribution
Beginning value	$447,406,572	—	—
Net contributions	449,686,572	0.00%	$2,280,000
Risk-free asset	451,067,710	0.30%	1,381,138
Asset category	466,122,089	3.33%	15,054,379
Benchmarks	467,329,262	0.28%	1,207,173
Investment managers	467,390,654	0.02%	61,392
Allocation effects	467,559,838	0.03%	169,184
Ending value	$467,559,838	3.96%	$20,153,266

1. **Net contributions.**

   Net contributions during September were a positive $2,280,000. Net contributions added to the starting value equals a value of $449,686,572.

2. **Risk-free asset.**

If the fund's starting value and its net external cash inflows are invested at the risk-free rate the fund value would have increased by 0.30%, an incremental increase of $1,381,138 above the value from the net contributions level, giving a total fund value of $451,067,710.

Professor's Note: The increment of $1,381,138 cannot be replicated by multiplying $449,686,572 by 0.30%, as the net $2,280,000 contribution was not a single start of the month cash flow. The composition of the net contribution is also unknown. There could have been a large contribution on day 1 and an almost equally large withdrawal just before month end.

The formulas from the previous pages are used to calculate the asset, benchmark, and manager effects.

3. **Asset category.**

This asset category level assumes that the fund's net contributions value is invested based on the fund sponsor's policy allocations to the specified asset category benchmarks. This is a pure index fund approach reflecting SAA. The policy allocations lead to a 3.33% increase above the risk-free rate, increasing the value of the fund by $15,054,379.

4. **Benchmarks.**

The benchmarks level assumes that the beginning value and external cash flows of the fund are passively invested in the aggregate of the managers' respective benchmarks. This is also a pure index fund approach but reflecting the sponsor's TAA decisions. The aggregate manager benchmark return was 0.28%, producing an incremental gain of $1,207,173. The difference between the manager benchmarks and the asset category benchmarks (aggregated) is also known as the "misfit return" or "style bias." For the Brice fund, the misfit return was 0.28%.

5. **Investment managers (value of active management).**

The investment managers level assumes that the beginning value and external cash flows of the fund invested are the actual results of the managers. This is not an index approach but still reflects sponsor decision making as the sponsor selects the managers. This incremental return reflects the value added by the managers. The aggregate actual return of the managers (using policy weights) exceeded the return on the aggregate manager investment style benchmark by 0.02%. In monetary terms, it has added $61,392.

6. **Allocation effects.**

This is a balancing "plug" figure. It is the difference between the fund's ending value and the value from the investment managers level. This is created if fund sponsors deviate slightly from their policy allocations. It was an incremental increase of $169,184 or +0.03%.

MICRO PERFORMANCE ATTRIBUTION

Micro performance attribution analyzes individual portfolios relative to designated benchmarks. The value-added return (portfolio return minus benchmark return) can be broken into three components: (1) pure sector allocation, (2) allocation/selection interaction, and (3) within-sector selection.

$$R_V = \underbrace{\sum_{j=1}^{S}\left(w_{P,j} - w_{B,j}\right)\left(R_{B,j} - R_B\right)}_{\text{pure sector allocation}} + \underbrace{\sum_{j=1}^{S}\left(w_{P,j} - w_{B,j}\right)\left(R_{P,j} - R_{B,j}\right)}_{\text{allocation/selection interaction}}$$

$$+ \underbrace{\sum_{j=1}^{S} w_{B,j}\left(R_{P,j} - R_{B,j}\right)}_{\text{within-sector selection}}$$

where:
R_V = value-added return
$w_{P,j}$ = portfolio weight of sector j
$w_{B,j}$ = benchmark weight of sector j
$R_{P,j}$ = portfolio return of sector j
$R_{B,j}$ = benchmark return of sector j
R_B = return on the portfolio's benchmark
S = number of sectors

> **For the Exam:** Spend the time to understand the micro attribution calculations and get past the notation; the concepts of the calculations are rather intuitive. The CFA text spends considerable time on both concept and calculation for micro attribution. Be ready for both conceptual, interpretation, and calculation questions.
>
> Pure sector allocation looks at whether the manager over- or underweighted a market sector that over- or underperformed the total return of the benchmark. It ignores the return of the stocks the manager selected so it purely captures the ability of the manager to emphasize outperforming sectors and avoid underperforming sectors.
>
> Within-sector selection does the opposite. It uses benchmark weights, so it ignores the manager's sector weighting decisions and only focuses on the manager's performance within a sector versus that of the benchmark within that sector. Essentially it measures the manager's stock picking skill.
>
> Adding the previous two components will not total to the portfolio incremental return in most situations. A joint allocation/selection interaction is needed that sums over-/ underweighting and stock selection.
>
> Joint effects are common in many models that break down return. They are mathematically necessary.

1. **Pure sector allocation.**

    Pure sector allocation assumes the manager holds the same sectors as in the benchmark and that within each sector the same securities are held in the same proportion as in the benchmark. The performance is attributed to the manager's decisions to hold each sector in a different weight in his portfolio relative to the weight of that sector in the benchmark.

> **Example: Pure sector allocation**
>
> One of the investment managers of the Giggs fund has the following results of a micro attribution analysis:
>
> Figure 2: Sector Weighting/Stock Selection Micro Attribution
>
> | Economic Sectors | Portfolio Sector Weight (%) | Benchmark Sector Weight (%) | Portfolio Sector Return (%) | Benchmark Sector Return (%) |
> |---|---|---|---|---|
> | Agriculture | 6.77 | 6.45 | −0.82 | −0.73 |
> | Capital goods | 8.52 | 8.99 | −3.28 | −4.34 |
> | Consumer durables | 36.22 | 37.36 | 1.96 | 1.98 |
> | Energy | 5.24 | 4.65 | 0.44 | 0.24 |
> | Financial | 18.53 | 16.56 | 2.98 | 2.22 |
> | Technology | 14.46 | 18.87 | 2.32 | −0.48 |
> | Utilities | 9.22 | 7.12 | 0.54 | −0.42 |
> | Cash and equivalents | 1.04 | 0.00 | 0.17 | — |
> | Portfolio + cash | 100.00 | 100.00 | 1.34 | 0.56 |
>
> Using data from Figure 2, **calculate** the performance impact due to the financial sector allocation.
>
> **Answer:**
>
> $$\begin{aligned} R_{FS\ Allocation} &= \left(w_{P,FS} - w_{B,FS}\right)\left(R_{B,FS} - R_B\right) \\ &= (0.1853 - 0.1656)(0.0222 - 0.0056) \\ &= (0.0197)(0.0166) = 0.000327 = 0.0327\% \end{aligned}$$

This example shows that the decision to overweight a sector that outperformed the overall benchmark resulted in a positive contribution to portfolio performance. Note that *underweighting* the sector would have produced a negative contribution.

The manager's goal should be for the two terms in the equation to have the same signs, either both positive or both negative:

- Overweight (+) an outperforming (+) sector → positive impact.
- Underweight (−) an underperforming (−) sector → positive impact.
- Underweight (−) an outperforming (+) sector → negative impact.
- Overweight (+) an underperforming (−) sector → negative impact.

2. **Within-sector selection return.**

   This calculates the impact on performance attributed only to security selection decisions. The within-sector selection return is assuming that the manager weights each sector in the portfolio in the same proportion as in the overall benchmark.

Example: Within-sector selection return

Using Figure 2 from the previous example, **calculate** the utilities within-sector allocation return.

Answer:

$$\text{utilities within-sector allocation return} = w_{B,utilities}(R_{P,utilities} - R_{B,utilities})$$

$$= 0.0712 \times [0.54\% - (-0.42\%)]$$

$$= +0.068\%$$

The positive contribution shows that the portfolio held utilities stocks that performed better than the utilities stocks contained in the sector benchmark.

---

3. **Allocation/selection interaction return.**

   This return involves the joint effect of assigning weights to both sectors and individual securities. A decision to increase the allocation of a particular security will also increase the weighting of the sector to which the security belongs.

Example: Allocation/selection interaction return

Using Figure 2 from the pure sector allocation example, **calculate** the allocation/selection interaction return for consumer durables.

Answer:

consumer durables allocation/selection interaction return

$$= (w_{P,durables} - w_{B,durables})(R_{P,durables} - R_{B,durables})$$

$$= [(0.3622 - 0.3736)(0.0196 - 0.0198)]$$

$$= (-0.0114)(-0.0002)$$

$$= 0.00000228 = 0.000228\%$$

Generally speaking, the allocation/selection interaction impact tends to be relatively small if the benchmark is appropriate. Thus, some analysts group the impact with the within-sector selection impact.

FUNDAMENTAL FACTOR MODEL MICRO ATTRIBUTION

LOS 31.m: Discuss the use of fundamental factor models in micro performance attribution.

It should be possible to construct multifactor models to conduct micro attribution. This involves combining economic sector factors with other fundamental factors (e.g., a company's size, its growth characteristics, its financial strength, etc.).

Constructing a suitable factor model involves the following:

- Identify the fundamental factors that will generate systematic returns.
- Determine the exposures of the portfolio and the benchmark to the fundamental factors at the start of the evaluation period. The benchmark could be the risk exposures of a style or custom index or a set of *normal* factor exposures that are typical of the manager's portfolio.
- Determine the manager's *active exposure* to each factor. The manager's active exposures are the difference between his *normal* exposures as demonstrated in the benchmark and his actual exposures.
- Determine the *active impact*. This is the added return due to the manager's active exposures.

The results of the fundamental factor micro attribution will indicate the source of portfolio returns, based on actual factor exposures versus the manager's normal factor exposures (e.g., sector rotation), the manager's ability to time the market (e.g., adjust the portfolio beta and/or duration in response to market expectations), and so on.

The results will look very similar to a *returns-based style analysis*, where the returns to the portfolio are regressed against the returns to several different indices to determine factor exposures. The primary difference between them is the use of other fundamental factors (e.g., management's use of leverage, market timing, sector rotation, and the size of the firm,) that would not ordinarily be used in a returns-based style analysis.

The strengths and limitations of the micro and fundamental factor model attributions are summarized in Figure 3.

Figure 3: Strengths and Limitations of Micro Attribution and Fundamental Factor Model Attribution

	Micro Attribution	*Fundamental Factor Model Attribution*
Strengths	Disaggregates performance effects of managers' decisions between sectors and securities. Relatively easy to calculate.	Identifies factors other than just security selection or sector allocation.
Limitations	The need to identify an appropriate benchmark with specified securities and weights at the start of the evaluation period. Security selection decisions will affect sector weighting (allocation/selection interaction).	Exposures to the factors need to be determined at the start of the evaluation period. Can prove to be quite complex, leading to potential spurious correlations.

FIXED-INCOME ATTRIBUTION: INTEREST RATE EFFECTS AND MANAGEMENT EFFECTS

LOS 31.n: Evaluate the effects of the external interest rate environment and active management on fixed-income portfolio returns.

LOS 31.o: Explain the management factors that contribute to a fixed-income portfolio's total return and interpret the results of a fixed-income performance attribution analysis.

For the Exam: LOS 31.n and LOS 31.o refer to evaluate, explain, and interpret. Past test questions on fixed income attribution models have followed the LOS and CFA text. Computers are used to simulate returns for the portfolio and break out components of return. The simulation mathematics are not covered. Focus on a conceptual understanding of each component and realize that these must sum up to the actual portfolio return as you will see in the example below. Questions may come down to nothing more than solving for the missing number, explaining one of the return components, or interpreting the relative performance of two or more fixed-income managers.

Attribution analysis of a fixed-income portfolio is different than that of equity. Duration and interest rates are typically the dominant factor in return. Therefore, the attribution focuses on simulations of what the *external interest rate environment* would have been expected to produce and the *manager's contribution.*

Changes in the external interest rate environment, consisting of shifts and twists in the Treasury yield curve, are beyond the individual manager's control and should neither penalize nor benefit the manager's evaluation. Therefore, the attribution begins with simulating what the portfolio would have done based on these external changes. The external interest rate effect is based on a term structure analysis of default-free securities (Treasury securities in the United States). The external interest rate effect can be subdivided into two components:

- First, a simulation of what the manager's benchmark would have returned if interest rates had moved in the manner of the forward curve. For example, if part of the benchmark is invested in 5 year securities yielding 4% and the 1-month forward rate for 4 year and 11 month securities is 4.1%, the expected return is calculated assuming rates do move to 4.1%. This must be done for all securities in the benchmark and aggregated. It is the **expected interest rate effect**. Notice it does not consider any actions of the manager or what actually happened to rates.
- Second, the benchmark return is simulated based on what actually happened to interest rates. The difference in simulated benchmark returns is due to changes in forward rates (i.e., change not in accord with starting forward rates). It is the **unexpected interest rate effect**. It still does not consider any actions of the manager.

The sum of these two effects is the **external interest rate effect** and is the return of a default-free benchmark return. The portfolio could have passively earned this return.

The next four simulations capture value added or lost versus the index by the actions of the manager.

- **Interest rate management effect** measures the manager's ability to anticipate changes in interest rates and adjust the portfolio duration and convexity accordingly. Each portfolio asset is priced as if it were a default-free bond (i.e., price each using Treasury forward rates). This is compared to another simulation, still using Treasury interest rates but including changes the manager made to duration and positioning on the yield curve. The difference is the interest rate management effect because it captures the consequences of the manager's changes to duration and curve positioning if only Treasury securities were used. It can be further subdivided into duration, convexity, and yield-curve shape effects if desired.
- **Sector/quality management effect** considers what happened to the yield spreads on the actual sectors and quality of assets held in the portfolio. For example, if the manager holds corporate bonds and corporate spreads narrow, the portfolio will outperform the previous Treasury-only simulation. These increments of value added or lost versus the previous Treasury-only simulation are aggregated for all non-Treasury sectors the manager holds to produce the sector/quality management effect. This effect does not look at the actual securities the manager used.
- **Security-selection effect** examines the actual securities selected by the manager. For example, if corporate bond spreads narrowed 20 basis points and the corporate bonds held by the manager narrowed more, the manager's selection effect is positive for corporate bonds. It is calculated as the total return of each security less all the previous components. It is analogous to security selection in equity attribution. The aggregate of all the individual security selection effects is the manager's security selection effect.

- **Trading effect** is a plug figure. The trading effect assumes any additional unexplained component of the portfolio return is due to the manager's trading activities. It is calculated as the total portfolio return less the other effects: the external interest rate effect, the interest rate management effect, the sector/quality management effect, and the security selection effect.

Example: Management factors

The table below outlines the performance attribution analysis for two fixed-income managers of the Helix fund for the year ended December 31, 2014:

Performance Attribution Analysis

	Alpha Asset Management	Beta Asset Management	Bond Portfolio Benchmark
1. Interest rate effect			
i. Expected	0.56	0.56	0.56
ii. Unexpected	0.66	0.66	0.66
Subtotal	1.22	1.22	1.22
2. Interest rate management effect			
iii. Duration	0.18	−0.17	0.00
iv. Convexity	−0.07	−0.07	0.00
v. Yield-curve change	0.10	0.18	0.00
Subtotal	0.21	−0.06	0.00
3. Other management effects			
vi. Sector	−0.08	1.17	0.00
vii. Bond selection	0.16	−0.13	0.00
viii. Transaction costs	0.00	0.00	0.00
Subtotal	0.08	1.04	0.00
4. Trading activity return	0.09	0.10	0.00
5. Total return	1.60	2.30	1.22

Alpha Asset Management states that its investment strategy is to outperform the index through active interest rate management and bond selection.

Beta Asset Management states its investment strategy is to immunize against interest rate exposure and to yield positive contribution through bond selection.

Assess whether both managers' positive performances were primarily through their stated objectives.

Answer:

Alpha's active management process yielded 38 basis points overall (subtotals of 2, 3, and 4). Twenty-one basis points were due to Alpha's interest rate management process (subtotal 2). Sixteen basis points were due to bond selection (category vii).

Thus, a substantial proportion of Alpha's positive contribution of 38 basis points came from its stated strategies of interest rate management and bond selection.

Although Beta has remained fairly neutral to interest rate exposure (–6 basis points), its main positive contribution has come from identifying undervalued sectors (117 basis points from category vi) rather than bond selection (–13 basis points from category vii).

Thus, the analysis seems to contradict Beta's stated aim of enhancing portfolio returns through bond selection.

RISK-ADJUSTED PERFORMANCE MEASURES

LOS 31.p: Calculate, interpret, and contrast alternative risk-adjusted performance measures, including (in their *ex post* forms) alpha, information ratio, Treynor measure, Sharpe ratio, and M^2.

The final stage of the performance evaluation process is performance *appraisal*. Performance appraisal is designed to assess whether the investment results are more likely due to skill or luck. Should we hire or fire the manager? **Risk-adjusted performance measures** are one set of tools to use in answering such questions. Each of the following is **ex post**, meaning the actual return of the portfolio or manager is used to assess how well the manager did on a risk-adjusted basis. Five commonly used measures are:

1. Alpha (also known as Jensen's ex post alpha or ex post alpha).

2. The information ratio (IR).

3. The Treynor measure.

4. The Sharpe ratio.

5. M^2 (Modigliani and Modigliani).

1. **Ex post alpha.**

   Alpha is the difference between the actual return and the return required to compensate for systematic risk. Alpha uses the ex post security market line (SML) as a benchmark to appraise performance. Positive alpha suggests superior performance but the sponsor may also be concerned with the variability of alpha over time.

©2016 Kaplan, Inc.

On an ex ante basis, the SML and CAPM project return to be:

$$\hat{R}_A = R_F + \beta_A \left(\hat{R}_M - R_F \right)$$

where:

$\hat{R}_A$ = expected return on the account (portfolio)
R_F = risk-free rate of return
$\hat{R}_M$ = expected return on the market
β_A = account's beta (systematic risk)

Using data on *actual returns* (i.e., historical rather than expected returns), a simple linear regression is used to calculate ex post alpha:

$$\alpha_A = R_{At} - \hat{R}_A$$

where:

α_A = ex post alpha on the account
R_{At} = actual return on the account in period *t*
$\hat{R}_A = R_F + \beta_A \left(\hat{R}_M - R_F \right)$ = predicted account return

> *Professor's Note: This may look mysterious but a Level III candidate will have done this a dozen times in the course of Levels I and II. Calculate the expected return of a portfolio given its beta, the market return, and the risk-free rate over a past period. Subtract the result from the actual return of the portfolio. The difference is alpha. Also remember that graphically, positive alpha means the portfolio plots above the SML and negative alpha plots below.*

2. **The Treynor measure.**

The Treynor measure is related to alpha by using beta, a systematic measure of risk. Visually, a portfolio or manager with positive alpha will plot above the SML. If a line is drawn from the risk-free return on the vertical axis through the portfolio, Treynor is the slope of that line. That means a portfolio with positive alpha will have a Treynor measure that is greater than the Treynor of the market. A portfolio with negative alpha will have a Treynor that is less than the Treynor of the market.

$$T_A = \frac{\overline{R}_A - \overline{R}_F}{\beta_A}$$

where:

$\overline{R}_A$ = average account return
$\overline{R}_F$ = average risk-free return
β_A = account beta

3. **The Sharpe ratio.**

While the previous two ratios only consider systematic risk, Sharpe uses total risk (standard deviation). Sharpe would be plotted against the CML, which also assesses risk as standard deviation. The Sharp ratio of the market is the slope of the CML. For any portfolio the line between the risk-free rate and the intersection of that portfolio's return and standard deviation is its CAL and the slope of that portfolio's CAL is its Sharpe ratio. A superior manager will have a higher Sharpe than the market and a steeper CAL than the CML.

Sharpe is similar to the Treynor measure in using excess return but the Sharpe ratio uses standard deviation for risk and Treynor uses beta.

$$S_A = \frac{\bar{R}_A - \bar{R}_F}{\sigma_A}$$

where:
$\bar{R}_A$ = average account return
$\bar{R}_F$ = average risk-free return
σ_A = standard deviation of account returns

4. **The M^2 measure** (from Modigliani and Modigliani).

M^2 also uses standard deviation as risk in the denominator and excess return in the numerator, which makes it very similar to Sharpe. M^2 measures the value added or lost relative to the market if the portfolio had the same risk (standard deviation) as the market. It measures the result of a hypothetical portfolio that uses leverage to increase risk and return if the portfolio has less risk than the market or lends at the risk-free rate to lower risk and return if the portfolio has more risk than the market:

$$M_P^2 = \bar{R}_F + \left(\frac{\bar{R}_P - \bar{R}_F}{\sigma_P} \right) \sigma_M$$

where:
$\bar{R}_P$ = average portfolio (account) return
$\bar{R}_F$ = average risk-free return
σ_P = standard deviation of portfolio (account) returns
σ_M = standard deviation of the market index

5. **The information ratio.**

The **information ratio** (IR) is quite similar to the Sharpe ratio in that excess return is measured against variability. For the IR, the excess return is the portfolio return less the return of an appropriate benchmark (rather than the risk-free rate). This excess return is also called **active return**. The denominator of the IR is the standard deviation of the excess return in the numerator (also called **active risk**).

$$IR_A = \frac{\text{active return}}{\text{active risk}} = \frac{\bar{R}_A - \bar{R}_B}{\sigma_{A-B}}$$

where:
$\bar{R}_A$ = average account return
$\bar{R}_B$ = average benchmark return
σ_{A-B} = standard deviation of excess returns measured as the difference between account and benchmark returns

Professor's Note: The Sharpe ratio and the IR are even more similar than they appear. Both use a form of excess return for the numerator, which is apparent from the formulas. Less obvious is that both use the standard deviation of their numerator for their denominator.

The Sharpe ratio uses the standard deviation of the portfolio in the denominator. However, because the standard deviation of the risk-free asset in a single period is zero with a zero correlation to the portfolio return, the standard deviation of the portfolio is equal to the standard deviation of excess return used in the numerator of the Sharpe ratio.

Example: Risk-adjusted performance appraisal measures

The data in the table below has been collected to appraise the performance of four asset management firms:

Performance Appraisal Data

	Fund 1	Fund 2	Fund 3	Fund 4	Market Index
Return	6.45%	8.96%	9.44%	5.82%	7.60%
Beta	0.88	1.02	1.36	0.80	1.00
Standard deviation	2.74%	4.54%	3.72%	2.64%	2.80%

The risk-free rate of return for the relevant period was 3%. **Calculate** and **rank** the funds using ex post alpha, Treynor measure, Sharpe ratio, and M^2.

Answer:

Evaluation Tool	Fund 1	Fund 2	Fund 3	Fund 4
Alpha	6.45 – 7.05 = **–0.60%**	8.96 – 7.69 = **1.27**	9.44 – 9.26 = **0.18**	5.82 – 6.68 = **–0.86**
Rank	**3**	**1**	**2**	**4**
Treynor	(6.45 – 3) / 0.88 = **3.92**	(8.96 – 3) / 1.02 = **5.84**	(9.44 – 3) / 1.36 = **4.74**	(5.82 – 3) / 0.80 = **3.53**
Rank	**3**	**1**	**2**	**4**
Sharpe	(6.45 – 3) / 2.74 = **1.26**	(8.96 – 3) / 4.54 = **1.31**	(9.44 – 3) / 3.72 = **1.73**	(5.82 – 3) / 2.64 = **1.07**
Rank	**3**	**2**	**1**	**4**
M^2	3 + (1.26 × 2.8) = **6.53%**	3 + (1.31 × 2.8) = **6.67%**	3 + (1.73 × 2.8) = **7.84%**	3 + (1.07 × 2.8) = **6.00%**
Rank	**3**	**2**	**1**	**4**

Note that the alpha and Treynor measures give the same rankings, and the Sharpe and M^2 measures give the same rankings. However, when comparing the alpha/Treynor rankings to the Sharpe/M^2 measures, funds 2 and 3 trade places.

Fund 2 has a much higher total risk (standard deviation) than Fund 3 but has a much lower beta. Relatively speaking, for Fund 2's total risk, a smaller proportion relates to systematic risk that is reflected in the low beta. Compared to Fund 3, it must have a bigger proportion of risk relating to non-systematic risk factors.

Hence, Fund 2 does better in the alpha and Treynor measures, as they only look at systematic risk (beta). It fairs less well when it comes to the Sharpe and M^2 measures that consider total risk.

Summary Points

Figure 4: Risk-Adjusted Measures

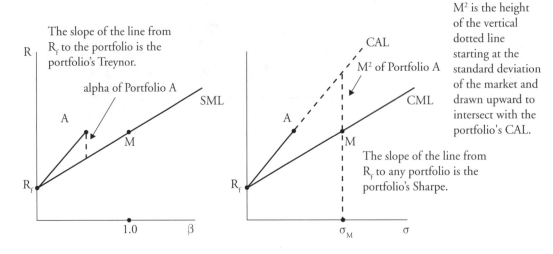

- Alpha and Treynor both measure risk as systematic risk (beta). They will agree in that a manager with positive alpha will have a Treynor in excess of the market Treynor. They may not always agree in relative ranking. A manager with the highest alpha may not have the highest Treynor.
- Superior (inferior) Sharpe will mean superior (inferior) M^2. Both measure risk as total risk (standard deviation).
- Both Alpha and Treynor are criticized because they depend on beta and assumptions of the CAPM. The criticisms include (1) the assumption of a single priced risk rather than some form of multifactor risk pricing and (2) the use of a market proxy, such as the S&P 500, to stand for the market. Roll's critique shows that small changes in what is assumed to be the market can significantly change the alpha and Treynor calculations and even reverse the conclusions of superior or inferior performance and rankings.
- Measures like M^2 that use a benchmark are also subject to the criticism the benchmark used may not be precisely replicable. M^2 uses the standard deviation of the market. As a related issue, transaction cost to replicate the market or a custom benchmark are not considered.
- Any ex post calculation is a sample of true results and actual results can be different in the future. Even if results do reflect true manager skill, the manager can change approach or style in the future.
- Alpha, Treynor, and Sharpe are the more widely used measures.
- Also remember from Levels I and II that the highest relative return measure does not necessarily mean the highest return. For example, a very low risk portfolio with low beta or standard deviation could have a higher alpha and Sharpe but a very risky portfolio with lower alpha and Sharpe can still have the higher absolute return.

LOS 31.q: Explain how a portfolio's alpha and beta are incorporated into the information ratio, Treynor measure, and Sharpe ratio.

Treynor is based on the portfolio's beta as the measure of risk. In other words, it considers only market-related (beta) risk. If the Treynor ratio is higher/lower than the market's Treynor, portfolio alpha will be positive/negative.

In contrast, the Sharpe ratio uses the portfolio's standard deviation. Portfolio standard deviation (total risk) includes both beta (market-related variability of return) risk and alpha (active management-related variability of return) risk.

The information ratio is similar to Sharpe in comparing excess return to standard deviation, but Sharpe defines excess return in relation to the risk-free rate and compares that excess to total risk, which includes both market volatility (beta) and any volatility added by active management (alpha). In contrast, the IR defines excess return versus a suitable benchmark. This benchmark reflects the suitable level of market risk for the investor. The risk measure in IR is the variability (standard deviation) of the value added only. Thus, IR is only reflecting the alpha-related risk.

QUALITY CONTROL CHARTS

LOS 31.r: Demonstrate the use of performance quality control charts in performance appraisal.

One way of evaluating performance results is through quality control charts. To construct a chart, three important assumptions are made about the distribution of the manager's value-added returns (i.e., the difference between the portfolio and benchmark returns):

1. The null hypothesis states the expected value-added return is zero.

2. Value-added returns are independent and normally distributed.

3. The investment process is consistent, producing more or less constant variability of the value-added returns (i.e., the distribution of the value-added returns about their mean is constant).

You will notice that these are assumptions we make in regression analysis. From these assumptions, a quality control chart is constructed, as in Figure 5.

Figure 5: Example Quality Control Chart

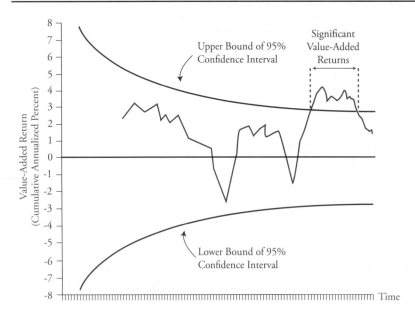

The manager's cumulative value-added return is plotted on the vertical axis, and time is plotted on the horizontal axis. You will notice that the center of the vertical axis is at zero, the event where the portfolio and benchmark returns are equal, so the value-added return is zero. The solid, horizontal line originating at zero can be thought of as the benchmark return, and any portfolio returns plotting off the horizontal line would represent those occasions when the portfolio and benchmark returns are not equal.

Management can plot the manager's cumulative value-added returns on the chart to determine whether they are randomly generated (happen by chance) or are derived through superior management. If deviations from the benchmark return are purely random, they should be distributed more or less randomly around the solid horizontal line (i.e., there will be no tendency for them to be positive or negative). If they tend to be consistently above or below the line, however, superior or inferior performance, respectively, could be indicated.

To this point, we have considered only the nominal value-added returns relative to the benchmark. We know from regression analysis, however, that we must also derive a measure of statistical significance (confidence). To do this, we calculate a *confidence interval* around the horizontal (zero value-added return) line. If the value-added return falls outside the confidence interval, we conclude that it is statistically different from zero.

The solid, cone-shaped-like lines surrounding the horizontal line in Figure 5 represent the *confidence interval*. The confidence interval is generated using the standard deviation of value-added returns and the empirical rule. For example, approximately 95% of all returns will fall within two standard deviations of the mean (zero in this case). When a value-added return falls outside the 95% confidence interval (see Figure 5), the null hypothesis is rejected. In other words, we say that the value-added return is statistically different from zero and, therefore, not the result of a random event.

MANAGER CONTINUATION POLICY

LOS 31.s: Discuss the issues involved in manager continuation policy decisions, including the costs of hiring and firing investment managers.

The costs of hiring and firing investment managers can be considerable because the fired manager's portfolios will have to be moved to the new manager(s). This can be quite expensive, both in time and money:

1. A proportion of the existing manager's portfolio may have to be liquidated if the new manager's style is significantly different.

2. Replacing managers involves a significant amount of time and effort for the fund sponsor.

As a result, some fund sponsors have a formalized, written manager continuation policy (MCP) which will include the goals and guidelines associated with the management review process:

- Replace managers only when justified (i.e., minimize unnecessary manager turnover).
  - Short periods of underperformance should not necessarily mean automatic replacement.

- Develop formal policies and apply them consistently to all managers.
- Use portfolio performance and other information in evaluating managers:
  - Appropriate and consistent investment strategies (i.e., the manager doesn't continually change strategies based upon near-term performance).
  - Relevant benchmark (style) selections.
  - Personnel turnover.
  - Growth of the account.

Implementing the MCP process usually involves:

1. Continual manager monitoring.

2. Regular, periodic manager review.

The manager review should be handled much as the original hiring interview, which should have included the manager's key personnel. Then, before replacing a manager, management must determine that the move will generate value for the firm (like a positive NPV project). That is, the value gained from hiring a new manager will outweigh the costs associated with the process.

Type I Errors and Type II Errors

LOS 31.t: Contrast Type I and Type II errors in manager continuation decisions.

Type I and Type II errors refer to incorrectly rejecting or failing to reject the null hypothesis, respectively. Stating the null hypothesis as the manager generates no value-added and the alternative hypothesis as the manager adds value, there are two potential statistical errors:

H_0: The manager adds no value.

H_A: The manager adds positive value.

Type I error—Rejecting the null hypothesis when it is true. That is, keeping managers who are not adding value.

Type II error—Failing to reject the null when it is false. That is, firing good managers who are adding value.

> **For the Exam:** To keep Type I and II errors straight, remember the phrase "Type I horn." That is, a Type I error is when you incorrectly reject the null hypothesis, H_0. Putting "ho" with the first letters of reject null, you get the word "horn."

KEY CONCEPTS

LOS 31.a

Fund sponsor's perspective: Performance evaluation improves the effectiveness of a fund's investment policy by acting as a feedback and control mechanism. It:

- Shows where the policy is effective and where it isn't.
- Directs management to areas of underperformance.
- Indicates the results of active management and other policy decisions.
- Indicates where other, additional strategies can be successfully applied.
- Provides feedback on the consistent application of the policies set forth in the IPS.

Investment manager's perspective: As with the fund sponsor's perspective, performance evaluation can serve as a feedback and control mechanism. Some investment managers may simply compare their reported investment returns to a designated benchmark. Others will want to investigate the effectiveness of each component of their investment process.

LOS 31.b

The three primary concerns to address when assessing the performance of an account are:

1. **The return performance of the account over the period.** This is addressed through performance measurement, which involves calculating rates of return based on changes in the account's value over specified time periods.

2. **How the manager(s) attained the observed performance.** This is addressed by performance attribution. This looks into the sources of the account's performance (e.g., sector or security selection) and the importance of those sources.

3. **Whether the performance was due to investment decisions.** This is addressed by performance appraisal. The objective is to draw conclusions regarding whether the performance was affected primarily by investment decisions, by the overall market, or by chance.

LOS 31.c

The **time-weighted rate of return** (TWRR) calculates the compounded rate of growth over a stated evaluation period of one unit of money initially invested in the account. It requires a set of subperiod returns to be calculated covering each period that has an external cash flow. The subperiod results are then compounded together:

$$R_p = (1 + R_{s1})(1 + R_{s2})(1 + R_{s3})(1 + R_{s4})...(1 + R_{sk}) - 1$$

The **money-weighted rate of return** (MWRR) is the internal rate of return (IRR) on all funds invested during the evaluation period, including the beginning value of the portfolio:

$$MV_1 = MV_0(1+R)^m + \sum_{i=1}^{n} CF_i(1+R)^{L(i)}$$

The MWRR, unlike the TWRR, is heavily influenced by the size and timing of cash flows. The TWRR is the preferred method unless the manager has control over the size and timing of the cash flows. The MWRR will be higher (lower) than the TWRR if funds are added prior to a period of strong (weak) performance.

LOS 31.d

The phrase "garbage in, garbage out" is quite appropriate for return calculations. That is, the calculated return is only as good (i.e., accurate) as the inputs. The following are potential problems relating to data quality:

- When accounts contain illiquid (infrequently priced) assets, estimates or educated guesses must sometimes be used to calculate returns.
- For many thinly-traded fixed-income securities, current market prices may not be available. Estimated prices may be derived from dealer quoted prices on securities with similar attributes. This is known as **matrix pricing**.
- Highly illiquid securities may be carried at cost or the price of the last trade, thus not reflecting the current price.
- Account valuations should include trade date accounting, including accrued interest and dividends.

LOS 31.e

Portfolio return, P, can be broken into returns due to market, style, and active management:

$$P = M + S + A$$

where:
P = portfolio return
M = market index return
S = return to style
A = return due to active management
S = $B - M$
B = portfolio benchmark return
A = $P - B$

LOS 31.f

A valid benchmark should meet the following criteria:

1. **Specified in advance:** The benchmark is known to both the investment manager and the fund sponsor. It is specified at the start of an evaluation period.

2. **Appropriate:** The benchmark is consistent with the manager's investment approach and style.

3. **Measurable:** Its value can be determined on a reasonably frequent basis.

4. **Unambiguous:** Clearly-defined identities and weights of securities constitute the benchmark.

5. **Reflective of current investment opinions:** The manager has current knowledge and expertise of the securities within the benchmark.

6. **Accountable:** The manager(s) should accept the applicability of the benchmark and be accountable for deviations in construction due to active management.

7. **Investable:** It is possible to replicate the benchmark and forgo active management.

There are seven primary types of benchmarks in use:
1. **Absolute:** An absolute benchmark is a return objective (e.g., aims to exceed a minimum return target).

2. **Manager universes:** The median manager or fund from a broad universe of managers or funds is used as the benchmark.

3. **Broad market indices:** There are several well-known broad market indices that are used as benchmarks (e.g., the S&P 500 for U.S. common stocks).

4. **Style indices:** Investment style indices represent specific portions of an asset category.

5. **Factor-model-based:** Factor models involve relating a specified set of factor exposures to the returns on an account.

6. **Returns-based:** Returns-based benchmarks are constructed using (1) the managed account returns over specified periods and (2) corresponding returns on several style indices for the same periods.

7. **Custom security-based:** A custom security-based benchmark reflects the manager's investment universe, weighted to reflect a particular approach.

LOS 31.g
The construction of a custom security-based benchmark entails the following steps:
Step 1: Identify the important elements of the manager's investment process.
Step 2: Select securities that are consistent with that process.
Step 3: Weight the securities (including cash) to reflect the manager's process.
Step 4: Review and adjust as needed to replicate the manager's process and results.
Step 5: Rebalance the custom benchmark on a predetermined schedule.

LOS 31.h
Using the median account as a benchmark has a number of drawbacks:
1. It fails several properties of a valid benchmark:
    *   It is impossible to identify the median manager in advance.
    *   It is ambiguous, as the median manager is unknown.
    *   The benchmark is not investable.
    *   It is impossible to verify the benchmark's appropriateness due to the ambiguity of the median manager.

2. Fund sponsors who choose to employ manager universes have to rely on the compiler's representations that the accounts within the universe have been screened, input data validated, and calculation methodology approved.

3. As fund sponsors will terminate underperforming managers, universes will be subject to "survivor bias." As consistently underperforming accounts will not survive, the median will be biased upwards. Without a valid reference point, evaluating manager performance using this benchmark becomes suspect.

LOS 31.i

Systematic bias: There should be minimal systematic bias in the benchmark relative to the account.

Tracking error: Tracking error is defined as the volatility of the excess return earned due to active management.

Risk characteristics: An account's exposure to systematic sources of risk should be similar to those of the benchmark over time.

Coverage: The coverage ratio is the market value of the securities that are in both the portfolio and the benchmark as a percentage of the total market value of the portfolio.

Turnover: Passively managed portfolios should utilize benchmarks with low turnover.

Positive active positions: An active position is the difference between the weight of a security or sector in the managed portfolio versus the benchmark.

LOS 31.j

The diversity of hedge funds has led to problems when designating a suitable benchmark. In most cases, hedge funds hold both short and long investment positions. This leads to performance measurement issues as well as administrative and compliance issues. Given these complications, other performance methods that may be more appropriate are:

1. **Value-added return:** One approach is to evaluate in terms of performance impact. A return can be calculated by summing up the performance impacts of the individual security positions, both long and short.

2. **Separate long/short benchmarks:** It may be possible to construct separate long and short benchmarks. These could then be combined in their relevant proportions to create an overall benchmark.

3. **The Sharpe ratio:** The confusion over exactly what constitutes a hedge fund, as well as the myriad strategies employed by hedge fund managers, has led to the popular use of the Sharpe ratio, which compares portfolio returns to a risk-free return rather than a benchmark.

LOS 31.k

The basic concept of performance attribution is to identify and quantify the sources of returns that are different from the designated benchmark. There are two basic forms of performance attribution:

1. Macro performance attribution is done at the fund sponsor level. The approach can be carried out in percentage terms (a rate-of-return metric) and/or in monetary terms (a value metric).

2. Micro performance attribution is used by both fund managers (to analyze the performance of the individual portfolio managers they use) and the portfolio managers themselves (to determine sources of excess returns). Note the distinction does not relate to who is carrying out the performance attribution, but rather to the variables being used.

There are three main inputs into the macro attribution approach:

1. **Policy allocations:** It is up to the sponsor to determine the asset categories and weights as well as to allocate the total fund among asset managers. As in any IPS development, allocations will be determined by the sponsor's risk tolerance, long-term expectations, and the liabilities (spending needs) the fund must meet.

2. **Benchmark portfolio returns:** A fund sponsor may use broad market indices as the benchmarks for asset categories and narrowly-focused indices for managers' investment styles.

3. **Fund returns, valuations, and external cash flows:** When using percentage terms, returns will need to be calculated at the individual manager level. This enables the fund sponsor to make decisions regarding manager selection.

If also using monetary values, account valuation and external cash flow data are needed to compute the value impacts of the fund sponsor's investment policy decision making.

LOS 31.l
Macro Attribution Analysis

There are six levels of investment policy decision-making, by which the fund's performance can be analyzed:

1. Net contributions.

2. Risk-free asset.

3. Asset categories.

4. Benchmarks.

5. Investment managers.

6. Allocation effects.

The levels represent investment strategies management can utilize to add value to the fund; these levels increase in risk, expected return, and tracking error as one progresses down the list.

Micro Attribution Analysis

Micro performance attribution consists of analyzing individual portfolios relative to designated benchmarks. The value-added return (portfolio return minus benchmark return) can be broken into three components: (1) pure sector allocation, (2) allocation/selection interaction, and (3) within-sector selection.

$$R_V = \underbrace{\sum_{j=1}^{S} \left(w_{P,j} - w_{B,j} \right) \left(R_{B,j} - R_B \right)}_{\text{pure sector allocation}} + \underbrace{\sum_{j=1}^{S} \left(w_{P,j} - w_{B,j} \right) \left(R_{P,j} - R_{B,j} \right)}_{\text{allocation/selection interaction}}$$

$$+ \underbrace{\sum_{j=1}^{S} w_{B,j} \left(R_{P,j} - R_{B,j} \right)}_{\text{within-sector selection}}$$

LOS 31.m

It should be possible to construct multifactor models to conduct micro attribution. This involves combining economic sector factors with other fundamental factors. Constructing a suitable factor model would involve the following:

- Identify the fundamental factors that will generate systematic returns.
- Determine the exposures of the portfolio and the benchmark to the fundamental factors at the start of the evaluation period.
- Determine the manager's active exposure to each factor.
- Determine the active impact. This is the added return due to the manager's active exposures.

The results of the fundamental factor micro attribution will indicate the source of portfolio returns, based upon actual factor exposures versus the manager's normal factor exposures (e.g., sector rotation), the manager's ability to time the market (e.g., adjust the portfolio beta and/or duration in response to market expectations), and so on.

LOS 31.n

Attribution analysis of a fixed-income portfolio amounts to comparing the return on the active manager's portfolio to the return on a passively managed, risk-free portfolio. The difference between the two can be attributed to the effects of the external interest rate environment and the manager's contribution.

1. Effect of the external interest environment:
    - Return on the default-free benchmark assuming no change in the forward rates.
    - Return due to the actual changes in interest rates.

2. Contribution of the management process:
    - Return from interest rate management.
    - Return from sector/quality management.
    - Return from the selection of specific securities.
    - Return from trading activity.

LOS 31.o

The manager's contribution to the portfolio return (i.e., the return to active management) can be divided into four components:

1. **Interest rate management effect:** The ability of the manager to predict changes in relevant interest rates.

2. **Sector/quality effect:** The ability of the manager to select and overweight (underweight) outperforming (underperforming) sectors and qualities.

3. **Security selection effect:** The ability of the manager to select superior securities to represent sectors.

4. **Trading activity:** The residual effect; assumed to measure the return to active trading (buying and selling) over the period.

LOS 31.p

The final stage of the performance evaluation process, performance appraisal, measures compare returns on a risk-adjusted basis. The following are five methods of performance appraisal in their ex post (historical) forms:

1. **Ex post alpha (Jensen's alpha):** Alpha is the difference between the account return and the return required to compensate for systematic risk. Alpha uses the ex post SML as a benchmark to appraise performance.

2. **Information ratio:** Excess return is measured against variability of excess return.

3. **The Treynor measure:** The Treynor measure calculates the account's excess return above the risk-free rate, relative to the account's beta (i.e., systematic risk).

4. **The Sharpe ratio:** Unlike the previous two methods, the Sharpe ratio calculates excess returns above the risk-free rate, relative to total risk measured by standard deviation.

5. **M^2:** Using the CML, M^2 compares the account's return to the market return if the two had equal risk.

LOS 31.q

Treynor considers only beta, market-related risk.

Sharpe is based on total portfolio risk (standard deviation of total return), which includes both beta (market related) risk and alpha (value added) related risk.

The information ratio considers only value added and its variability. It is based only on alpha risk.

LOS 31.r
Quality control charts plot managers' performance relative to a benchmark, with a statistical confidence interval.

The manager's value-added return is plotted on the vertical axis, and time is plotted on the horizontal axis. The center of the vertical axis is where the portfolio and benchmark returns are equal, so the value-added return is zero. The solid, horizontal line originating at zero can be thought of as the benchmark return, and any portfolio returns plotting off the horizontal line would represent those occasions when the portfolio and benchmark returns are not equal.

Management can plot the manager's value-added returns on the chart to determine whether they are randomly generated or are derived through superior management. If they tend to be consistently above or below the line, this could indicate superior or inferior performance, respectively.

LOS 31.s
Some fund sponsors have a formalized, written manager continuation policy (MCP) which includes the goals and guidelines associated with the management review process:
- Replace managers only when justified (i.e., minimize unnecessary manager turnover).
  - Short periods of underperformance should not necessarily mean automatic replacement.
- Develop formal policies and apply them consistently to all managers.
- Use portfolio performance and other information in evaluating managers:
  - Appropriate and consistent investment strategies (i.e., the manager doesn't continually change strategies based upon near term performance).
  - Relevant benchmark (style) selections.
  - Personnel turnover.
  - Growth of the account.

LOS 31.t
Type I and Type II errors refer to incorrectly rejecting or failing to reject the null hypothesis, respectively. Stating the null hypothesis as the manager generates no value-added and the alternative hypothesis as the manager adds value, there are two potential statistical errors:

H_0: The manager adds no value.

H_A: The manager adds positive value.

Type I error—Rejecting the null hypothesis when it is true. That is, keeping managers who are returning no value-added.

Type II error—Failing to reject the null when it is false. That is, firing good managers who are adding value.

CONCEPT CHECKERS

1. The Helix account was valued at $6,000,000 at start of the month. At the month-end, its value is $6,380,000. The account received a contribution of $80,000.

    Calculate the rate of return for the month under the following conditions:
    (a) The contribution was received at the start of the month.
    (b) The contribution was received at the end of the month.

2. The Genesis account is valued at $1,000,000 at the start of the month and $1,200,000 at the end. During the month, there was a cash inflow of $30,000 on day 11 and $20,000 on day 17. The values of the account are $1,050,000 and $1,150,000 on days 11 and 17, respectively. **Calculate** the time-weighted rate of return (assuming 30 days in the month).

3. The Pygmalion account is valued at $750,000 at the start of the month. On day 22, a contribution of $20,000 is made. At the end of the month, the account is worth $1,266,513. Assuming 30 days in a month, the daily MWRR is *closest* to:
    A. 1.5%.
    B. 1.7%.
    C. 1.9%.

4. Answer the following questions relating to rate of return calculations:

   (a) **Outline** the advantages and disadvantages of the time-weighted rate of return and the money-weighted rate of return.

   (b) If daily valuations are unavailable, **describe** a method that is an approximate estimate to the time-weighted rate of return.

   (c) **Discuss** circumstances where there could be significant differences between the time-weighted and money-weighted rates of return.

5. Rhombus Asset Management runs a U.S. small-cap equity portfolio. The portfolio generated an 8.9% return during 2005. Rhombus uses the Russell 2000® Index as the most appropriate benchmark. The Russell 2000® Index yielded 9.1% over the same evaluation period. The Wilshire 5000, a broad U.S. equity market index, yielded 8.5% over the same evaluation period.

   Calculate Rhombus Asset Management's return due to style and due to active management. **Assess** Rhombus's performance compared to the benchmark and to the market.

6. **List** and **discuss** the seven characteristics for a benchmark to effectively evaluate management performance.

7. Hexagon PLC is an investment management company based in London. It manages portfolios consisting of European equities only. It states that its benchmark is to beat the median manager. **Discuss** the validity of the median manager benchmark approach.

8. **Discuss** the problems associated with applying traditional performance measurement and evaluation techniques to a long-short hedge fund and **suggest** alternative measures that may be more appropriate.

9. **Distinguish** between macro and micro attribution, including their inputs.

10. The following is an extract from a micro attribution analysis of one of the investment managers of the Hiatus fund:

Economic Sectors	Portfolio Weight (%)	Sector Benchmark Weight (%)	Portfolio Return (%)	Sector Benchmark Return (%)
Energy	8.38	7.72	3.55	3.32
Financial	15.48	13.42	1.66	1.10
Technology	17.89	22.01	3.21	3.18

*The overall benchmark return was 2.32%.

Using the above table, **calculate** and **evaluate**:

(i) The pure sector allocation return for the energy sector.

(ii) The within-sector selection return for the financial sector.

(iii) The allocation/selection interaction return for the technology sector.

11.   (i) **Explain** management factors contributing to a fixed-income portfolio's total return.

     (ii) Delta Asset Management states that its investment strategy is to outperform the index through active interest rate management and identifying undervalued sectors. Kappa Asset Management states its investment strategy is to immunize against interest rate exposure and to yield positive contribution through bond selection. Using the data in the table, **assess** whether both managers' positive performance was primarily through their stated objectives.

	Delta Asset Management	Kappa Asset Management	Bond Portfolio Benchmark
1. Interest rate effect			
i. Expected	0.49	0.49	0.49
ii. Unexpected	0.59	0.59	0.59
Subtotal	1.08	1.08	1.08
2. Interest rate management effect			
iii. Duration	−0.12	0.23	0.00
iv. Convexity	−0.02	−0.03	0.00
v. Yield-curve change	0.10	0.16	0.00
Subtotal	−0.04	0.36	0.00
3. Other management effects			
vi. Sector	1.02	0.04	0.00
vii. Bond selection	0.08	0.23	0.00
viii. Transaction costs	0.00	0.00	0.00
Subtotal	1.10	0.27	0.00
4. Trading activity return	0.05	0.07	0.00
5. Total return	2.19	1.78	1.08

12. The following data has been collected to appraise the following four funds:

	Fund A	Fund B	Fund C	Fund D	Market Index
Return	8.25%	7.21%	9.44%	10.12%	8.60%
Beta	0.91	0.84	1.02	1.34	1.00
Standard deviation	3.24%	3.88%	3.66%	3.28%	3.55%
Tracking error*	0.43%	0.62%	0.33%	1.09%	

* Tracking error is the standard deviation of the difference between the Fund Return and the Market Index Return.

The risk-free rate of return for the relevant period was 4%. **Calculate** and **rank** the funds using the following methods:

(i) Jensen's alpha

(ii) Treynor measure

(iii) Sharpe ratio

(iv) M^2

(v) Information ratio

Compare and **contrast** the methods and **explain** why the ranking differs between methods.

13. The Solus fund is in the process of implementing a Manager Continuation Policy in order to avoid excessive manager turnover yet remove inferior managers as required. At the moment, Solus believes it is being a bit too conservative and retaining managers even though they are producing weak performance. **State** and **explain** the type of statistical error Solus is currently making. Briefly **explain** the other kind of error Solus could make.

14. For a given portfolio over a particular time period, an analyst is given beginning market value, ending market value, and a specified cash flow. All of the given values are positive with a positive return for the year. The analyst represents the return for the period calculated as if the one cash flow came at the beginning of the period with the symbol R_B and represents the return calculated as if the cash flow came at the end of the period with the symbol R_E. Based only on the given information:
   A. $R_B > R_E$.
   B. $R_B = R_E$.
   C. $R_B < R_E$.

15. For a passively-managed portfolio, with respect to managing the portfolio and choosing the best benchmark, a manager would want a:
   A. low coverage ratio of the chosen benchmark, which has a low turnover ratio.
   B. low coverage ratio of the chosen benchmark, which has a high turnover ratio.
   C. high coverage ratio of the chosen benchmark, which has a low turnover ratio.

16. **Specify** one way each for how fundamental factor model micro attribution is similar to and different from a returns-based style analysis.

17. In calculating the Treynor and Sharpe measures for a given portfolio, other things constant, lowering unsystematic risk will *most likely*:
    A. increase both the Treynor measure and Sharpe measures.
    B. increase the Treynor measure but not the Sharpe measure.
    C. increase the Sharpe measure but not the Treynor measure.

18. A standard deviation measure appears in:
    A. the Sharpe measure but not the information ratio.
    B. the information ratio but not the Sharpe measure.
    C. both the information ratio and the Sharpe measure.

19. An analyst examines a quality control chart that depicts a manager's value-added return. The manager's value-added return is plotted on the vertical axis over time, which is on the horizontal axis. Above and below the horizontal axis are two confidence interval bounds. The analyst will say that the manager has *added* significant value when the plot of the manager's performance is:
    A. above zero only.
    B. below zero and below the lower bound of the 95% confidence interval.
    C. above zero and above the upper bound of the 95% confidence interval.

For more questions related to this topic review, log in to your Schweser online account and launch SchweserPro™ QBank; and for video instruction covering each LOS in this topic review, log in to your Schweser online account and launch the OnDemand video lectures, if you have purchased these products.

ANSWERS – CONCEPT CHECKERS

1. If the contribution of $80,000 had been at the start of the month:

$$r_t = \frac{\$6,380,000 - (\$6,000,000 + \$80,000)}{\$6,000,000 + \$80,000} \times 100 = 4.93\%$$

If the $80,000 contribution had occurred at the month end:

$$r_t = \frac{(\$6,380,000 - \$80,000) - \$6,000,000}{\$6,000,000} \times 100 = 5.00\%$$

2. Calculating rates of return for each subperiod:

Subperiod 1 (days 1–11)

$r_{t,1}$ = [($1,050,000 – $30,000) – $1,000,000] / $1,000,000 = 0.02

Subperiod 2 (days 12–17)

$r_{t,2}$ = [($1,150,000 – $20,000) – $1,050,000] / $1,050,000 = 0.0762

Subperiod 3 (days 18–30)

$r_{t,3}$ = ($1,200,000 – $1,150,000) / $1,150,000 = 0.0435

Compounding the returns together to calculate an overall time-weighted rate of return:

TWRR = (1 + 0.02)(1 + 0.0762)(1 + 0.0435) − 1 = 0.1455 = 14.55%

3. **B** For the daily MWRR, the following equation needs to be solved:

$1,266,513 = \$750,000(1 + R)^{30} + \$20,000(1 + R)^{8}$

Using a trial and error process, the closest rate of return that equates the above formula is R = 0.017. (Note: Most calculators are unable to solve for an IRR when the time intervals between cash flows are unequal. If you are asked to perform a MWRR calculation on the exam, the time intervals will be equal.)

$\$750,000(1.017)^{30} + \$20,000(1.017)^{8} = \$1,266,513$

4. **TWRR**

    (a) The following outlines advantages and disadvantages of the TWRR and the MWRR:

    Advantages

    (i) The TWRR is not influenced by external cash flow activity. Therefore, it reflects what return an investor would achieve if he had placed the funds in the account at the start of the evaluation period.

    (ii) As most investment managers have very little control over external cash activity, the TWRR would be an appropriate measure.

Disadvantages

    (i) Account valuations are needed for every date an external cash flow takes place.

    (ii) Administration costs may be higher as, potentially, daily valuations are required.

MWRR

Advantages

    (i) The MWRR would be more appropriate if the investment manager retains control over external cash flows.

    (ii) Only valuations at the start and end of the evaluation period are required.

Disadvantages

    (i) The MWRR is sensitive to the size and timing of external cash flows.

    (ii) If an investment manager has little or no control over the size or timing of external cash flows, the TWRR would be more appropriate.

(b) The TWRR can be approximated by calculating the MWRR over frequent time intervals and then chain-link those returns over the evaluation period. This process is known as the linked internal rate of return (LIRR).

(c) If the external cash flows are relatively large compared to the account's value, and the account's performance is varying considerably, there can be a significant difference between the TWRR and MWRR.

If funds are invested into an account prior to a period of strong (weak) performance, then the MWRR will be higher (lower) than the TWRR as the contribution is being invested just prior to the subperiod earning a high (low) growth rate.

5.   Style return = B – M = 9.1% – 8.5% = +0.6%

Active management return = P – B = 8.9% – 9.1% = –0.2%

The positive style return tells us small-cap stocks outperformed the market as a whole.

However, the negative active management return tells us Rhombus has underperformed its benchmark for the evaluation period in question. Consistently underperforming the benchmark would bring Rhombus's investment management skills under question.

6.   The following criteria are required from a benchmark to effectively evaluate performance:
- *Specified in advance.* The benchmark is known and specified at the start of an evaluation period.
- *Appropriate.* The benchmark is consistent with the manager's investment style.
- *Measurable.* It can be calculated on a reasonably frequent basis.
- *Unambiguous.* The identities and weights of securities constituting the benchmark are clearly defined.
- *Reflective of current investment opinions.* The manager has current knowledge of the securities within the benchmark.
- *Accountable.* The investment manager should be aware of and accept accountability of the constituents and performance of the benchmark (i.e., the manager exhibits ownership).
- *Investable.* It is possible to replicate the benchmark and forgo active management.

7. The median manager is not a valid benchmark because that manager cannot be specified in advance and is not investable. It is not a passive alternative to active management. The only benchmark characteristic it meets is it can be measured after the fact.

8. Problems with using traditional techniques to assess long-short hedge funds include:
   - It is possible for MV_0 to be zero for a long-short portfolio, making the return calculation nonsensical.
   - Many hedge funds use an "absolute return" approach, which makes relative performance comparisons with a traditional benchmark less useful.

   Alternative performance methods that can be used instead:

   A. Value-added return.

   This method evaluates in terms of performance impact:

   value-added return = portfolio return – benchmark return

   To replicate a zero net asset hedge fund, the value-added return on a long-short portfolio will be where the active weights sum to zero. Although the active weights sum to zero, a return can be calculated by summing up the performance impacts of the individual security positions, both long and short.

   B. Creating separate long/short benchmarks.

   It may be possible to use either a returns-based or security-based benchmark approach to construct separate long and short benchmarks. The benchmarks could then be combined in their relevant proportions to create an appropriate overall benchmark.

   C. The Sharpe ratio.

   The Sharpe ratio measures the excess return over a risk-free rate of return, relative to volatility (risk) of returns. A hedge fund's Sharpe ratio can be compared to that of a universe of other similar hedge funds.

9. (i) Macro attribution is performance attribution carried out at the fund sponsor level. Micro attribution is performance attribution carried out at the investment manager level (i.e., to attribute the performance of an individual manager). The distinction relates to the decision variables being used, not who is carrying out the attribution analysis, as micro attribution is often employed by fund managers and portfolio managers.

   (ii) Macro attribution analysis uses a value metric that uses account valuation and external cash flow data to calculate rates of return and dollar impacts. Micro performance attribution analysis uses a rate of return metric that calculates percentage returns at the level of the individual manager account.

   (iii) There are three inputs into both approaches:

   Macro attribution:
   1. Policy allocations.
   2. Benchmark portfolio returns.
   3. Fund returns, valuations, and external cash flows.

   Micro attribution:
   1. Pure sector allocation.
   2. Allocation selection.
   3. Within-sector selection.

10. (i)   Pure energy sector allocation = [(0.0838 – 0.0772) × (3.32% – 2.32%)] = 0.0066%

This shows that the decision to overweight a sector that performed better than the overall benchmark resulted in a positive contribution to portfolio performance.

(ii)   Financial sector within-sector allocation return = 0.1342 × (1.66% – 1.10%) = +0.0752%

The positive contribution shows that the Hiatus portfolio held financial stocks that performed better than the financial stocks contained in the sector benchmark.

(iii)   Technology sector allocation/selection interaction return = [(0.1789 – 0.2201) × (3.21% – 3.18%)] = –0.0012%

Underweighting the portfolio in the technology sector when the fund performed better than the sector benchmark has led to a negative contribution.

11. (i)   There are four management factors contributing to a fixed-income portfolio's return:

1.   Interest rate management effect—this indicates how well the manager predicts interest rate changes.

2.   Sector/quality effect—this effect measures the manager's ability to select the best issuing sectors and quality groups.

3.   Security selection effect—this measures how the return of a specific security within its sector relates to the average performance of the sector.

4.   Trading activity—this encompasses the effect of sales and purchases of bonds over a given period.

(ii)   **Delta**

Delta has yielded an overall positive contribution of 111 basis points through active management (subtotals 2, 3, and 4). Most of this positive contribution has come from sector management (102 basis points). Delta actually made a negative contribution of –4 basis points from active interest rate management.

Thus, the statement that Delta's strategy is to outperform the index through active interest rate management (incorrect) and identifying undervalued sectors (correct) appears to be only partially correct.

Kappa

Kappa has yielded 70 basis points overall through active management. This has primarily come from active interest rate management (36 basis points) and bond selection (23 basis points).

Thus, the statement that Kappa's strategy is to immunize against interest rate exposure (incorrect) and to yield positive contribution through bond selection (correct) is also partially correct.

12.   Jensen's alpha and the Treynor measure will give the same ranking:

	Fund A	Fund B	Fund C	Fund D
Alpha	8.25% – 8.19% = +0.06%	7.21% – 7.86% = –0.65%	9.44% – 8.69% = +0.75%	10.12% – 10.16% = –0.04%
Ranking	2	4	1	3
Treynor	(8.25 – 4) / 0.91 = 4.67	(7.21 – 4) / 0.84 = 3.82	(9.44 – 4) / 1.02 = 5.33	(10.12 – 4) / 1.34 = 4.57
Ranking	2	4	1	3

The Sharpe ratio and M^2 will give the same ranking:

	Fund A	Fund B	Fund C	Fund D
Sharpe	(8.25 – 4) / 3.24 = 1.31	(7.21 – 4) / 3.88 = 0.83	(9.44 – 4) / 3.66 = 1.49	(10.12 – 4) / 3.28 = 1.87
Ranking	3	4	2	1
M^2	4 + [(8.25 – 4) / 3.24] 3.55 = 8.65%	4 + [(7.21 – 4) / 3.88] 3.55 = 6.95%	4 + [(9.44 – 4) / 3.66] 3.55 = 9.29%	4 + [(10.12 – 4) / 3.28] 3.55 = 10.64%
Ranking	3	4	2	1

The notable change in ranking between Alpha/Treynor and Sharpe/M^2 is Fund D. Fund D has a relatively low total risk (standard deviation of 3.28%) but a relatively high beta (1.34). This implies that Fund D has a high proportion of systematic risk but very little non-systematic risk.

	Fund A	Fund B	Fund C	Fund D
IR	(8.25% – 8.60%) / 0.43% = –0.81	(7.21% – 8.60%) / 0.62% = –2.24	(9.44% – 8.60%) / 0.33% = 2.55	(10.12% – 8.60%) / 1.09% = 1.39
Ranking	3	4	1	2

The ranks based upon the information ratio are similar to that of the Sharpe and M^2 measures. This is because the measure of risk in the denominator is related to other measures of dispersion, and the information ratio uses the average return in the numerator, as do the other measures.

13.   Solus is currently making a **Type I error**. A Type I error is incorrectly rejecting the null hypothesis. In management assessment, the null hypothesis is, "The manager contributes no value-added returns," or, "The manager's value-added returns are zero." Rejecting the null would imply that the manager generates positive value-added returns. The error is that inferior managers are kept when they should be removed.

        The other type of error Solus could make is a **Type II error**, which is failing to reject the null hypothesis when it is false. This is when good managers are removed when they should have been kept.

14. C   The cash flow is subtracted out of the numerator in both cases. If the cash flow comes at the beginning of the period, it is added to the denominator and decreases the measure of return even more.

15. C   The coverage ratio is the market value of the securities that are in both the portfolio and the benchmark, specified as a percentage of the total market value of the portfolio. The higher the coverage ratio, the more closely the manager is replicating the benchmark. Benchmark turnover is the proportion of the benchmark's total market value that is bought or sold (turned over) during periodic rebalancing. Passively-managed portfolios should utilize benchmarks with low turnover.

16.   The methods are *similar* in that they both use the following initial steps in constructing a suitable factor model:
        * Identify the fundamental factors that will generate systematic returns.
        * Determine the exposures of the portfolio and the benchmark to the fundamental factors.
        * Determine the performance of each of the factors.

        In this way, the fundamental factor model micro attribution results will look very similar to a returns-based style analysis and can be determined the same way (e.g., the returns to the portfolio are regressed against the returns to several different indices to determine the factor exposures).

        The primary *difference* between them is the use of other fundamental factors (e.g., management's use of leverage, market timing, sector rotation, the size of the firm, and so on) that would not ordinarily be used in a returns-based style analysis.

17. C   The Treynor measure uses only systematic risk (i.e., beta) in the denominator, so lowering the unsystematic risk of the asset in question will have no affect on the Treynor measure. The Sharpe ratio uses standard deviation, which includes both unsystematic and systematic risk. Lowering unsystematic risk, therefore, will lower the denominator and increase the Sharpe ratio.

18. C   The Sharpe measure uses the standard deviation of the returns in the denominator, and the information ratio uses the standard deviation of the excess return. Although they measure standard deviation differently, they both incorporate a standard deviation measure.

19. **C**   A quality control chart combines the average value added and its standard deviation to generate a confidence interval that can be used to determine statistical significance. The upper and lower confidence interval bounds are indicated with lines on the quality control chart. When the value added is above the upper bound of the confidence interval (i.e., outside the confidence interval), it means that we can reject the null hypothesis that the value was achieved by chance. We can conclude that the manager added value to the portfolio with her trading strategies.

You have now finished the Performance Evaluation topic section. To get immediate feedback on how effective your study has been for this material, log in to your Schweser online account and take the self-test for this topic area. Questions are more exam-like than typical Concept Checkers or QBank questions; a score of less than 70% indicates that your study likely needs improvement. These tests are timed and allow three minutes per question.

Overview of the Global Investment Performance Standards

Study Session 18

Exam Focus

GIPS material is usually tested as one item set for 5% of the exam. Just to keep things interesting, it is occasionally included in the constructed response morning section of the exam. You may recall that GIPS was part of ethics at Level I. This is not true at Level III; GIPS questions will be separate from and in addition to the 10 to 15% ethics weight.

GIPS falls pretty far down the list of favorite topics for most candidates. Like ethics, you must know the concepts and principles, then apply them to specific situations to identify compliance or non-compliance. There are a surprising number of calculation issues. To prepare for GIPS:

- **Read the SchweserNotes or the CFA text.**
- **Watch the OnDemand video lecture.**
- **Immediately work the Schweser practice questions <u>and</u> CFA end-of-chapter questions.**

There are a couple of pitfalls to watch out for:

- A popular myth is to read the actual 2010 GIPS document from the CFA Institute website instead of the assigned material. It will not provide the end-of-chapter questions you are expected to have worked and can mislead you on what is actually in the assigned material.
- Like ethics, it is easy to make up questions that cannot be answered. Exam questions are designed to test your understanding of the assigned material and not hypothetical real-world situations that would require additional research or delve into the sub-issues that can arise in GIPS. The CFA Institute devotes an entire website to GIPS and its real-world application issues, something you can peruse at leisure after the exam.

Read the assigned material, work the expected questions, and there is every reason to do well on this section of the exam.

The Creation and Evolution of the Gips Standards

The Global Investment Performance Standards (GIPS®) contain ethical and professional standards for the presentation of investment performance results. The GIPS are a *voluntary* set of standards. They are based on the fundamental principles of full disclosure and fair representation of performance results. When investment management firms comply with the GIPS, clients, prospective clients, and consultants are better equipped to fairly assess historical investment performance.

The GIPS are not all-encompassing because there is no practical way for a set of standards to address every possible situation a firm may face. The GIPS should, therefore, be viewed as a *minimum* set of investment performance presentation standards. Investment management firms should always include additional information in their performance presentations that would help current and prospective clients better understand the reported performance results.

Recognizing the need for one globally accepted set of investment performance presentation standards, CFA Institute [formerly Association for Investment Management and Research (AIMR)] sponsored and funded the Global Investment Performance Standards Committee to develop and publish a single global standard by which all firms calculate and present performance to clients and prospective clients. As a result of this initiative, the AIMR Board of Governors formally endorsed GIPS on February 19, 1999, as the worldwide standard. This was not the first time that such a unified approach had been conceived: as far back as 1966, Peter O. Dietz published a description for pension fund investment performance,[1] and in 1980, Wilshire Associates was involved in the establishment of the Trust Universe Comparison Service, a database of portfolio returns for which members produced unified return calculations. Later, in 1993, AIMR published the Performance Presentation Standards, effectively the precursor to today's GIPS.

Since 1999, the Investment Performance Council (IPC), the replacement of the GIPS Committee, has developed the standards further. The IPC's purpose is "to promote the adoption and implementation of a single investment performance presentation standard throughout the world as the common method for calculating and presenting investment performance." As such, the IPC issued revised GIPS standards that were adopted by the CFA Institute Board of Governors on February 4, 2005, and became effective on January 1, 2006. The latest edition of the GIPS was adopted by the GIPS Executive Committee on January 29, 2010.

OBJECTIVES, KEY CHARACTERISTICS, AND SCOPE OF THE GIPS

LOS 32.a: Discuss the objectives, key characteristics, and scope of the GIPS standards and their benefits to prospective clients and investment managers.

GIPS Objectives

- Establish global, industry-wide best practices for the calculation and presentation of investment performance, so that performance presentations for GIPS-compliant firms can be compared regardless of their country location.
- Facilitate the accurate and unambiguous presentation of investment performance results to current and prospective clients.
- Facilitate a comparison of the historical performance of investment management firms so that clients can make educated decisions when hiring new managers.
- Encourage full disclosure and fair global competition without barriers to entry.
- Encourage self-regulation.

---

1. Peter O. Dietz, *Pension Funds: Measuring Investment Performance* (New York: The Free Press, 1966).

GIPS Characteristics

- The GIPS are voluntary, minimum standards for performance presentation.
- The GIPS contain requirements that must be followed and recommendations that are considered industry best practice and should be followed but are not required. Firms must meet all requirements on a firm-wide basis in order to claim compliance.
- Only investment management firms may claim compliance; individuals may not claim GIPS compliance.
- The GIPS provide a minimum standard where local or country-specific laws, regulation, or industry standards may not exist.
- The GIPS require managers to include all actual fee-paying, discretionary portfolios in composites defined according to similar strategy and/or investment objective.
- Firms must present a minimum of five years of GIPS-compliant history or since inception if less than five years. After presenting at least five years of compliant history, the firm must add annual performance each year going forward, up to ten years, at a minimum.
- Firms may link years of noncompliant performance but must present only compliant data for periods beginning on or after January 1, 2000.
- Firms must use prescribed calculation and presentation methods and include required disclosures in presentations.
- The GIPS rely on the integrity of input data. The accuracy of input data is critical to the accuracy of the performance presentation.
- The GIPS must be applied with the goal of full disclosure and fair representation of investment performance. Meeting the objective of full and fair disclosure will likely require more than compliance with the minimum requirements of the GIPS.
- If an investment firm applies the GIPS in a performance situation that is not addressed specifically by the standards or that is open to interpretation, disclosures other than those required by the GIPS may be necessary. To fully explain the performance included in a presentation, firms are encouraged to present all relevant supplemental information.
- In cases in which applicable local or country-specific laws or regulations conflict with the GIPS, the standards require firms to comply with the local law or regulation and make full disclosure of the conflict.
- Firms are encouraged to develop monitoring processes and controls for maintaining GIPS compliance.
- Firms must document the policies used to ensure the existence and ownership of client assets.
- January 1, 2011, is the effective date of the 2010 edition of the GIPS. Presentations that include performance for periods beginning on or after January 1, 2011, must comply with the 2010 version of the GIPS.

Scope of the GIPS

Firms from any country may come into compliance with the GIPS. Compliance with the standards will facilitate a firm's participation in the investment management industry on a global level.

For periods prior to January 1, 2006, firms are granted reciprocity, so that if pre-2006 data are presented in compliance with a previous edition of the GIPS or a Country Version of GIPS (CVG), such data may continue to be shown as compliant with the revised GIPS.

Benefits to Managers and Clients

The benefits to existing and prospective clients derive from the underlying purpose of the GIPS—the ability to compare the performance of firms operating in different countries with different sets of established practices. With the increase in global investing and the accompanying increase in global competition comes the need for a standardized method for calculating and presenting investment results. The GIPS ensure that performance data are complete and fairly presented so that existing and prospective clients can have greater confidence in comparative investment results.

In addition to a more reliable measure of past investment performance results, the GIPS provide managers with the ability to compete fairly in foreign markets. Firms located in countries with little or no regulation can compete on an even basis with regulated countries by presenting performance results that have been verified through GIPS compliance. Simply put, investors can place more confidence in GIPS-compliant performance results. In addition to external benefits to GIPS compliance, firms can identify weaknesses in internal management controls during the implementation of GIPS.

GIPS COMPLIANCE

LOS 32.b: Explain the fundamentals of compliance with the GIPS standards, including the definition of the firm and the firm's definition of discretion.

GIPS compliance must be on a *firm-wide basis.* How a firm defines itself, therefore, is critically important because it determines total firm assets as well as the policies and practices that must be performed in compliance with the GIPS. *Total firm assets* are defined as the total fair value of all assets the firm manages, including non-fee-paying and non-discretionary portfolios. Also included in the definition are assets delegated to sub-advisers, as long as the firm has selected the sub-advisers. Assets managed by sub-advisers not selected by the firm are not included in total firm assets.

How a firm defines *discretion* is also of paramount importance. If (according to the firm's definition of discretion) a portfolio is deemed discretionary, it is considered sufficiently free of client-mandated constraints such that the manager is able to pursue its stated strategy, objectives, or mandate. The GIPS require that all actual, fee-paying discretionary portfolios are included in at least one composite.[2]

Definition of the Firm[3]

A **firm** is defined as:

"an investment firm, subsidiary, or division held out to clients or potential clients as a distinct business entity."

---

2. Actual means that the portfolio is assets under management, not a model or simulated portfolio. A composite is a portfolio or group of portfolios managed to the same investment strategy or mandate.
3. CFA Program 2017 Curriculum, Volume 6, Level III.

A **distinct business entity** is defined as:

> "a unit, division, department, or office that is organizationally or functionally separated from other units, divisions, departments, or offices and that retains discretion over the assets it manages and that should have autonomy over the investment decision-making process."

Fundamentals of Compliance

To claim compliance with GIPS, the firm must meet all requirements. Partial compliance is not acceptable. The firm must also meet the ethical intent of GIPS. Technical compliance that violates the intent is a violation of GIPS.

- Firms must establish, update on a timely basis, and document policies and procedures for meeting GIPS. This includes policies for error correction. Manuals and handbooks are proper documentation.
- A firm may not assert that calculations are in accord with GIPS unless it is a firm in compliance with GIPS, making a performance presentation to an individual firm client.
- Firms cannot claim partial compliance with GIPS or in compliance "except for."
- Only investment management firms can claim compliance with GIPS, not a pension plan sponsor or a consultant.

While not required, it is recommended the firm:

- Comply with the GIPS recommendations as well as the requirements.
- Have compliance verified by an independent third party.
- Adopt a broad definition of the firm that includes all parts of the firm that operate as the same brand without regard to location or name used by the unit.
- Provide an annual GIPS compliant report to all existing clients for the composites in which that client's performance is included. This will likely require an explanation whenever the client's return is below the composite's return.

INPUT DATA REQUIREMENTS AND RECOMMENDATIONS

LOS 32.c: Explain the requirements and recommendations of the GIPS standards with respect to input data, including accounting policies related to valuation and performance measurement.

GIPS Input Data Requirements (Standards 1.A.1–7)

- **Standard 1.A.1.** All data and information necessary to support the firm's performance presentation, including calculations, must be stored and maintained.

  Discussion: Current and prospective clients as well as auditors and regulators should be able to confirm valuations and recreate return calculations.

Study Session 18
Cross-Reference to CFA Institute Assigned Reading #32 – Overview of the Global Investment Performance Standards

Study Session 18

- **Standard 1.A.2.** For periods beginning on or after January 1, 2011, portfolios must be valued at fair value according to GIPS principles. Cost or book values are not permitted.

  Discussion: Fair value is the price, including any earned income, at which willing and knowledgeable participants would trade. These should be observable prices for identical investments trading in active markets. For thinly traded securities or other assets for which current market prices are not readily available, firms should use recognized and justifiable methods for estimating fair value.

- **Standard 1.A.3.** Portfolio valuation.
  - Prior to January 1, 2001, portfolios must be valued at least quarterly.
  - Beginning on or after January 1, 2001, at least monthly.
  - Beginning on or after January 1, 2010, at least monthly and on the date of all large external cash flows.

  Discussion: What constitutes a *large cash flow* is not defined by the GIPS. Firms must define *large* either on a value or percentage basis for each portfolio or composite. A large cash flow is generally one that has the potential to distort valuations and, hence, return calculations.

- **Standard 1.A.4.** For periods beginning January 1, 2010, firms must value portfolios as of the calendar month-end or the last business day of the month.

  Discussion: Prior to this date, there is more flexibility, depending on the firm's reporting cycle.

- **Standard 1.A.5.** For periods beginning January 1, 2005, firms must use trade-date accounting.

  Discussion: The use of trade-date accounting establishes the true economic value of an asset and improves the accuracy of performance measurements. The result of this requirement is that an asset will be shown (along with changes in cash balances) on the date of trade rather than settlement date. Settlement date accounting, which is valid for periods prior to 2005, would not for instance show an asset that was purchased just before the period end if the settlement date was in the following period. Note that pre-2005 performance results calculated using settlement date accounting will *not* need to be recalculated.

- **Standard 1.A.6.** Accrual accounting must be used for fixed-income securities and all other assets that accrue interest income. Market values of fixed-income securities must include accrued income.

  Discussion: When a fixed-income security or other asset that accrues interest is sold, the amount of the accrued interest at the sale date is calculated and paid by the purchaser. Thus, to measure performance fairly and accurately, accrued interest (received or paid) must be accounted for in both beginning and ending portfolio valuations.

- **Standard 1.A.7.** For periods beginning January 1, 2006, composites must have consistent beginning and ending annual valuation dates. Unless the composite is reported on a non-calendar fiscal year, the beginning and ending valuation dates must be at calendar year-end (or on the last business day of the year).

  Discussion: The valuation dates given for each composite must be the same each year, and either December 31 (or the previous Friday if that was the last working day of the year) or the last working day of the corporate accounting year.

GIPS Input Data Recommendations (Standards 1.B.1–4)

- **Standard 1.B.1.** Rather than only at large external cash flows, portfolios should be valued at each external cash flow.

- **Standard 1.B.2.** Valuations should be obtained from an independent third party.

  Discussion: To avoid disagreements between managers and custodians and to make fair and accurate representation of performance, firms should utilize qualified third-party valuators.

- **Standard 1.B.3.** Dividends from equities should be accrued as of the ex-dividend date.

- **Standard 1.B.4.** When presenting net-of-fees returns, firms should accrue investment management fees.

  Discussion: Performance may be presented gross or net of management fees (see *Disclosures* discussed later). If data is shown net of fees, part-year performance should accrue the appropriate percentage.

CALCULATION METHODOLOGY REQUIREMENTS AND RECOMMENDATIONS

LOS 32.d: Discuss the requirements of the GIPS standards with respect to return calculation methodologies, including the treatment of external cash flows, cash and cash equivalents, and expenses and fees.

GIPS Calculation Methodology *Requirements*

GIPS requires comparable calculation methods by all firms to facilitate comparison of results. Returns must be calculated on a total return basis using beginning and ending fair value (Standard 2.A.1). If there are no client contributions or withdrawals (ECFs), this is simply (EV – BV) / BV.

- Beginning and ending portfolio value must include income earned, realized gain and loss, and unrealized gain and loss. For fixed income securities, both beginning and ending values must include accrued interest. (It is recommended, but not required, that stock dividends be included in portfolio value as of the ex-dividend date).

When there are ECFs, the calculations are more complex, and time-weighted (geometrically compounded) computations must be used to link periodic rates of return (Standard 2.A.2).

- Beginning January 1, 2001, firms must value portfolios and compute periodic returns at least monthly.
  - Prior to that date, quarterly valuation was allowed.
  - Less frequent valuation provisions may apply to real estate and private equity. (If relevant, this is covered in the special provisions for RE and PE.)
- Beginning January 1, 2010, GIPS requires firms to also value portfolios on the date of any large external cash flow (ECF) and time weight the subperiod returns.

- The firm is responsible for determining what constitutes a large ECF. The definition is normally a percentage (ECF / portfolio value). A large ECF is defined as any ECF that is large enough that it may distort the computed return. The firm's definition of large is composite specific and can consider practical realities. It can be higher for illiquid than for liquid markets.

- Once the valuation frequency policy by composite is adopted, it must be followed. More or less frequent valuation to determine subperiod returns is prohibited. This prevents firms from cherry-picking the periods in an effort to find the most favorable (highest) return calculation.

- Prior to 2010, firms could use approximations of time-weighted return to deal with large ECFs.

- Technically, those older methods can still be used but only if the firm can document that they do not materially differ from true time-weighted return with subperiods determined by the date of large ECFs.

- BV and EV must include the value of any cash and cash equivalents the manager chooses to hold in the portfolio (Standard 2.A.3). This cash represents a manager decision, as does any other holding. This requirement applies even if the firm uses another manager to manage the cash equivalents.

  - If the cash and cash equivalent position is due to client activity and large enough to prevent the manager from implementing the intended strategy, other provisions of GIPS apply.

- All return calculations must be gross of fees. This means after actual trading expenses but before all other fees (Standard 2.A.4). Estimated trading expense is not allowed. Note that this will normally occur in trade settlement, as sale proceeds (purchase cost) are normally reduced (increased) for actual transaction costs. Instead of gross-of-fee returns, firms may report net-of-fee returns, which are gross returns minus the account investment management fee.

  - Bundled fees (Standard 2.A.5) may make gross-of-fee reporting difficult. A bundled fee is any fee that includes some combination of trading expense, management fee, and other fees. Other fees are anything other than trading and management fees. If trading and management expenses cannot be separated out of the bundled fee, deduct the entire bundled fee. If the bundled fee includes trading but not management, label the result gross-of-fee. If the bundled fee includes both trading and management fees, label the result net-of-fee. What is included in the bundled fee must be fully disclosed.

- When the firm controls the timing of ECFs, time-weighted return cannot be used, and internal rate of return (IRR) must be used for return computations. (If relevant, this is covered in the special provisions for RE and PE.)

Example: Time-weighted rate of return

The Rooney account was $2,500,000 at the start of the month and $2,700,000 at the end. During the month, there was a cash inflow of $45,000 on day 7 and $25,000 on day 19. The values of the Rooney account are $2,555,000 and $2,575,000 (inclusive of the cash flows for the day) on day 7 and day 19, respectively. **Calculate** the time-weighted rate of return (assuming 30 days in the month).

Answer:

First, calculate three subperiod returns using the rate of return calculation when external cash flows occur at the end of the evaluation period:

Subperiod 1 (days 1–7)

$$r_{t,1} = \frac{\left[(\$2,555,000 - \$45,000) - \$2,500,000\right]}{\$2,500,000} = 0.004 = 0.4\%$$

Subperiod 2 (days 8–19)

$$r_{t,2} = \frac{\left[(\$2,575,000 - \$25,000) - \$2,555,000\right]}{\$2,555,000} = -0.002 = -0.2\%$$

Subperiod 3 (days 20–30)

$$r_{t,3} = \frac{(\$2,700,000 - \$2,575,000)}{\$2,575,000} = 0.049 = 4.9\%$$

Second, compound the returns together (chain-link) to calculate an overall time-weighted rate of return:

$$\text{TWRR} = (1 + 0.004)(1 - 0.002)(1 + 0.049) - 1 = 0.051 = 5.1\%$$

Older Computation Methods

Prior to January 1, 2005, ECFs could be treated as if they occurred in the middle of the time period (the original Dietz method). After January 1, 2005, until the current rules took effect on January 1, 2010, two methods were allowed to approximate time-weighted return:

- ECFs could be daily weighted (the modified Dietz method).
- The modified internal rate of return could be used. (MIRR is simply IRR, and *modified* refers to using IRR as an approximation for time-weighted return.)

Example: Older methods of approximating TWRR for GIPS

Based on the previous data in the Rooney account, calculate the approximations of TWRR.

Original Dietz:

- Total ECFs were +45,000 + 25,000 for a net +ECF of 70,000.

  (EV – BV – ECF) / (BV + 0.5(Net ECF))

  (2,700,000 – 2,500,000 – 70,000) / (2,500,000 + .5(70,000))

  130,000 / 2,535,000 = 5.13%

Modified Dietz:

- The numerator is the same as for original Dietz: 130,000.
- The denominator is the BV plus each ECF time weighted for the remainder of the full time period:

  2,500,000 was available for the full month

  + 45,000 received on day 7 is available for (30 – 7) / 30 of the month

  + 45,000((30 – 7) / 30) = 34,500 ≈ 45,000(0.77)

  + 25,000 received on day 19 is available for (30 – 19) / 30 of the month

  + 25,000((30 – 19) / 30) = 9,167 ≈ 25,000(0.37)

  130,000 / (2,500,000 + 34,500 + 9,167) = 5.11%

MIRR:

- This must be solved by trial and error to find the r that equates the EV to the FV of the BV and ECFs. Like modified Dietz, each ECF is weighted for the portion of the month it is available. (The ,000 are dropped to simplify, and the remainder of month periods are calculated to two decimal places.)

  $2,700 = 2,500(1 + r) + 45(1 + r)^{0.77} + 25(1 + r)^{0.37}$

  r = MIRR = 5.11%

Professor's Note: The previously calculated true TWRR was 5.1%, making the older approximations methods very close. This is not surprising, given that the ECFs were relatively small. Unless ECFs are relatively large and the path of returns varies significantly by subperiod, the methods will produce similar results.

The old methods are covered in the CFA text and are easy enough once you grasp the concept. Solving for MIRR by trial and error is not an LOS and not specifically covered in the CFA text.

COMPOSITE RETURNS AND ASSET-WEIGHTED RETURNS

LOS 32.e: Explain the requirements and recommendations of the GIPS standards with respect to composite return calculations, including methods for asset-weighting portfolio returns.

GIPS requires firms to report performance by composite, where a composite is a group of accounts with similar objectives (Standards 2.A.6 and 7). The return of the composite is the weighted average monthly return of the accounts in the composite. (Prior to January 1, 2010, quarterly returns could be used.)

Weights can be based on either beginning of period account value or beginning of period plus weighted average ECFs for the period. End of period account values cannot be used, as that would increase the relative weighting of the accounts with the higher relative return for the period.

It is also allowable to aggregate total beginning and ending market value and aggregate all the ECFs of the composite. Then, directly calculate the return of the composite as if it were all one account.

Professor's Note: The formulas for computing weighted average can look intimidating. Of course, by now, you have computed weighted average dozens of times in the course of CFA exam prep; this is no different. One weighted average is like another weighted average.

Example: Comparison of composite returns calculation methods

Using the data presented in portfolios A and B, **calculate** the composite return using the (1) beginning market value-weighted method, (2) beginning market value plus cash flow method, and (3) aggregate return method.

Figure 1: Portfolio A

Date	Market Value ($)	Cash Flow ($)	Market Value After Cash Flow ($)
03/31/05	500,000		
04/10/05	515,000	100,000	615,000
04/18/05	650,000		
04/30/05	665,000		
	Monthly return = 11.32%		

Figure 2: Portfolio B

Date	Market Value ($)	Cash Flow ($)	Market Value After Cash Flow ($)
03/31/05	250,000		
04/10/05	256,000		
04/18/05	265,000	–35,000	230,000
04/30/05	235,000		

Monthly return = 8.26%

Answer:

Beginning market value method:

$$R_{BMV} = \frac{(500,000 \times 0.1132) + (250,000 \times 0.0826)}{500,000 + 250,000} = 10.30\%$$

Beginning market value plus cash flows method:

$$W_{Port\,A} = \frac{30-10}{30} = 0.67 \quad W_{Port\,B} = \frac{30-18}{30} = 0.40$$

$$R_{BMV+CF} = \frac{\begin{Bmatrix} [500,000 + (100,000 \times 0.67)] \times 0.1132 \\ + [250,000 + (-35,000 \times 0.40)] \times 0.0826 \end{Bmatrix}}{\begin{Bmatrix} [500,000 + (100,000 \times 0.67)] \\ + [250,000 + (-35,000 \times 0.40)] \end{Bmatrix}} = 10.42\%$$

Aggregate method:

$$W_{Port\,A} = \frac{30-10}{30} = 0.67$$

$$W_{Port\,B} = \frac{30-18}{30} = 0.40$$

$$R_{BMV+CF} = \frac{(665,000 + 235,000) - (500,000 + 250,000) - [100,000 + (-35,000)]}{500,000 + 250,000 + (100,000 \times 0.67) + (-35,000 \times 0.40)}$$

$$= 10.59\%$$

GIPS Calculation Methodology *Recommendations*

- **Standard 2.B.1.** Returns should be calculated net of non-reclaimable withholding taxes on dividends, interest, and capital gains. Reclaimable withholding taxes should be accrued.

Discussion: This Standard is similar to 2.A.4 stated previously. Foreign investments often have a tax on income or gains that is deducted at the source. It is often possible to reclaim this amount by applying to the relevant tax authorities. If the withheld tax is reclaimable, it should be accrued until recovered; if the tax is not reclaimable, it should be treated like a transactions cost.

DISCRETIONARY PORTFOLIOS

LOS 32.f: Explain the meaning of "discretionary" in the context of composite construction and, given a description of the relevant facts, determine whether a portfolio is likely to be considered discretionary.

- **Standard 3.A.1.** All actual, fee-paying, discretionary portfolios must be included in at least one composite. Although non-fee-paying discretionary portfolios may be included in a composite (with appropriate disclosures), nondiscretionary portfolios must not be included in a firm's composites.

Discussion: From the wording of this Standard, it is clear that the notion of "discretionary" is key to a portfolio because it determines whether the portfolio *must* be included in at least one composite or if it *must not* be included in any composite.

The Investment Performance Council defines discretion as "the ability of the firm to implement its intended strategy." A client may place significant constraints on the manager—for instance, the investment policy statement (IPS) may specify limits on sectors, credit ratings, durations, et cetera. Furthermore, there may be total restrictions on certain transactions, such as the purchase of "unethical" or foreign investments, or the sale of specified stocks. These restrictions *do not* automatically remove the discretionary nature of the portfolio.

A portfolio becomes nondiscretionary when the manager is no longer able to implement the intended investment strategy. If for instance the liquidity requirements are so great that much of the value must be in cash, or if the portfolio has minimal tracking limits from an index portfolio, then the description of "discretionary" is really no longer appropriate.

Standard 3.A.1 also demonstrates that by including all fee-paying discretionary portfolios in at least one composite, managers cannot cherry-pick their best performing portfolios to present to prospective clients. Firms are permitted to include a portfolio in more than one composite, provided it satisfies the definition of each composite.

Non-fee-paying portfolios may be included in the firm's composites, but if they are, firms are required to disclose the percentage of composite assets represented by non-fee-paying portfolios. If the firm includes non-fee-paying portfolios in its composites, those portfolios are subject to the same rules as fee-paying portfolios.

If a portfolio's status changes from discretionary to nondiscretionary, the portfolio may not be removed from a composite retroactively. However, the portfolio must be removed going forward.

CONSTRUCTING COMPOSITES: MANDATES, STRATEGIES, AND STYLES

LOS 32.g: Explain the role of investment mandates, objectives, or strategies in the construction of composites.

- **Standard 3.A.4.** Composites must be defined according to similar investment objectives and/or strategies. Composites must include all portfolios that meet the composite definition. The full composite definition must be made available on request.

  Discussion: Composites should be defined such that clients are able to compare the performance of one firm to another. Composites must be representative of the firm's products and be consistent with the firm's marketing strategy.

  - Firms are not permitted to include portfolios with different investment strategies or objectives in the same composite.
  - Portfolios may not be moved into or out of composites except in the case of valid, documented, client-driven changes in investment objectives or guidelines or in the case of the redefinition of the composite.

  Generic definitions such as "equity" or "fixed income" may be too broad to enable clients to make comparisons, so qualifiers such as sector, benchmark, capitalization (e.g., large, mid, small), style (e.g., value, growth, blend), or even risk-return profile may be useful. However, too many qualifiers could result in a plethora of similar composites, each containing a very small number of portfolios.

CONSTRUCTING COMPOSITES: ADDING PORTFOLIOS AND TERMINATING PORTFOLIOS

LOS 32.h: Explain the requirements and recommendations of the GIPS standards with respect to composite construction, including switching portfolios among composites, the timing of the inclusion of new portfolios in composites, and the timing of the exclusion of terminated portfolios from composites.

- **Standard 3.A.2.** Composites must include only assets under management within the defined firm.
- **Standard 3.A.3.** Firms are not permitted to link simulated or model portfolios with actual performance.

  Discussion: Simulated, back-tested, or model portfolio results do not represent the returns of actual assets under management and, thus, may not be included in composites performance results.

- **Standard 3.A.5.** Composites must include new portfolios on a timely and consistent basis after the portfolio comes under management.

   Discussion: For each individual composite, firms should have a policy for the inclusion of new portfolios. Ideally, the policy will prescribe inclusion of a new portfolio in a composite at the start of the next full performance measurement period.

   Recognizing that situations exist where firms may need time to invest the assets of a new portfolio, the Standards allow some discretion on this issue. For example, it will likely take longer to add a new portfolio to an emerging markets fixed-income portfolio than it will take to add portfolio assets to a developed market government bond portfolio, or a client may deposit the asset for a new portfolio over a period of time. In any case, firms must establish a policy for the inclusion of new portfolios on a composite-by-composite basis and apply it consistently.

- **Standard 3.A.6.** Terminated portfolios must be included in the historical returns of the appropriate composites up to the last full measurement period that the portfolio was under management.

   Discussion: Retaining the performance of a terminated portfolio through its final full period helps alleviate the effects of survivorship bias. For example, if the portfolio was in the composite for one quarter and the performance for the composite for that quarter is reported, the performance of the terminated portfolio must be included. However, presenting an annual return for a terminated portfolio with less than a full year's performance (e.g., creating an annual return from less than four quarterly returns) is not allowed. This would be equivalent to presenting simulated performance. (See Standard 3.A.3.)

- **Standard 3.A.7.** Portfolios must not be switched from one composite to another unless documented changes in client guidelines or the redefinition of the composite make it appropriate. The historical record of the portfolio must remain with the original composite.

   Discussion: Even if investment strategies change over time, firms usually do not change the definition of a composite. Rather, changes in strategy typically result in the creation of a new composite. In the rare case that it is deemed appropriate to redefine a composite, the firm must disclose the date and nature of the change. Changes to composite definitions must not be applied retroactively.

- **Standard 3.A.9.** If a firm sets a minimum asset level for portfolios to be included in a composite, no portfolios below that asset level can be included in that composite. Any changes to a composite-specific minimum asset level are not permitted to be applied retroactively.

   Discussion: If a composite specifies a minimum size for portfolios, the minimum size must be applied on a consistent basis. Because portfolios may drop below the minimum for a short period, the IPC Guidance Statement on Composite Definition recommends that a policy be put in place to identify percentage or period of breaches after which a portfolio should be removed from the composite. For instance, a portfolio may have to be removed after falling more than 10% below the limit or after being below the limit at the start of three successive periods.

   Note that the performance history for a composite may not be adjusted as a result of a constituent portfolio being removed, and composite definitions may not be changed retroactively.

- **Standard 3.A.10.** A portfolio could receive a significant external cash flow (defined as a cash flow large enough that the portfolio temporarily does not reflect the composite's style). The recommendation is to put the cash in a temporary new account that is not part of the composite until the funds are invested in accordance with the style. At that time the temporary new account should be merged into the existing account. Only if this is not possible should the account be temporarily removed from the composite until the account again reflects the composite style.

  Discussion: The intent is to prevent the client contribution from creating a cash drag and disrupting the ability of the manager to implement the intended style. Either the temporary account or removal should be temporary and only for a period of time long enough for the manager to make investments that reflect the composite's style.

  Example:

  Account #207 invests in illiquid, fixed income securities. The account receives a large cash infusion on April 12 that cannot be invested quickly at reasonable prices. It is expected to take 60 days for the funds to be reasonably invested.

  Best Solution:

  Place the funds in a new, temporary, subaccount (call it 207T) until the funds are invested. Continue to report results for 207 in its appropriate composite. Results for 207T will not be reported in any composite. Once 207T is invested in accord with account objectives, 207T will be merged into 207 and affect future results for 207. (Note that the client will need to receive reports showing the results of 207T and 207 to comply with general reporting requirements under the Standards of Professional Conduct. Subaccount 207T is only excluded from GIPS reporting.)

  Alternative Solution:

  The funds could be placed directly into 207 and 207 results would be excluded from the composite results until the funds are invested in accord with client objectives. GIPS composite results are based on monthly results so if the investments are completed by June 15, account 207 will be excluded from the composite for months April, May, and June. (Note that the client will need to receive reports showing the results of 207 to comply with general reporting requirements under the Standards of Professional Conduct. Account 207 is temporarily excluded from GIPS reporting.)

- **Standard 3.B.2.** To remove the effect of significant cash flows, firms should use temporary new accounts.

  Discussion: Significant cash flows are external cash flows directed by a client that are large enough to disrupt the management of the composite. In the case of significant inflows, the firm is encouraged to create a separate account until the funds can be invested according to the composite strategy. The inclusion of the new securities in the composite should be managed according to the firm's established policy on the inclusion of new portfolios. When the client directs a significant withdrawal, the firm is encouraged to establish a securities account separate from the composite until the securities can be liquidated and the cash distributed.

CARVE-OUTS

LOS 32.i: Explain the requirements of the GIPS standards for asset class segments carved out of multi-class portfolios.

- **Standard 3.A.8.** For periods beginning on or after January 1, 2010, carve-outs must not be included in a composite unless the carve-out is actually managed separately with its own cash balance. Prior to that date, firms could do internal computations to simulate the results of dividing the portfolio into subaccounts.

  Carve out accounting is optional and used if an investment management firm wishes to report the results of portions of an account that follows a multiple-strategy objective.

Example:

DVE Asset Management manages portfolios that include four styles: (1) domestic equity, (2) international equity, (3) fixed income, and (4) balanced portfolios that include all three asset segments. DVE maintains composites for each of these four investment styles. Within DVE there are separate teams that manage each of the three asset segments (the first three styles). One of the accounts, the BJ Foundation (BJF), is a balanced account that has a strategic objective to invest one-third in each of the three asset segments. BJF results are reported as part of the Balanced Composite and DVE would like to also report the domestic equity results of BJF as part of the Domestic Equity Composite.

Solution:

DVE should set up an account for BJF domestic equity and manage it as a separate account. If, for example, BJF is a $30 million portfolio, then $10 million (one-third of the $30 million) should be placed in the BJF domestic equity account and the performance of this separate subaccount can be included in the Domestic Equity Composite. If the managers of the BJF domestic equity account hold cash in that account, it will affect the total return calculation that is included in the domestic equity composite for BJF. The results of the entire $30 million BJF account must continue to be included in the Balanced Composite (and reported to the client). (Note that DVE could also set up separate subaccounts for BJF international equity and fixed income as well if desired and report each of these subaccount performances in their respective asset segment composites.)

DISCLOSURE REQUIREMENTS AND RECOMMENDATIONS

LOS 32.j: Explain the requirements and recommendations of the GIPS standards with respect to disclosure, including fees, the use of leverage and derivatives, conformity with laws and regulations that conflict with the GIPS standards, and noncompliant performance periods.

GIPS REQUIRED DISCLOSURES

- **Standard 4.A.1.** Once a firm has met all the requirements of the GIPS standards, the firm must disclose its compliance with the GIPS standards using one of the following compliance statements.

  For firms that are verified:

  [Insert name of firm] claims compliance with the Global Investment Performance Standards (GIPS®) and has prepared and presented this report in compliance with the GIPS standards. [Insert name of firm] has been independently verified for the periods [insert dates]. The verification report(s) is/are available upon request.

  Verification assesses whether (1) the firm has complied with all the composite construction requirements of the GIPS standards on a firm-wide basis, and (2) the firm's policies and procedures are designed to calculate and present performance in compliance with the GIPS standards. Verification does not ensure the accuracy of any specific composite presentation.

  For composites of a verified firm that have also had a performance examination:

  [Insert name of firm] claims compliance with the Global Investment Performance Standards (GIPS®) and has prepared and presented this report in compliance with the GIPS standards. [Insert name of firm] has been independently verified for the periods [insert dates].

  Verification assesses whether (1) the firm has complied with all the composite construction requirements of the GIPS standards on a firm-wide basis, and (2) the firm's processes and procedures are designed to calculate and present performance in compliance with the GIPS standards. The [insert name of composite] composite has been examined for the periods [insert dates]. The verification and examination reports are available upon request.

  For firms that have not been verified:

  [Insert name of firm] claims compliance with the Global Investment Performance Standards (GIPS®) and has prepared and presented this report in compliance with the GIPS standards. [Insert name of firm] has not been independently verified.

- **Standard 4.A.2.** Firms must disclose the definition of "firm" used to determine the total firm assets and firm-wide compliance.
- **Standard 4.A.3.** Firms must disclose the composite description.
- **Standard 4.A.4.** Firms must disclose the benchmark description.

- **Standard 4.A.5.** When presenting gross-of-fees returns, firms must disclose if any other fees are deducted in addition to the direct trading expenses.
- **Standard 4.A.6.** When presenting net-of-fees returns, firms must disclose a) if any other fees are deducted in addition to the investment management fee and direct trading expenses, b) if model or actual investment management fees are used, and c) if returns are net of performance-based fees.
- **Standard 4.A.7.** Firms must disclose the currency used to express performance.
- **Standard 4.A.8.** Firms must disclose which measure of internal dispersion is used.
- **Standard 4.A.9.** Firms must disclose the fee schedule appropriate to the compliant presentation.
- **Standard 4.A.10.** Firms must disclose the composite creation date.
- **Standard 4.A.11.** Firms must disclose that the firm's list of composite descriptions is available upon request.
- **Standard 4.A.12.** Firms must disclose that policies for valuing portfolios, calculating performance, and preparing compliant presentations are available upon request.
- **Standard 4.A.13.** Firms must disclose the presence, use, and extent of leverage, derivatives, and short positions, if material, including a description of the frequency of use and characteristics of the instruments sufficient to identify risks.

Discussion: It is important that prospective clients understand how leverage or derivatives affected past performance and could affect future performance (i.e., risk and return). Many clients may never have dealt with some of these complex strategies, so a clear and comprehensive description is essential. For instance, a manager may use equity or debt futures to adjust the beta or duration of a portfolio. The description of the strategy should highlight possible differences in performance between the derivative and the underlying assets, such as rollover, basis, or call risk.

An example of an acceptable disclosure under this Standard is as follows: "Eurodollar CD futures are used occasionally to hedge against adverse interest rate changes. The positions are not leveraged."

- **Standard 4.A.14.** Firms must disclose all significant events that would help a prospective client interpret the compliant presentation.
- **Standard 4.A.15.** For any performance presented for periods prior to January 1, 2000, that does not comply with the GIPS standards, firms must disclose the periods of non-compliance.

Discussion: In order to claim compliance with the GIPS, performance presentations for periods beginning January 1, 2000, must be GIPS-compliant. For periods prior to January 1, 2000, firms may present performance results that do not comply with the Standards as long as they disclose the periods of non-compliance.

- **Standard 4.A.16.** If the firm is redefined, the firm must disclose the date of, description of, and reason for the redefinition.
- **Standard 4.A.17.** If a composite is redefined, the firm must disclose the date of, description of, and reason for the redefinition.
- **Standard 4.A.18.** Firms must disclose any changes to the name of a composite.
- **Standard 4.A.19.** Firms must disclose the minimum asset level, if any, below which portfolios are not included in a composite. Firms must also disclose any changes to the minimum asset level.

- **Standard 4.A.20.** Firms must disclose relevant details of the treatment of withholding tax on dividends, interest income, and capital gains, if material. Firms must also disclose if benchmark returns are net of withholding taxes if this information is available.
- **Standard 4.A.21.** For periods beginning January 1, 2011, firms must disclose and describe any known material differences in the exchange rates or valuation sources used among the portfolios within a composite and between the composite and the benchmark. For periods prior to January 1, 2011, firms must disclose and describe any known inconsistencies in the exchange rates used among the portfolios within a composite and between the composite and the benchmark.
- **Standard 4.A.22.** If the compliant presentation conforms with laws and/or regulations that conflict with the requirement of the GIPS standards, firms must disclose this fact and disclose the manner in which the local laws and regulations conflict with the GIPS standards.
- **Standard 4.A.23.** For periods prior to January 1, 2010, if carve-outs are included in a composite, firms must disclose the policy used to allocate cash to the carve-outs.
- **Standard 4.A.24.** If a composite contains portfolios with bundled fees, firms must disclose the types of fees that are included in the bundled fee.
- **Standard 4.A.25.** Beginning January 1, 2006, firms must disclose the use of a sub-adviser and the periods a sub-adviser was used.
- **Standard 4.A.26.** For periods prior to January 1, 2010, firms must disclose if any portfolios were not valued at calendar month end or on the last business day of the month.
- **Standard 4.A.27.** For periods beginning January 1, 2011, firms must disclose the use of subjective unobservable inputs for valuing portfolio investments if the portfolio investments valued using subjective unobservable inputs are material to the composite.
- **Standard 4.A.28.** For periods beginning January 1, 2011, firms must disclose if the composite's valuation hierarchy materially differs from the recommended hierarchy in the GIPS Valuation Principles.
- **Standard 4.A.29.** If the firm determines no appropriate benchmark for the composite exists, the firm must disclose why no benchmark is presented.
- **Standard 4.A.30.** If the firm changes the benchmark, the firm must disclose the date of, description of, and reason for the change.
- **Standard 4.A.31.** If a custom benchmark or combination of multiple benchmarks is used, the firm must disclose the benchmark components, weights, and rebalancing process.
- **Standard 4.A.32.** If the firm has adopted a significant cash flow policy for a specific composite, the firm must disclose how the firm defines a significant cash flow for that composite and for which periods.
- **Standard 4.A.33.** Firms must disclose if the 3-year annualized ex post standard deviation of the composite and/or benchmark is not presented because 36 monthly returns are not available.
- **Standard 4.A.34.** If the firm determines that the 3-year annualized ex post standard deviation is not relevant or appropriate, the firm must a) describe why ex post standard deviation is not relevant or appropriate and b) describe the additional risk measure presented and why it was selected.
- **Standard 4.A.35.** Firms must disclose if the performance from a past firm or affiliation is linked to the performance of the firm.

GIPS Recommended Disclosures

- **Standard 4.B.1.** Firms should disclose material changes to valuation policies and/or methodologies.
- **Standard 4.B.2.** Firms should disclose material changes to calculation policies and/or methodologies.
- **Standard 4.B.3.** Firms should disclose material differences between the benchmark and the composite's investment mandate, objective, or strategy.
- **Standard 4.B.4.** Firms should disclose the key assumptions used to value portfolio investments.
- **Standard 4.B.5.** If a parent company contains multiple defined firms, each firm within the parent company should disclose a list of the other firms contained within the parent company.
- **Standard 4.B.6.** For periods prior to January 1, 2011, firms should disclose the use of subjective unobservable inputs for valuing portfolio investments if the portfolio investments valued using subjective unobservable inputs are material to the composite.
- **Standard 4.B.7.** For periods prior to January 1, 2006, firms should disclose the use of a sub-adviser and the periods a sub-adviser was used.
- **Standard 4.B.8.** Firms should disclose if a composite contains proprietary assets.

GIPS Presentation and Reporting Requirements

LOS 32.k: Explain the requirements and recommendations of the GIPS standards with respect to presentation and reporting, including the required timeframe of compliant performance periods, annual returns, composite assets, and benchmarks.

LOS 32.l: Explain the conditions under which the performance of a past firm or affiliation must be linked to or used to represent the historical performance of a new or acquiring firm.

LOS 32.m: Evaluate the relative merits of high/low, range, interquartile range, and equal-weighted or asset-weighted standard deviation as measures of the internal dispersion of portfolio returns within a composite for annual periods.

After constructing composites, gathering input data, calculating returns, and determining the necessary disclosures, firms must integrate this information in presentations based on the guidelines set out in GIPS for presenting the investment performance results. No finite set of guidelines can cover all potential situations or anticipate future developments in investment industry structure, technology, products, or practices. When appropriate, firms have the responsibility to include information not covered by the Standards.

- **Standard 5.A.1.** The following items must be reported for each composite presented:

  a. At least five years of annual performance (or a record for the period since firm or composite inception if the firm or composite has been in existence less than five years) that meets the requirements of the GIPS standards; after presenting five years of performance, the firm must present additional annual performance up to a minimum of ten years.

  b. Annual returns for all years clearly identified as gross- or net-of-fees.

  c. For composites with a composite inception date beginning on or after January 1, 2011, when the initial period is less than a full year, firms must present returns from the composite inception through the initial year-end.

  d. For composites with a termination date of January 1, 2011, or later, returns from the last annual period through the termination date.

  e. Annual returns for a benchmark, which reflects the mandate, objective, or strategy of the portfolio.

  f. The number of portfolios in the composite at each year-end. If the composite contains *five portfolios or less,* the number of portfolios is not required.

  g. The amount of assets in the composite at the end of each annual period.

  h. Either total firm assets or composite assets as a percentage of firm assets at each annual period end.

  i. A measure of dispersion of individual portfolio returns for each annual period. If the composite contains *five portfolios or less* for the full year, a measure of dispersion is not required.

Internal dispersion is a measure of the range of returns for only those portfolios that are included in the composite over the entire period. Portfolios added to or removed from a composite during the period are not included in that period's calculation of internal dispersion.

Example: Internal dispersion

The following figure illustrates the structure of a composite during 2014. An *X* indicates that the portfolio was included in the composite for the quarter. If a cell is blank, the portfolio was not included in the composite for the entire quarter. **Determine** which portfolios should be contained in the internal dispersion measure for 2014.

Figure 3: Composite Structure, 2014

Portfolio	Quarter 1	Quarter 2	Quarter 3	Quarter 4
A	X	X	X	X
B	X	X	X	
C	X	X	X	X
D		X	X	X
E	X	X	X	X
F			X	X

Answer:

Based on the information contained in the previous figure, Portfolios A, C, and E would be included in the internal dispersion measure for 2014. Portfolios B, D, and F should be excluded from the calculation of the composite's 2014 internal dispersion because they do not have an entire year of performance results. Note that this is only three portfolios to include in the dispersion calculation. Unless there are other portfolios with a full year of data to include in the calculation, no dispersion will be reported. Six or more are required to report dispersion.

The GIPS Handbook identifies the following acceptable methods for calculating internal dispersion:

- The range of annual returns.
- The high and low annual returns.
- Interquartile range.
- The standard deviation of equal-weighted annual return.
- The asset-weighted standard deviation of annual returns.

The **range** of annual returns and the **high and low** annual returns are the simplest and most easily understood measures of dispersion. The advantages of these measures include simplicity, ease of calculation, and ease of interpretation. Disadvantages include the fact that an extreme value can skew the data, and they do not stand alone as adequate risk measures.

The **interquartile range** is the middle 50% of a population, excluding the top 25% and bottom 25%. Hence, it measures the part of the population between the bottom of the first quartile and the bottom of the third quartile.

The **standard deviation** across equally weighted portfolios is the most widely accepted measure of dispersion within a composite. It is calculated as:

$$\sigma_C = \sqrt{\frac{\sum_{i=1}^{n}[R_i - MEAN(R)]^2}{n-1}}$$

where:
R_i = return on portfolio i
$MEAN(R)$ = equal-weighted mean (composite) return
n = number of portfolios

 Professor's Note: The use of either n or n – 1 in the denominator can be supported, and firms are encouraged to disclose how they calculate standard deviation.

The *standard deviation with asset-weighted composite* returns is calculated in the following manner:

$$\text{dispersion} = \sqrt{\sum_{i=1}^{n} w_i \left(R_i - C_{ASSET}\right)^2}$$

where:
R_i = unweighted return on portfolio i
w_i = market weight of portfolio i relative to the market value of the composite
C_{ASSET} = composite's asset-weighted return, or $C_{ASSET} = \sum w_i R_i$

- **Standard 5.A.2.** For periods beginning on or after January 1, 2011, firms must present for each annual period:

  a. Three-year annualized ex post standard deviation using monthly returns for the composite and benchmark.

  b. An additional 3-year ex post risk measure if management feels standard deviation is inappropriate. The firm must match the periodicity of calculated returns used for the composite and benchmark.

- **Standard 5.A.3.** Firms may link non-GIPS-compliant returns to their compliant history so long as the firms meet the disclosure requirements for noncompliant performance and only compliant returns are presented for periods after January 1, 2000.

- **Standard 5.A.4.** Returns of portfolios and composites for periods of less than one year must not be annualized.

  Discussion: The annualizing of partial-year returns is essentially the simulation of returns over a period, which is not allowed.

- **Standard 5.A.5.** For periods beginning on or after January 1, 2006, and ending prior to January 1, 2011, if a composite includes carve-outs, the presentation must include the percentage of the composite that is composed of carve-outs for each annual period.

- **Standard 5.A.6.** If a composite contains any non-fee-paying portfolios, the firm must present, as of the end of each annual period, the percentage of the composite assets represented by the non-fee-paying portfolios.

  Discussion: An example of a non-fee-paying portfolio is one that is managed on a *pro bono* basis. Portfolios that are non-fee-paying do not have to be included in any composite, and the firm need not make any disclosures regarding such portfolios.

- **Standard 5.A.7.** If a composite includes bundled-fee portfolios, the firm must present, as of the end of each annual period, the percentage of the composite assets represented by bundled-fee portfolios.

- **Standard 5.A.8.**

  a. Generally a performance track record of a composite *must* stay with the firm where it was generated. The record is not "portable," but if a past firm or affiliation is acquired and if three other conditions are met, the past record must be linked to and used by the new or acquiring firm. The three conditions are:

     i. Substantially all the investment decision makers are employed by the new firm (e.g., research department, portfolio managers, and other relevant staff);

     ii. The decision-making process remains substantially intact and independent within the new firm; and

     iii. The new firm has records that document and support the reported performance.

  b. If a firm acquires another firm or affiliation, the firm has one year to bring any noncompliant assets into compliance.

  Discussion: If ownership of the firm changes, through acquisition by a larger firm or other means, and the assets, managers, and management process remain substantially the same, the firm's composites are considered to have continued as if nothing happened.

  For most *new affiliations* or *newly formed entities*, however, performance results of a prior firm cannot be used to represent a historical record. For example, when a manager leaves a firm to start or join another firm, the manager cannot present the old firm's past performance in the new firm's composite. The composite record is assumed to remain with the old firm because that firm *owns* the strategy and process.

GIPS PRESENTATION AND REPORTING RECOMMENDATIONS

- **Standard 5.B.1.** Firms should present gross of fees returns.
- **Standard 5.B.2.** Firms should present:
  a. Cumulative returns for composite and benchmarks for all periods.

  b. Equal-weighted mean and median returns for each composite.

    c.   Quarterly and/or monthly returns.

    d.   Annualized composite and benchmark returns for periods greater than 12 months.

- **Standard 5.B.3.** For periods prior to January 1, 2011, the 3-year annualized ex post standard deviation of monthly returns for each year for the composite and its benchmark.
- **Standard 5.B.4.** For each year in which an annualized ex post standard deviation is present for the composite and the benchmark, corresponding annualized return should be presented.
- **Standard 5.B.5.** For each year that annualized composite and benchmark returns are reported, the corresponding annualized standard deviation of monthly returns for the composite and benchmark.
- **Standard 5.B.6.** Additional ex post composite risk measures.
- **Standard 5.B.7.** Firms should present more than ten years of annual performance in the compliant presentation.
- **Standard 5.B.8.** Firms should comply with GIPS for all historical periods.
- **Standard 5.B.9.** Firms should update compliant presentations quarterly.

REAL ESTATE AND PRIVATE EQUITY—INTRODUCTION

LOS 32.n: Identify the types of investments that are subject to the GIPS standards for real estate and private equity.

Most of the GIPS provisions we have discussed thus far apply to real estate and private equity, and there are some exceptions as well as additional standards for the two asset classes.

The GIPS standards relating to real estate and private equity are fairly complex due to the nature of the investments. Before describing the Standards, let us first consider exactly which investments are covered by the provisions. (The GIPS, in fact, describe investments that should *not* be included in the asset classes.)

For **real estate**, the following investment types would fall under the *general provisions* of the GIPS standards (as opposed to the provisions dealing directly with real estate and private equity):

- Publicly traded real estate securities, including any listed securities issued by public companies.
- Mortgage-backed securities (MBS).
- Private debt investments, including commercial and residential loans where the expected return is solely related to contractual interest rates without any participation in the economic performance of the underlying real estate.

Note that publicly traded securities include Real Estate Investment Trusts (REITs) and mortgage-backed securities (MBS). If a portfolio consists of real estate plus other investments, the carve-out provisions of GIPS (Standard 3.A.8) would apply.

The exclusions to the definitions of **private equity** are *open-end* and *evergreen* funds, both of which are covered by the general provisions of the GIPS. Because redemptions and subscriptions may be made after the funds' inceptions, open-end and evergreen funds do not have fixed levels of capital with a set number of investors.

LOS 32.o: Explain the provisions of the GIPS standards for real estate and private equity.

GIPS REAL ESTATE REQUIREMENTS

For assets meeting the GIPS definition of real estate, the following additional provisions apply.

- **Standard 6.A.1.** Beginning January 1, 2011, real estate investments must be valued in accordance with the definition of fair value and the GIPS valuation principles.
- **Standards 6.A.2 and A.3.** For periods prior to January 1, 2008, real estate investments must be valued at market value at least once every 12 months. For periods beginning January 1, 2008, real estate investments must be valued at least quarterly. For periods on or after January 1, 2010, firms must value portfolios as of the end of each quarter or the last business day of each quarter using fair value principles.
- **Standards 6.A.4 and A.5.** For periods prior to January 1, 2012, real estate investments must have an external valuation done at least once every three years. External valuation means an outside, independent party certified to perform such valuations. "Certified" would mean licensed or otherwise recognized as qualified to perform such work. For periods beginning January, 1, 2012, real estate investments must have an external valuation done at least once every 12 months or if a client agreement states otherwise, at least once every three years.
- **Standards 6.A.6 and A.7.** Beginning January 1, 2006, real estate portfolio returns must be calculated at least quarterly after the deduction of transaction costs during the period. Transaction costs include actual financial, investment banking, legal, and advisory fees incurred for recapitalization, restructuring, buying, and selling properties.
- **Standard 6.A.8.** Beginning January, 1, 2011, income and capital component returns must be calculated separately using geometrically linked time-weighted rates of return.
- **Standard 6.A.9.** Composite returns, including component returns, must be calculated at least quarterly by asset-weighting the individual portfolio returns using time-weighted rates of return.
- **Standard 6.A.10.a.** The firm must provide a description of discretion. Discretion in real estate exists if the firm has sole or sufficient discretion to make major decisions regarding the investments.
- **Standards 6.A.10.b–e.** In regard to valuation methods used, the firm must disclose the internal valuation methods used and the frequency of external valuation. Beginning January 1, 2011, disclose material changes in valuation approach and differences in internal and external valuation and the reason for the difference.
- **Standards 6.A.11 and 6.A.15.** On or after January 1, 2006, GIPS compliant and non-compliant performance may not be linked. Prior to this date, any such linking must be disclosed.

Professor's Note: Standards 6.A.12 and 6.A.13 are not discussed in the CFA reading.

- **Standard 6.A.14.** In addition to the total return, the capital return and income return components must be disclosed, must sum to the total return, and must be clearly identified as gross or net of fees.

  Core real estate may earn most of its return from income while opportunistic real estate may earn more return from capital return. In either case, disclosing the components of return provides clients with information about the nature of the investment. The firm:

  - May present total return and component returns gross-of-fees (management), net-of-fees, or both ways. If only gross total return is presented, gross component returns must be presented. If only net total return is presented, net component returns must be presented. If both gross and net total returns are presented, then at least gross component returns must be presented.
  - For any quarterly return, the income and capital return components must sum to the total return (allowing for rounding differences). If the firm calculates monthly returns, the monthly component returns will sum to the monthly total return. However, the geometrically linked monthly component returns will not sum to the geometrically linked monthly total returns.

Figure 4: Hypothetical Real Estate Return Presentation

	Income Return	*Capital Return*	*Total Return*
January	1.00%	1.00%	2.00%
February	1.00%	1.00%	2.00%
March	1.00%	1.00%	2.00%
1st Quarter	3.03%	3.03%	6.12%

The quarterly return is found by *geometrically linking* the monthly returns:

$$R_{\text{quarterly component returns}} = 1.01^3 - 1 = 0.0303 = 3.03\%$$

$$R_{\text{quarterly total return}} = (1.02)^3 - 1 = 0.0612 = 6.12\%$$

- **Standard 6.A.16.a.** Composites with more than five portfolios must disclose the high and low of the portfolio time-weighted rates of return as the internal dispersion number.
- **Standard 6.A.16.b.** The percentage of composite assets valued using an external valuator as of the end of each annual period.

Recommended Items

Firms should disclose the accounting methods used for the portfolios (e.g., GAAP or IFRS) and at the end of each year any material differences in valuations for performance reporting versus financial reporting.

Both gross- and net-of-fee reporting is recommended along with the component returns for the benchmark and the percentage of value of the composite that is not real estate (if any).

Closed-End Fund Reporting

- **Standards 6.A.17 and 6.A.18.** Since inception rates of return (SI-IRR) must be reported using at least quarterly rates of return. This is the IRR of the cash flows since the start of the portfolio. Time periods less than a year are not annualized and periods longer than a year are annualized.

	Quarter	Value
Invested December 31, 2015	0	$100,000*
Invested March 31, 2016	1	$200,000
Distributed June 30, 2016	2	$10,000
Value as of September 30, 2016	3	$295,000

> * It is recommended the cash flows be done on a daily basis and at least quarterly must be used. GIPS allow flexibility in the exact calculation method used as long as the method is used consistently and fairly represents results.

  Using the cash flow functions of the calculator or by trial and error, the quarterly periodic IRR is 0.7209%. This is less than one year of data; therefore, the three-quarter geometrically linked return must be reported as 2.18% (= $1.007209^3 - 1$).

- **Standards 6.A.19 and 6.A.22.** Composites must be defined by grouping accounts with similar objective, strategy, et cetera, and **vintage year**. Vintage year can be determined by either (1) year of first drawdown or capital call (i.e., when investors first contribute funds) or (2) when investor-contributed capital is closed and legally enforceable (i.e., when all investors to the fund have legally committed to the amount they must contribute).

Disclosures

- **Standard 6.A.20.** The final liquidation date for liquidated composites.
- **Standard 6.A.21.** The frequency of cash flows used in the SI-IRR calculation.
- **Standard 6.A.23.** On or after January 1, 2011, periods less than a year must present net-of-fees SI-IRR and reporting must continue until liquidation of the composite.

Presentation and reporting

- **Standard 6.A.24.** Firms must report the benchmark SI-IRR results and, for comparison, may wish to report composite gross-of-fees SI-IRR. If this is done, then gross- and net-of-fees composite results must be shown for all reporting periods.

- **Standard 6.A.25.** At the end of each reporting period, the firm must disclose the following (these provisions also apply to private equity):
  - **Committed capital and since-inception paid-in-capital.** These are respectively the amount of capital the investor must contribute and how much of that has been contributed to date.
  - **Distributions.** What has been paid back to investors.
  - **TVPI (the investment multiple).** The ratio of total value to since-inception paid-in-capital; total value is the residual value (value of the portfolio at the end of the period) plus since-inception distributions.
  - **DPI (the realization multiple).** The ratio of since-inception distributions to paid-in-capital.
  - **PIC multiple.** The ratio of paid-in-capital to committed capital.
  - **RVPI (the unrealized multiple).** The ratio of residual value to paid-in-capital.
- **Standard 6.A.26.** The SI-IRR of the benchmark through each annual period end. The benchmark must:
  1. Reflect the investment mandate, objective, or strategy of the composite.
  2. Be presented for the same time period as presented for the composite.
  3. Be the same vintage year as the composite.

PRIVATE EQUITY REQUIREMENTS

Input data:

- **Standards 7.A.1 and 7.A.2.** Private equity assets must be valued at least annually, at fair value, and according to GIPS Valuation Principles.

Calculation methodology:

- **Standards 7.A.3 and 7.A.4.** Annualized since-inception internal rate of return (SI-IRR).

  SI-IRR must be calculated using daily or monthly cash flows prior to January 1, 2011.

  Beginning January 1, 2011, the SI-IRR must be calculated using daily cash flows. Stock distributions must be valued at the time of the distribution and included as cash flows.

- **Standard 7.A.5 and 7.A.6.** Net-of-fees returns must be calculated with consideration given to management fees and carried interest.

  All returns must be calculated after deducting transaction expenses for the period.

- **Standard 7.A.7.** For fund of funds, all returns must be net of all partnership fees, fund fees, expenses, and carried interest.

Composite construction:

- **Standard 7.A.8.** Throughout the life of the composite, composite definitions must remain consistent.
- **Standard 7.A.9.** Primary funds must be included in at least one composite defined by vintage year and investment strategy, mandate, or objective.
- **Standard 7.A.10.** Fund of funds must be included in at least one composite defined by vintage year and/or investment strategy, mandate, or objective.

Carried interest is an incentive fee earned by the manager. Generally, these are not paid until the investors have received back an amount equal to their contributed capital. They are essentially a deduction for an accrued fee to be paid.

Required disclosures:

- **Standards 7.A.11 and 7.A.12.** Vintage year and definition of the vintage year for the composite.

  The liquidation date for liquidated composites.

- **Standards 7.A.13 and 7.A.14.** Valuation methodology used for the most recent period, and starting January 1, 2011, any material changes in methodology or policies.
- **Standard 7.A.15.** Industry guidelines that have been followed in addition to the GIPS guidelines.
- **Standard 7.A.16.** The benchmark used and the return calculation methodology applied to the benchmark.
- **Standard 7.A.17.** The frequency of cash flows if daily cash flows are not used in calculating the SI-IRR prior to January 1, 2011.
- **Standards 7.A.18 and 7.A.19.** If any other fees are deducted in addition to transaction expenses when presenting gross-of-fees returns.

  If any other fees are deducted in addition to investment management fees and transaction expenses when presenting net-of-fees returns.

- **Standard 7.A.20.** Any periods of non-compliance prior to January 1, 2006.

Presentation and reporting:

- **Standard 7.A.21.** Beginning January 1, 2011, firms must present both the net-of-fees and gross-of-fees annualized SI-IRR of the composite for each year since inception and through the final liquidation date.

  Discussion: SI-IRR is the *since inception internal rate of return*. Remember that the IRR is the interest rate that makes the net present value (NPV) of the investment equal to zero. It is the IRR calculation example we did under closed-end fund reporting for Standards 6.A.17 and 18. The calculations must be performed and reported starting with the first period after initial client contributions and continue until the private equity investment is liquidated.

- **Standard 7.A.22.** Beginning January 1, 2011, for fund of funds composites, firms must present the SI-IRR of the underlying investments grouped by vintage year as well as the other measures required by Standard 7.A.23. All measures must be presented gross of the fund of funds investment management fees and for the most recent annual accounting period.
- **Standard 7.A.23.** For each period presented, firms must report:

  a. Since-inception paid-in capital.

  b. Cumulative committed capital.

  c. Since-inception distributions.

  d. Total value to paid-in capital (investment multiple or TVPI).

  e. Cumulative distributions to paid-in capital (realization multiple or DPI).

    f.   Paid-in capital to committed capital (PIC multiple).

    g.   Residual value to paid-in capital (unrealized multiple or RVPI).

Discussion: These are discussed in real estate.

- **Standard 7.A.24.** If a benchmark is shown, the cumulative annualized SI-IRR for the benchmark that reflects the same strategy and vintage year of the composite must be presented for the same periods for which the composite is presented. If no benchmark is shown, the presentation must explain why no benchmark is disclosed.

  Discussion: The **vintage year** is the year in which the private equity fund first draws down (calls for) capital. The economic conditions the year a fund starts significantly affects future performance, making vintage year an important disclosure item.

- **Standard 7.A.25.** For fund of funds composites, if a benchmark is presented, it must be of the same vintage year and investment objective, strategy, or mandate as the underlying investments.
- **Standard 7.A.26.** Beginning January 1, 2011, fund of funds composites must present the percentage of composite assets invested in direct investments.
- **Standard 7.A.27.** Beginning January 1, 2011, primary fund composites must present the percentage of composite assets invested in fund investment vehicles (instead of direct investments) as of the end of each annual period-end.
- **Standard 7.A.28.** Prior to January 1, 2006, firms may present non-GIPS-compliant performance.

GIPS PRIVATE EQUITY RECOMMENDATIONS

- **Standard 7.B.1–B.3.** Valuation should be done at least quarterly for private equity investments. For periods before January 1, 2011, the SI-IRR should be calculated using daily cash flows. Firms should disclose and explain any material differences between valuations used in performance reporting and those used in financial reporting as of the end of each annual reporting period.

WRAP FEE/SEPARATELY MANAGED ACCOUNTS

LOS 32.p: Explain the provisions of the GIPS standards for Wrap fee/ Separately Managed Accounts.

These GIPS provisions were adopted January 1, 2006, and apply to **wrap fee/separately managed accounts** (WFSMAs) where a GIPS-compliant investment manager serves as the subadvisor to a sponsor. For example:

Sponsor B is the client's (end user's) investment advisor and typically provides investment services such as overall portfolio advice, recordkeeping, and reporting; everything except the individual security management. Sponsor B is the client's manager but uses subadvisor K who has discretion and authority to manage the underlying assets. The client's investment advisor (sponsor B) charges the client a single bundled fee that covers all expenses including subadvisor K's fee as well as custody, trading, and administrative fees. There can be other types of bundled fees or subadvisor relationships but the following WFSMA provisions only apply when an intermediary (sponsor) exists between the investment management firm and the sponsor's client.

Professor's Note: The CFA text does not illustrate these other types of relationships and there is no reason to expect a "trick" question where you must identify such situations. But suppose manager G hires advisor M as a subadvisor to G and pays M for this advice. G can follow or not follow the advice of M and G has full responsibility and discretion for how the advice is used in any of G's client portfolios. The normal provisions of GIPS apply but not the special WFSMA provisions. M, the subadvisor, does not have discretion to mange underlying client assets.

These specific WFSMA provisions apply where the underlying investment management firm has discretion to manage the client portfolio and a bundled fee is charged by the sponsor. All of the normal provisions of GIPS still apply with the following being particularly important: (1) the performance results of the end user client must be computed, documented, and verified. The underlying investment manager may choose to rely on the sponsor to do so (with due diligence to verify the sponsor's ability) or maintain her own tracking and shadow accounting of the account's performance. (2) Returns must be calculated after actual trading expenses. If the trading expenses cannot be identified and separated from the bundled wrap fee, the entire bundled fee including the trading expenses must be deducted from the return. (3) All of the fees that are included in the bundled fee must be disclosed. (4) Composite results must disclose the percentage of composite assets made up of portfolios with bundled fees.

This treatment of WFSMA portfolios can cause concern for management firms. The GIPS require investment management firms to include WFSMA portfolios in an appropriate composite according to their written policies for inclusion. Thus, they must decide whether to create composites containing only WFSMAs or include WFSMAs in other composites containing non-wrap fee accounts. If firms include WFSMAs in composites containing non-WFSMA accounts and are unable to isolate the direct trading expenses from the sponsor's bundled fees, the resulting WFSMA returns could bring down the reported performance of the composites. Remember that in GIPS, gross of fees means before management fees but after direct trading expenses. This could put the firm at a competitive disadvantage when presenting the performance of a composite to current and potential non-wrap fee clients because the large bundled fee would cause reported results to appear low in relation to accounts that do not have the bundled fee. Offsetting this concern is the ability to show more assets under management in the composite than if the WFSMA was in a totally separate composite.

The additional provisions of this section are the following:

- Include the performance of actual WFSMAs in appropriate composites and then use the composite results for presentations to prospective new WFSMA prospects.
- If the composite presentation includes time periods when WFSMA accounts were not included, the details of when this occurred must be disclosed.
- If any non-GIPS-compliant results prior to January 1, 2006, are included, this must be disclosed. After January 1, 2006, (the adoption date of these provisions) non-compliant results cannot be included.

- If an investment management firm manages assets for more than one sponsor using the same investment style, the composite presentation to prospective clients must include the results of all WFSMAs that follow that style (regardless of sponsor). The composite is style specific, not sponsor specific, and results must be after the entire wrap fee.
- In addition, a sponsor-specific composite may also be produced if desired. In this case, the sponsor's name must be disclosed. For this sponsor-specific composite, the entire wrap fee does not have to be deducted; but, if it is not deducted, this must be disclosed and the presentation must be labeled as only for the use of that sponsor (to discourage the sponsor from using it for prospective WFSMA client presentations). The intent is that the sponsor is not to use the report for marketing to clients but only as part of any internal review of the manager's performance.

GIPS VALUATION PRINCIPLES

LOS 32.q: Explain the requirements and recommended valuation hierarchy of the GIPS Valuation Principles.

For periods beginning on or after January 1, 2011, the GIPS require firms to use *fair values*.

In simple terms, this means that if the investment is a regularly traded security, the recent reported trading price is used as fair value (i.e., what is more generally referred to as market value). If that is not available (due perhaps to the asset being infrequently traded, transaction prices not being reported, or a private investment with no transactions occurring), then fair value establishes a hierarchy for what to use instead. The hierarchy is in descending order of usage. A method lower in the hierarchy is used only when all methods higher in the hierarchy are unavailable. The fair value hierarchy is:

1. "Market value" (e.g., for an actively traded stock or bond use the last trade price.)

2. Quoted prices for less actively traded identical or very similar investments (e.g., a stock trades infrequently, the last available price is a week old, and there is no material evidence indicating the price would have changed; another example is a dealer quote for a stock that has not recently traded).

3. Using market-based inputs to estimate price (e.g., using P/E or dividend yield for comparable and actively traded securities to infer a price estimate or using a YTM for similar actively traded bonds to price a bond that has not traded).

4. Price estimates based on inputs that are not directly observable (e.g., a discounted free cash flow price estimate based on projected cash flows and assumed discount rate).

Real estate and private equity (as defined for GIPS reporting) will generally fall well down the valuation hierarchy. GIPS provides additional guidance for these assets.

Real estate valuation principles

- The GIPS require that real estate investments be valued externally by outside sources following accepted industry and governmental valuation standards.
- The amount of the external valuator's fee must not be based on the resulting value.
- Although appraisal standards allow reporting values in ranges, the GIPS recommend a single value be reported for returns purposes.
- The firm should rotate external valuators every three to five years.

Private equity valuation principles:

- The valuation methodology utilized must be "the most appropriate for a particular investment based on the nature, facts, and circumstances of the investment."
- When valuing private enterprises, the process should consider:
  - Reliable appraisal data.
  - Comparable enterprise or transaction data.
  - The enterprise's stage of development.
  - Additional characteristics unique to the enterprise.

Other miscellaneous GIPS valuation requirements are:

- If local laws or regulations related to valuation conflict with the GIPS, firms are required to follow the local laws or regulations and disclose the conflict.
- Firms must disclose their portfolio valuation policies and hierarchy.
- For periods beginning on or after January 1, 2011, firms must disclose any subjective valuation if the portfolio is a significant portion of the composite.
- Firms must disclose if the valuation hierarchy used to value composites differs from the GIPS recommended hierarchy.

Firms must always follow the intent of GIPS and not mechanical rules. The intent is to indicate what the investment is "worth." If the mechanical following of the valuation hierarchy some how created a misrepresentation of true value, the firm should follow the intent and disclose the issue. Generally, firms should follow standard industry and governmental valuation guidelines as closely and consistently as possible in an effort to obtain the best possible value estimates. Firms must also document valuation policies followed and disclose those policies to prospective clients. Firms are recommended to provide the input data to prospective clients as well, so they can feel comfortable relying on the presented values and returns.

GIPS ADVERTISING GUIDELINES

LOS 32.r: Determine whether advertisements comply with the GIPS Advertising Guidelines.

In addition to the GIPS report, firms may also present a more abbreviated report following the GIPS Advertising Guidelines if they wish. This provision is intended to assist firms in their marketing efforts by allowing limited GIPS information to be presented without the rather cumbersome full GIPS report being presented. The most significant caveat of this provision is that it must be clear the full GIPS report is available as well.

All advertisements that include a claim of compliance with the GIPS Advertising Guidelines must include the following:

1. A description of the firm.

2. How an interested party can obtain a presentation that complies with the requirements of GIPS standards and/or a list and description of all firm composites.

3. The GIPS Advertising Guidelines compliance statement:

    [Insert name of firm] claims compliance with the Global Investment Performance Standards (GIPS®).

    The briefest of the three full compliance statements is shown below for comparison. A full statement must still be used in the GIPS report.

    (Insert name of firm) claims compliance with the Global Investment Performance Standards (GIPS®) and has prepared and presented this report in compliance with the GIPS standards. (Insert name of firm) has not been independently verified.

All advertisements that include a claim of compliance with the GIPS Advertising Guidelines and that present performance results must also include the following information (the relevant information must be taken/derived from a presentation that adheres to the requirements of the GIPS standards):

4. A description of the composite being advertised.

5. One of the following sets of total returns:

    a. 1-, 3-, and 5-year annualized composite returns through the most recent period.

    b. Period-to-date composite performance results in addition to 1-, 3-, and 5-year cumulative annualized composite returns with the end-of-period date clearly identified (or annualized period since composite inception if inception is greater than one and less than five years). Periods of less than one year are not permitted to be annualized. The annualized returns must be calculated through the same period of time as presented in the corresponding compliant presentation.

    c. Period-to-date composite returns in addition to five years of annual composite returns calculated through the same period of time as presented in the corresponding compliant presentation.

6. Whether performance is shown gross and/or net of investment management fees.

7. The benchmark total return for the same periods for which the composite return is presented and a description of that benchmark. (The appropriate composite benchmark return is the same benchmark total return as presented in the corresponding GIPS-compliant presentation.) If no benchmark is presented, the advertisement must disclose why no benchmark is presented.

8. The currency used to express returns.

9. Describe the extent and use of leverage, derivatives, and short selling in sufficient detail to identify the risks involved.

10. When presenting noncompliant performance information for periods prior to January 1, 2000, in an advertisement, firms must disclose the period(s) and which specific information is not in compliance with the GIPS standards.

The Advertising Guidelines also suggest that firms may present other information, though this supplemental information should be of equal or lesser prominence than the required information described previously.

GIPS Verification

LOS 32.s: Discuss the purpose, scope, and process of verification.

Once a firm claims compliance with the GIPS, it is responsible for its claim of compliance and for maintaining its compliance. In doing so, the firm may *voluntarily* hire an independent third party to verify its claim of compliance, which adds credibility to the firm's claim of compliance.

The *primary purpose of verification* is to increase the level of confidence that a firm claiming GIPS compliance did, indeed, adhere to the Standards on a firm-wide basis.

Verification involves the review of an investment management firm's performance-measurement processes and procedures by an *independent third-party verifier*. Upon completion of verification, a verification report is issued that must confirm the following:

- The investment firm has complied with all the composite construction requirements of GIPS on a firm-wide basis.
- The firm's processes and procedures are designed to calculate and present performance results in compliance with the GIPS.

Without such a report from the verifier, the firm cannot assert that its claim of compliance with GIPS has been verified.

Other noteworthy aspects of GIPS verification include the following:

- A single verification report is issued to the entire firm; *GIPS verification cannot be carried out for a single composite*.
- Verification cannot be partial: it is all or nothing. In other words, verification cannot enable a firm to claim that its performance presentation is in compliance with GIPS "except for ..."
- Verification is not a requirement for GIPS compliance, but it is *strongly encouraged*.
- The initial minimum period for which verification can be performed is one year of a firm's presented performance. The recommended period over which verification is performed will be that part of the firm's track record for which GIPS compliance is claimed.
- After performing the verification, the verifier may conclude that the firm is not in compliance with GIPS or that the records of the firm cannot support a complete verification. In such situations, the verifier must issue a statement to the firm clarifying why a verification report was not possible.

AFTER-TAX RETURNS

LOS 32.t: Discuss challenges related to the calculation of after-tax returns.

Reporting after-tax return data is extremely complex and, if reported, is part of supplemental information. As of January 1, 2011, responsibility for advising firms on after-tax reporting was shifted to the GIPS country sponsors who assist firms in adapting GIPS to a specific country. Firms that claim particular ability to manage portfolios in a tax-sensitive manner and maximize after-tax returns may want to present after-tax composite results to support this claim and gain a competitive advantage.

> *Professor's Note: It might seem surprising that you cannot just report the average after-tax return of the clients, but consider three issues: (1) clients have no reason to share their personal tax return with the manager; (2) if they do, it is highly confidential information; and (3) if after-tax client returns were averaged, there is no way to explain the tax rules applied and therefore no way for prospective clients to relate the reported returns to their specific tax situations.*

Two methods for incorporating the effects on returns are the pre-liquidation method and the mark-to-liquidation method:

- The *pre-liquidation* method calculates after-tax returns based on income earned and gains and losses actually recognized over the period through asset sales. This method ignores unrealized gains and losses, generally understating tax liability (gains are more likely in the long run) and overstating after-tax return.
- The *mark-to-liquidation* method assumes all gains, whether recognized or not, are taxed each period. This method ignores the value of tax deferral, overstating tax liability and understating after-tax return.

Neither method measures the portfolio's true economic value. To measure a portfolio's true economic value would require numerous assumptions about the size, timing, and recognition of future investment results as well as tax laws and the client's tax status. Of course, future tax liabilities will depend on the initial cost of securities that are sold as well as the length of the investment period, as most tax regimes make a distinction between long- and short-term capital gains. Under GIPS, the responsibility falls on the firm to make and disclose reasonable assumptions to use if the firm wishes to report supplemental after-tax composite returns.

After-Tax Benchmark Returns

If the firm presents after-tax portfolio returns, they must also present appropriate after-tax benchmark returns. The appropriate after-tax benchmark should exhibit all the characteristics of a valid benchmark plus be reflective of the client's tax status. Generally, index providers do not present after-tax returns. The portfolio manager is left with this complicated task.[4] To estimate the after-tax returns on an index, the manager must consider:

- The way the provider constructed the index, such as price, equal, or market value weighting.
- The rebalancing policy followed by the index provider.
- The effects of taxable events such as price changes, dividends, splits, et cetera, associated with each of the component firms.

As an alternative to using an index as a benchmark and trying to estimate the after-tax index returns, the manager can consider using mutual funds or exchange-traded funds as benchmarks. Unfortunately, mutual funds that track indices are subject to licensing fees, and their returns can differ from the index. In addition, their tax effects are driven by the trading actions of the manager and redemptions and deposits by shareholders. Because they are not subject to taxes related to investors' deposits or redemptions, exchange traded funds may make better after-tax benchmarks.

The most accurate after-tax benchmark may be the use of a custom security-based benchmark that adjusts the components and value of the benchmark to reflect the client's actions and tax status. Alternatively, managers can construct *shadow portfolios*, paper portfolios used as benchmarks constructed from mutual funds or exchange traded funds, and then adjust the shadow portfolios to reflect the client's transactions.

Firms must also adjust for the effect of client-directed actions in order to accurately report the results of the firm's management decisions. A client with multiple managers may direct a manager to sell a high tax basis holding to generate a tax loss (tax loss harvesting). The client can then use the loss on his tax return to shelter other gains. The manager cannot take the full benefit of this loss in reporting after-tax results because the sale was not a manager decision. In such cases, firms should disclose the percentage effect of such loss harvesting on reported after-tax return.

The challenges of after-tax composite return reporting are considerable. Firms must have the mathematical skills, data collection, technological, and human resources to undertake such supplemental reporting.

 Professor's Note: The CFA text is specific in stating it will not cover the mathematics.

---

4.   Some index providers present returns net of withholding taxes on dividends.

GIPS: SAMPLE PERFORMANCE PRESENTATION ANALYSIS

LOS 32.u: Identify and explain errors and omissions in given performance presentations and recommend changes that would bring them into compliance with GIPS standards.

Example: Evaluating a performance presentation

Equity Investors, the equity management unit of Manhattan Investment Management, Incorporated (MIMI), has prepared the following performance presentation for its equity growth composite for use in its marketing materials to prospective clients. MIMI manages equity, fixed-income, and balanced portfolios for retail clients to a variety of investment strategies. **Evaluate** the presentation in the figure below, and **identify** any errors or omissions that would prevent Equity Investors from claiming compliance with the GIPS.

Figure 5: Equity Investors Equity Growth Composite

Year	Composite Return (%)	Number of Portfolios	Dispersion (%)	Total Assets at End of Period ($US 000s)	Percentage of Firm Assets	Total Firm Assets ($US 000s)
2006	16.49	19	4.7	235	19	1,237
2007	13.81	24	6.1	365	20	1,825
2008	28.20	27	8.8	400	25	1,600
2009	7.96	26	1.9	410	22	1,864
2010	9.83	32	4.5	470	27	1,741

Equity Investors has prepared and presented this report in compliance with the Global Investment Performance Standards (GIPS®).

Notes:

1. Equity Investors is defined as the equity management unit of Manhattan Investment Management, Incorporated. Equity Investors manages all dedicated equity portfolios for Manhattan Investment Management, Incorporated.
2. The Equity Growth Composite was created in February 2006.
3. Performance results are presented gross of management, wrap, and custodial fees but after all trading commissions.
4. Trade date prices, expressed in U.S. dollars, are used to calculate performance results.
5. The Equity Growth Composite includes all portfolios managed to the firm's equity growth strategy. The composite also includes the equity growth segments of the balanced portfolios managed by another unit of Manhattan Investment Management, Incorporated.
6. Dispersion is measured as the standard deviation of monthly composite returns.

Answer:

1. The equity management unit of a larger investment management firm usually does not satisfy one of the options for defining a firm. In the case of Equity Investors, it is affiliated with the parent company, Manhattan Investment Management, Incorporated, as indicated by the source of the carve-out returns. Thus, Equity Investors may not define itself as a firm. (GIPS Standard 0.A.12)

2. The Equity Growth Composite includes the carve-out returns of the equity growth segment of the firm's balanced composites. The GIPS require that cash be allocated to carve-out returns prior to 2010. The Standards also require disclosure of (1) the method by which cash is allocated to carve-out returns and (2) the percentage of each composite represented by the carve-outs. Starting in 2010 the carve-out must be managed separately with its own cash balance. (Standard 3.A.8, Standard 4.A.23, Standard 5.A.5)

3. The firm did not report an internal measure of dispersion of the composite's portfolio returns about the composite's aggregate return. The dispersion reported in Equity Investor's presentation is an external measure of dispersion, which is a recommended disclosure, but not required.

4. The compliance statement is incorrect. (GIPS Standard 4.A.1)

5. When wrap fees are present, performance results should have been presented net of all wrap fees. (Standard 8.A.6)

6. The presentation does not include a benchmark return. (Standard 5.A.1.e)

7. The firm failed to disclose that a complete list and description of the firm's composites is available upon request. (Standard 4.A.11)

GIPS: Bringing a Presentation Into Compliance

With reference to the preceding example, the following changes will bring the presentation into compliance with the GIPS.

1. Because it is now assumed that Equity Investors is affiliated with MIMI, it does not satisfy the options for firm definition under GIPS, and the definition of the firm for this presentation must be revised. An appropriate firm definition for this presentation would be as follows: "Equity Investors is the equity management unit of Manhattan Investment Management, Incorporated. Manhattan Investment Management, Incorporated, is an investment firm that manages equity, fixed-income, and balanced portfolios for retail clients. Manhattan Investment Management, Incorporated, is registered with the United States Securities and Exchange Commission" (GIPS Standard 0.A.12). Defining the firm as Manhattan Investment Management, Incorporated, will necessitate the revision of all reported figures that are linked to firm assets. Cash must be allocated to the carve-out returns of the growth equities of the firm's balanced composites, and the method used to allocate cash to the carve-outs must be disclosed. An acceptable disclosure in this case would be as follows: "Prior to 2010 Equity Investor's Equity Growth Composite included all dedicated equity growth portfolios and the equity growth segments of Manhattan Investment Management's balanced portfolios. Starting in 2010 the carve-out was managed separately with its own cash account. Cash was allocated to the carve-out segment returns on a pro rata basis based on the market weight of growth equities in the

balanced portfolios." The presentation must also include the percentage of each composite the carve-out represents. (Standard 3.A.8, Standard 4.A.23, Standard 5.A.5)

2. The firm must report an internal measure of dispersion of the composite's portfolio returns about the composite's aggregate return for each year in the presentation. The dispersion reported in Equity Investor's presentation is an external measure of dispersion, which may be included as supplemental information. For periods prior to January 1, 2011, firms should present the 3-year annualized ex post standard deviation of monthly returns of the composite and the benchmark as of the end of each annual period. (Standard 5.A.1.i, Standard 5.B.3)

3. An acceptable compliance statement in this presentation would be as follows: "Manhattan Investment Management, Incorporated, claims compliance with the Global Investment Performance Standards (GIPS®) and has prepared and presented this report in compliance with the GIPS standards. Manhattan Investment Management, Incorporated, has not been independently verified." (GIPS Standard 4.A.1)

4. The wrap fees should have been deducted. Performance results presented to prospective wrap fee clients should be net of wrap fees. (Standard 8.A.6)

5. The presentation should include the total return for an appropriate benchmark for each year. For the composite reported in this presentation, the return on the Dow-Jones U.S. Growth Index may be an appropriate benchmark return. (Standard 5.A.1.e)

6. The firm must disclose that the firm's list of composite descriptions is available upon request. (Standard 4.A.11)

GIPS: Writing a Compliant Presentation

An example of a GIPS-compliant performance presentation is provided in Figure 6.

 Professor's Note: The first six column headings are required. The presentation must include one of the last two, either % of Firm Assets or Total Firm Assets.

Figure 6: Firm XZX, Dedicated Equity Composite, March 1, 2006–December 31, 2010

Year	Total Return (%)	Benchmark Return	Number of Portfolios	Composite Dispersion (%)	Total Assets at End of Period (€ millions)	% of Firm Assets	Total Firm Assets (€ millions)
2006	19.54	18.23	29	4.8	183	65	282
2007	12.81	11.75	34	5.9	329	75	439
2008	17.30	18.56	37	8.5	346	72	481
2009	11.86	11.20	36	1.7	333	68	490
2010	7.59	8.50	42	3.5	284	63	451

GIPS-Compliant Performance Presentation

XZX Investment Management Firm claims compliance with the Global Investment Performance Standards (GIPS®) and has prepared and presented this report in compliance with the GIPS standards. XZX Investment Management Firm has not been independently verified.

Notes:

1. XZX Investment Management Firm is a dedicated equity portfolio manager that invests entirely in German securities. XZX Investment Management Firm is defined as an independent investment management firm that is not affiliated with any parent organization.
2. The benchmark composition is 100% DAX 100. The annualized compound composite return is 13.7%; the annualized compound benchmark return is 13.6%.
3. Valuations are computed using euros and are obtained from Reuters.
4. The dispersion of annual returns is measured by the standard deviation among asset-weighted portfolio returns for portfolios that were in the composite over the entire year.
5. Performance results are presented before management and custodial fees but after all trading commissions. The management fee schedule is contained in the appendix to this report.
6. This composite was created in March 2006. No modifications to the composite as presented here have occurred as a result of changes in personnel or for any other reason at any time. A complete list of firm composites and performance results is available upon request.
7. Policies for valuing portfolios, calculating performance, and preparing compliant presentations are available upon request.

KEY CONCEPTS

LOS 32.a

Recognizing the need for one globally accepted set of investment performance presentation standards, CFA Institute (formerly Association for Investment Management and Research) sponsored and funded the Global Investment Performance Standards Committee to develop and publish a single global standard by which all firms calculate and present performance to clients and prospective clients. As a result of this initiative, the AIMR Board of Governors formally endorsed the GIPS on February 19, 1999, as the worldwide standard. The latest edition of the GIPS is the 2010 GIPS Standards effective January 1, 2011.

GIPS objectives:
- Establish global, industry-wide best practices for the calculation and presentation of investment performance.
- Facilitate the accurate and unambiguous presentation of investment performance results to current and prospective clients.
- Facilitate a comparison of the historical performance of investment management firms.
- Encourage full disclosure and fair global competition without barriers to entry.
- Encourage self-regulation.

GIPS characteristics:
- Voluntary minimum standards for performance presentation.
- Firms must meet all requirements on a firm-wide basis in order to claim compliance.
- Only investment management firms may claim compliance.
- Provide a minimum standard where local or country-specific laws, regulation, or industry standards may not exist.
- Require managers to include all actual fee-paying discretionary portfolios in composites defined according to similar strategy and/or investment objective.
- Firms must present a minimum of five years of GIPS-compliant history or since inception if less than five years. After presenting at least five years of compliant history, the firm must add annual performance each year going forward up to ten years, at a minimum.
- Firms may link years of noncompliant performance but must present only compliant data for periods beginning on or after January 1, 2000.
- Firms must use prescribed calculation and presentation methods and include required disclosures in presentations.
- Meeting the objective of full and fair disclosure will likely require more than compliance with the minimum requirements of the GIPS.
- To fully explain the performance included in a presentation, firms are encouraged to present all relevant supplemental information.
- In cases in which applicable local or country-specific laws or regulations conflict with the GIPS, the standards require firms to comply with the local law or regulation and make full disclosure of the conflict.
- Firms are encouraged to develop monitoring processes and controls for maintaining GIPS compliance.

- Firms must document the policies used to ensure the existence and ownership of client assets.
- January 1, 2011, is the effective date of the 2010 edition of the GIPS. Presentations that include performance for periods beginning on or after January 1, 2011, must comply with the 2010 version of the GIPS.

Scope of the GIPS:

Firms from any country may come into compliance with the GIPS. Compliance with the standards will facilitate a firm's participation in the investment management industry on a global level.

For periods prior to January 1, 2006, firms are granted reciprocity, so that if pre-2006 data are presented in compliance with a previous edition of the GIPS or a Country Version of GIPS (CVG), such data may continue to be shown as compliant with the revised GIPS.

The benefits to existing and prospective clients derive from the ability to compare the performance of firms operating in different countries with different sets of established practices. The GIPS ensure that performance data are complete and fairly presented so that existing and prospective clients can have greater confidence in comparative investment results.

LOS 32.b

GIPS compliance must be on a firm-wide basis. Total firm assets are defined as the total fair value of all assets the firm manages, including non-fee-paying and non-discretionary portfolios. Also included in the definition are assets delegated to sub-advisers, as long as the firm has selected the sub-advisers. If (according to the firm's definition of discretion) a portfolio is deemed discretionary, it is considered sufficiently free of client-mandated constraints such that the manager is able to pursue its stated strategy, objectives, or mandate.

A **firm** is defined as "an investment firm, subsidiary, or division held out to clients or potential clients as a distinct business entity."

A **distinct business entity** is defined as "a unit, division, department, or office that is organizationally or functionally separated from other units, divisions, departments, or offices and that retains discretion over the assets it manages and that should have autonomy over the investment decision-making process."

Firms must meet all the requirements of GIPS and the ethical intent. Partial compliance is not acceptable. Policies and procedures must be developed, maintained, and documented to meet the requirements.

LOS 32.c

GIPS input data requirements
- **Standard 1.A.1.** All data and information necessary to support the firm's performance presentation, including calculations, must be stored and maintained.
- **Standard 1.A.2.** For periods beginning on or after January 1, 2011, portfolios must be valued at fair value according to GIPS principles. Cost or book values are not permitted.
- **Standard 1.A.3.** Portfolio valuation.
  - Prior to January 1, 2001, portfolios must be valued at least quarterly.

♦ Beginning on or after January 1, 2001, at least monthly.
♦ Beginning on or after January 1, 2010, at least monthly and on the date of all large external cash flows.

- **Standard 1.A.4.** For periods beginning January 1, 2010, firms must value portfolios as of the calendar month-end or the last business day of the month.
- **Standard 1.A.5.** For periods beginning January 1, 2005, firms must use trade-date accounting.
- **Standard 1.A.6.** Accrual accounting must be used for fixed-income securities and all other assets that accrue interest income. Market values of fixed-income securities must include accrued income.
- **Standard 1.A.7.** For periods beginning January 1, 2006, composites must have consistent beginning and ending annual valuation dates. Unless the composite is reported on a non-calendar fiscal year, the beginning and ending valuation dates must be at calendar year-end (or on the last business day of the year).

GIPS input data recommendations
- **Standard 1.B.1.** Rather than only at large external cash flows, portfolios should be valued at each external cash flow.
- **Standard 1.B.2.** Valuations should be obtained from an independent third party.
- **Standard 1.B.3.** Dividends from equities should be accrued as of the ex-dividend date.
- **Standard 1.B.4.** When presenting net-of-fees returns, firms should accrue investment management fees.

LOS 32.d

GIPS calculation methodology requirements
- **Standard 2.A.1.** Total returns must be used.
- **Standard 2.A.2.** Time-weighted rates of return that adjust for external cash flows must be used. Periodic returns must be geometrically linked. External cash flows must be treated in a consistent manner with the firm's documented, composite-specific policy in order to determine when portfolios in the composite require revaluation. For periods beginning January 1, 2010, firms must value portfolios on the date of all large external cash flows.

Cash and cash equivalents
- **Standard 2.A.3.** Returns from cash and cash equivalents held in portfolios must be included in total return calculations.

Fees and expenses
- **Standard 2.A.4.** All returns must be calculated after the deduction of the actual trading expenses incurred during the period. Estimated trading expenses are not permitted.
- **Standard 2.A.5.** If the actual direct trading expenses cannot be identified and segregated from a bundled fee:

  1. When calculating gross-of-fees returns, returns must be reduced by the entire bundled fee or the portion of the bundled fee that includes the direct trading expenses. The use of estimated trading expenses is not permitted.

  2. When calculating net-of-fees returns, returns must be reduced by the entire bundled fee or the portion of the bundled fee that includes the direct trading expenses and the investment management fee. The use of estimated trading expenses is not permitted.

LOS 32.e

- **Standard 2.A.6.** Composite returns must be calculated by asset-weighting the individual portfolio returns using beginning-of-period values or a method that reflects both beginning-of-period values and external cash flows.
- **Standard 2.A.7.** For periods beginning January 1, 2006, firms must calculate composite returns by asset-weighting the individual portfolio returns at least quarterly. For periods beginning on or after January 1, 2010, composite returns must be calculated by asset-weighting the individual portfolio returns at least monthly.

GIPS calculation methodology recommendations

- **Standard 2.B.1.** Returns should be calculated net of non-reclaimable withholding taxes on dividends, interest, and capital gains. Reclaimable withholding taxes should be accrued.

LOS 32.f

- **Standard 3.A.1.** All actual fee-paying discretionary portfolios must be included in at least one composite. Although non-fee-paying discretionary portfolios may be included in a composite (with appropriate disclosures), nondiscretionary portfolios must not be included in a firm's composites.

The IPC defines discretion as "the ability of the firm to implement its intended strategy." A client may place significant constraints on the manager; for instance, the investment policy statement (IPS) may specify limits on sectors, credit ratings, durations, et cetera. Furthermore, there may be total restrictions on certain transactions, such as the purchase of "unethical" or foreign investments, or the sale of specified stocks. These restrictions *do not* automatically remove the discretionary nature of the portfolio.

A portfolio becomes nondiscretionary when the manager is no longer able to implement the intended investment strategy. If, for instance, the liquidity requirements are so great that much of the value must be in cash, or if the portfolio has minimal tracking limits from an index portfolio, then the description of "discretionary" is really no longer appropriate.

LOS 32.g

- **Standard 3.A.4.** Composites must be defined according to similar investment objectives and/or strategies. Composites must include all portfolios that meet the composite definition. The full composite definition must be made available on request.

LOS 32.h

- **Standard 3.A.2.** Composites must include only assets under management within the defined firm.
- **Standard 3.A.3.** Firms are not permitted to link simulated or model portfolios with actual performance.
- **Standard 3.A.5.** Composites must include new portfolios on a timely and consistent basis after the portfolio comes under management.
- **Standard 3.A.6.** Terminated portfolios must be included in the historical returns of the appropriate composites up to the last full measurement period that the portfolio was under management.

- **Standard 3.A.7.** Portfolios must not be switched from one composite to another unless documented changes in client guidelines or the redefinition of the composite make it appropriate. The historical record of the portfolio must remain with the appropriate composite.
- **Standard 3.A.9.** If a firm sets a minimum asset level for portfolios to be included in a composite, no portfolios below that asset level can be included in that composite. Any changes to a composite-specific minimum asset level are not permitted to be applied retroactively.
- **Standard 3.A.10.** Firms that wish to remove portfolios from composites in cases of significant cash flows must define *significant* on an ex-ante composite-specific basis and must consistently follow the composite-specific significant cash flow policy.
- **Standard 3.B.2.** As an alternative to temporarily removing the account from the composite, the firm can direct the significant cash flow into a temporary new account until the funds are invested.

LOS 32.i

- **Standard 3.A.8.** For periods beginning on or after January 1, 2010, carve-outs must not be included in a composite unless the carve-out is actually managed separately with its own cash balance.

LOS 32.j

GIPS required disclosures

- **Standard 4.A.1.** Once a firm has met all the requirements of the GIPS standards, the firm must disclose its compliance with the GIPS standards using one of the following compliance statements.

For firms that are verified:

[Insert name of firm] claims compliance with the Global Investment Performance Standards (GIPS®) and has prepared and presented this report in compliance with the GIPS standards. [Insert name of firm] has been independently verified for the periods [insert dates]. The verification report(s) is/are available upon request.

Verification assesses whether (1) the firm has complied with all the composite construction requirements of the GIPS standards on a firm-wide basis, and (2) the firm's policies and procedures are designed to calculate and present performance in compliance with the GIPS standards. Verification does not ensure the accuracy of any specific composite presentation.

For composites of a verified firm that have also had a performance examination:

[Insert name of firm] claims compliance with the Global Investment Performance Standards (GIPS®) and has prepared and presented this report in compliance with the GIPS standards. [Insert name of firm] has been independently verified for the periods [insert dates].

Verification assesses whether (1) the firm has complied with all the composite construction requirements of the GIPS standards on a firm-wide basis, and (2) the firm's processes and procedures are designed to calculate and present performance in compliance with the GIPS standards. The [insert name of composite] composite has been examined for the periods [insert dates]. The verification and examination reports are available upon request.

For firms that have not been verified:

[Insert name of firm] claims compliance with the Global Investment Performance Standards (GIPS®) and has prepared and presented this report in compliance with the GIPS standards. [Insert name of firm] has not been independently verified.

- **Standard 4.A.2.** Firms must disclose the definition of "firm" used to determine the total firm assets and firm-wide compliance.
- **Standard 4.A.3.** Firms must disclose the composite description.
- **Standard 4.A.4.** Firms must disclose the benchmark description.
- **Standard 4.A.5.** When presenting gross-of-fees returns, firms must disclose if any other fees are deducted in addition to the direct trading expenses.
- **Standard 4.A.6.** When presenting net-of-fees returns, firms must disclose: a) if any other fees are deducted in addition to the investment management fee and direct trading expenses; b) if model or actual investment management fees are used; and c) if returns are net of performance-based fees.
- **Standard 4.A.7.** Firms must disclose the currency used to express performance.
- **Standard 4.A.8.** Firms must disclose which measure of internal dispersion is used.
- **Standard 4.A.9.** Firms must disclose the fee schedule appropriate to the compliant presentation.
- **Standard 4.A.10.** Firms must disclose the composite creation date.
- **Standard 4.A.11.** Firms must disclose that the firm's list of composite descriptions is available upon request.
- **Standard 4.A.12.** Firms must disclose that policies for valuing portfolios, calculating performance, and preparing compliant presentations are available upon request.
- **Standard 4.A.13.** Firms must disclose the presence, use, and extent of leverage, derivatives, and short positions, if material, including a description of the frequency of use and characteristics of the instruments sufficient to identify risks.
- **Standard 4.A.14.** Firms must disclose all significant events that would help a prospective client interpret the compliant presentation.
- **Standard 4.A.15.** For any performance presented for periods prior to January 1, 2000, that does not comply with the GIPS standards, firms must disclose the periods of non-compliance.
- **Standard 4.A.16.** If the firm is redefined, the firm must disclose the date of, description of, and reason for the redefinition.
- **Standard 4.A.17.** If a composite is redefined, the firm must disclose the date of, description of, and reason for the redefinition.
- **Standard 4.A.18.** Firms must disclose any changes to the name of a composite.
- **Standard 4.A.19.** Firms must disclose the minimum asset level, if any, below which portfolios are not included in a composite. Firms must also disclose any changes to the minimum asset level.
- **Standard 4.A.20.** Firms must disclose relevant details of the treatment of withholding tax on dividends, interest income, and capital gains, if material. Firms must also disclose if benchmark returns are net of withholding taxes if this information is available.
- **Standard 4.A.21.** For periods beginning on or after January 1, 2011, firms must disclose and describe any known material differences in the exchange rates or valuation sources used among the portfolios within a composite and between the composite and the benchmark. For periods prior to January 1, 2011, firms must disclose and describe any known inconsistencies in the exchange rates used among the portfolios within a composite and between the composite and the benchmark.

- **Standard 4.A.22.** If the compliant presentation conforms with laws and/or regulations that conflict with the requirement of the GIPS standards, firms must disclose this fact and disclose the manner in which the local laws and regulations conflict with the GIPS standards.
- **Standard 4.A.23.** For periods prior to January 1, 2010, if carve-outs are included in a composite, firms must disclose the policy used to allocate cash to the carve-outs.
- **Standard 4.A.24.** If a composite contains portfolios with bundled fees, firms must disclose the types of fees that are included in the bundled fee.
- **Standard 4.A.25.** Beginning on January 1, 2006, firms must disclose the use of a sub-adviser and the periods a sub-adviser was used.
- **Standard 4.A.26.** For periods prior to January 1, 2010, firms must disclose if any portfolios were not valued at calendar month end or on the last business day of the month.
- **Standard 4.A.27.** For periods beginning January 1, 2011, firms must disclose the use of subjective unobservable inputs for valuing portfolio investments if the portfolio investments valued using subjective unobservable inputs are material to the composite.
- **Standard 4.A.28.** For periods beginning on January 1, 2011, firms must disclose if the composite's valuation hierarchy materially differs from the recommended hierarchy in the GIPS Valuation Principles.
- **Standard 4.A.29.** If the firm determines no appropriate benchmark for the composite exists, the firm must disclose why no benchmark is presented.
- **Standard 4.A.30.** If the firm changes the benchmark, the firm must disclose the date of, description of, and reason for the change.
- **Standard 4.A.31.** If a custom benchmark or combination of multiple benchmarks is used, the firm must disclose the benchmark components, weights, and rebalancing process.
- **Standard 4.A.32.** If the firm has adopted a significant cash flow policy for a specific composite, the firm must disclose how the firm defines a significant cash flow for that composite and for which periods.
- **Standard 4.A.33.** Firms must disclose if the 3-year annualized ex post standard deviation of the composite and/or benchmark is not presented because 36 monthly returns are not available.
- **Standard 4.A.34.** If the firm determines that the 3-year annualized ex post standard deviation is not relevant or appropriate, the firm must: a) describe why ex post standard deviation is not relevant or appropriate; and b) describe the additional risk measure presented and why it was selected.
- **Standard 4.A.35.** Firms must disclose if the performance from a past firm or affiliation is linked to the performance of the firm.

GIPS recommended disclosures
- **Standard 4.B.1.** Firms should disclose material changes to valuation policies and/or methodologies.
- **Standard 4.B.2.** Firms should disclose material changes to calculation policies and/or methodologies.
- **Standard 4.B.3.** Firms should disclose material differences between the benchmark and the composite's investment mandate, objective, or strategy.
- **Standard 4.B.4.** Firms should disclose the key assumptions used to value portfolio investments.

- **Standard 4.B.5.** If a parent company contains multiple defined firms, each firm within the parent company should disclose a list of the other firms contained within the parent company.
- **Standard 4.B.6.** For periods prior to January 1, 2011, firms should disclose the use of subjective unobservable inputs for valuing portfolio investments if the portfolio investments valued using subjective unobservable inputs are material to the composite.
- **Standard 4.B.7.** For periods prior to January 1, 2006, firms should disclose the use of a sub-adviser and the periods a sub-adviser was used.
- **Standard 4.B.8.** Firms should disclose if a composite contains proprietary assets.

LOS 32.k,l,m

GIPS presentation and reporting requirements

- **Standard 5.A.1.** The following items must be reported for each composite presented:

  a. At least five years of annual performance (or a record for the period since firm or composite inception if the firm or composite has been in existence less than five years) that meets the requirements of the GIPS standards; after presenting five years of performance, the firm must present additional annual performance up to a minimum of ten years.

  b. Annual returns for all years clearly identified as gross- or net-of-fees.

  c. For composites with a composite inception date beginning on or after January 1, 2011, when the initial period is less than a full year, firms must present returns from the composite inception through the initial year-end.

  d. For composites with a termination date of January 1, 2011, or later, returns from the last annual period through the termination date.

  e. Annual returns for a benchmark, which reflects the mandate, objective, or strategy of the portfolio.

  f. The number of portfolios in the composite at each year-end. If the composite contains *five portfolios or less,* the number of portfolios is not required.

  g. The amount of assets in the composite at the end of each annual period.

  h. Either total firm assets or composite assets as a percentage of firm assets at each annual period end.

  i. A measure of dispersion of individual portfolio returns for each annual period. If the composite contains *five portfolios or less* for the full year, a measure of dispersion is not required.

- **Standard 5.A.2.** For periods beginning on or after January 1, 2011, firms must present for each annual period:

  a. Three-year annualized ex post standard deviation using monthly returns for the composite and benchmark.

  b. An additional 3-year ex post risk measure if management feels standard deviation is inappropriate. The firm must match the periodicity of calculated returns used for the composite and benchmark.

- **Standard 5.A.3.** Firms may link non-GIPS-compliant returns to their compliant history so long as the firms meet the disclosure requirements for noncompliant performance and only compliant returns are presented for periods after January 1, 2000.

- **Standard 5.A.4.** Returns of portfolios and composites for periods of less than one year must not be annualized.

- **Standard 5.A.5.** For periods beginning on or after January 1, 2006, and ending prior to January 1, 2011, if a composite includes carve-outs, the presentation must include the percentage of the composite that is composed of carve-outs for each annual period.
- **Standard 5.A.6.** If a composite contains any non-fee-paying portfolios, the firm must present, as of the end of each annual period, the percentage of the composite assets represented by the non-fee-paying portfolios.
- **Standard 5.A.7.** If a composite includes bundled-fee portfolios, the firm must present, as of the end of each annual period, the percentage of the composite assets represented by bundled-fee portfolios.
- **Standard 5.A.8.**

   a. Performance track records of a past firm or affiliation must be linked to or used to represent the historical record of the new or acquiring firm on a composite-specific basis if:

       i. Substantially all the investment decision makers are employed by the new firm (e.g., research department, portfolio managers, and other relevant staff).

       ii. The decision-making process remains substantially intact and independent within the new firm.

       iii. The new firm has records that document and support the reported performance.

   b. If a firm acquires another firm or affiliation, the firm has one year to bring any noncompliant assets into compliance.

GIPS presentation and reporting recommendations

- **Standard 5.B.1.** Firms should present gross of fees returns.
- **Standard 5.B.2.** Firms should present:
   a. Cumulative returns for composite and benchmarks for all periods.
   b. Equal-weighted mean and median returns for each composite.
   c. Quarterly and/or monthly returns.
   d. Annualized composite and benchmark returns for periods greater than 12 months.

- **Standard 5.B.3.** For periods prior to January 1, 2011, the 3-year annualized ex post standard deviation of monthly returns for each year for the composite and its benchmark.
- **Standard 5.B.4.** For each year in which an annualized ex post standard deviation is present for the composite and the benchmark, corresponding annualized return should be presented.
- **Standard 5.B.5.** For each year that annualized composite and benchmark returns are reported, the corresponding annualized standard deviation of monthly returns for the composite and benchmark.
- **Standard 5.B.6.** Additional ex post composite risk measures.
- **Standard 5.B.7.** Firms should present more than ten years of annual performance in the compliant presentation.
- **Standard 5.B.8.** Firms should comply with the GIPS for all historical periods.
- **Standard 5.B.9.** Firms should update compliant presentations quarterly.

LOS 32.n

For real estate, the following investment types would fall under the *general provisions* of the GIPS (as opposed to the provisions dealing directly with real estate and private equity):

- Publicly traded real estate securities, including any listed securities issued by public companies.
- Mortgage-backed securities (MBS).
- Private debt investments, including commercial and residential loans where the expected return is solely related to contractual interest rates without any participation in the economic performance of the underlying real estate.

Note that publicly traded securities include Real Estate Investment Trusts (REITs). If a portfolio consists of real estate plus other investments, the carve-out provisions of GIPS (Standard 3.A.8) would apply.

The exclusions to the definitions of private equity are *open-end* and *evergreen* funds, both of which are covered by the general provisions of the GIPS. Because redemptions and subscriptions may be made after the funds' inceptions, open-end and evergreen funds do not have fixed levels of capital with a set number of investors.

LOS 32.o

GIPS Real Estate Requirements

- **Standard 6.A.1.** Beginning January 1, 2011, real estate investments must be valued in accordance with the definition of fair value and the GIPS valuation principles.
- **Standards 6.A.2 and A.3.** For periods prior to January 1, 2008, real estate investments must be valued at market value at least once every 12 months. For periods beginning January 1, 2008, real estate investments must be valued at least quarterly. For periods on or after January 1, 2010, firms must value portfolios as of the end of each quarter or the last business day of each quarter using fair value principles.
- **Standards 6.A.4 and A.5.** For periods prior to January 1, 2012, real estate investments must have an external valuation done at least once every three years. External valuation means an outside, independent party certified to perform such valuations. For periods beginning January, 1, 2012, real estate investments must have an external valuation done at least once every 12 months or if a client agreement states otherwise, at least once every three years.
- **Standards 6.A.6 and A.7.** Beginning January 1, 2006, real estate portfolio returns must be calculated at least quarterly after the deduction of transaction costs during the period.
- **Standard 6.A.8.** Beginning January, 1, 2011, income and capital component returns must be calculated separately using geometrically linked time-weighted rates of return.
- **Standard 6.A.9.** Composite returns, including component returns, must be calculated at least quarterly by asset-weighting the individual portfolio returns using time-weighted rates of return.
- **Standard 6.A.10.a.** The firm must provide a description of discretion. Discretion in real estate exists if the firm has sole or sufficient discretion to make major decisions regarding the investments.
- **Standards 6.A.10.b–e.** The firm must disclose the internal valuation methods used and the frequency of external valuation. Beginning January 1, 2011, disclose

material changes in valuation approach and differences in internal and external valuation and the reason for the difference.

- **Standards 6.A.11 and 6.A.15.** On or after January 1, 2006, GIPS compliant and non-compliant performance may not be linked. Prior to this date, any such linking must be disclosed.

Standards 6.A.12 and 6.A.13 are not discussed in the CFA reading.

- **Standard 6.A.14.** In addition to the total return, the capital return and income return components must be disclosed, must sum to the total return, and must be clearly identified as gross or net of fees.
    - May present total return and component returns gross-of-fees (management), net-of-fees, or both ways.
    - For any quarterly return, the income and capital return components must sum to the total return (allowing for rounding differences). If the firm calculates monthly returns, the monthly component returns will sum to the monthly total return.

  The quarterly return is found by *geometrically linking* the monthly returns.

- **Standard 6.A.16.a.** Composites with more than five portfolios must disclose the high and low of the portfolio time-weighted rates of return as the internal dispersion number.
- **Standard 6.A.16.b.** The percentage of composite assets valued using an external valuator as of the end of each annual period.

Closed-End Fund Reporting

- **Standards 6.A.17 and 6.A.18.** Since inception rates of return (SI-IRR) must be reported using at least quarterly rates of return. Time periods less than a year are not annualized and periods longer than a year are annualized.
- **Standards 6.A.19 and 6.A.22.** Composites must be defined by grouping accounts with similar objective, strategy, et cetera, and vintage year.

Disclosures

- **Standard 6.A.20.** The final liquidation date for liquidated composites.
- **Standard 6.A.21.** The frequency of cash flows used in the SI-IRR calculation.
- **Standard 6.A.23.** On or after January 1, 2011, periods less than a year must present net-of-fees SI-IRR and reporting must continue until liquidation of the composite.

Presentation and reporting

- **Standard 6.A.24.** Firms must report the benchmark SI-IRR results and, for comparison, may wish to report composite gross-of-fees SI-IRR.
- **Standard 6.A.25.** At the end of each reporting period, the firm must disclose the following:
    - **Committed capital and since-inception paid-in-capital.**
    - **Distributions.**
    - **TVPI (the investment multiple).** The ratio of total value to since-inception paid-in-capital; total value is the residual value (value of the portfolio at the end of the period) plus since-inception distributions.
    - **DPI (the realization multiple).** The ratio of since-inception distributions to paid-in-capital.
    - **PIC multiple.** The ratio of paid-in-capital to committed capital.
    - **RVPI (the unrealized multiple).** The ratio of residual value to paid-in-capital.

- **Standard 6.A.26.** The SI-IRR of the benchmark through each annual period end. The benchmark must:
    1. Reflect the investment mandate, objective, or strategy of the composite.
    2. Be presented for the same time period as presented for the composite.
    3. Be the same vintage year as the composite.

Private Equity Requirements
Input data:
- **Standards 7.A.1 and 7.A.2.** Private equity assets must be valued at least annually, at fair value, and according to GIPS Valuation Principles.

Calculation methodology:
- **Standards 7.A.3 and 7.A.4.** Annualized since-inception internal rate of return (SI-IRR).

    SI-IRR must be calculated using daily or monthly cash flows prior to January 1, 2011.

    Beginning January 1, 2011, the SI-IRR must be calculated using daily cash flows. Stock distributions must be valued at the time of the distribution and included as cash flows.

- **Standard 7.A.5 and 7.A.6.** Net-of-fees returns must be calculated with consideration given to management fees and carried interest.

    All returns must be calculated after deducting transaction expenses for the period.

- **Standard 7.A.7.** For fund of funds, all returns must be net of all partnership fees, fund fees, expenses, and carried interest.

Composite construction:
- **Standard 7.A.8.** Throughout the life of the composite, composite definitions must remain consistent.
- **Standard 7.A.9.** Primary funds must be included in at least one composite defined by vintage year and investment strategy, mandate, or objective.
- **Standard 7.A.10.** Fund of funds must be included in at least one composite defined by vintage year and/or investment strategy, mandate, or objective.

Required disclosures:
- **Standards 7.A.11 and 7.A.12.** Vintage year and definition of the vintage year for the composite.

    The liquidation date for liquidated composites.

- **Standards 7.A.13 and 7.A.14.** Valuation methodology used for the most recent period, and starting January 1, 2011, any material changes in methodology or policies.
- **Standard 7.A.15.** Industry guidelines that have been followed in addition to the GIPS guidelines.
- **Standard 7.A.16.** The benchmark used and the return calculation methodology applied to the benchmark.
- **Standard 7.A.17.** The frequency of cash flows if daily cash flows are not used in calculating the SI-IRR prior to January 1, 2011.

- **Standards 7.A.18 and 7.A.19.** If any other fees are deducted in addition to transaction expenses when presenting gross-of-fees returns.

  If any other fees are deducted in addition to investment management fees and transaction expenses when presenting net-of-fees returns.

- **Standard 7.A.20.** Any periods of non-compliance prior to January 1, 2006.

Presentation and reporting:

- **Standard 7.A.21.** Beginning January 1, 2011, firms must present both the net-of-fees and gross-of-fees annualized SI-IRR of the composite for each year since inception and through the final liquidation date.

  SI-IRR is the *since inception internal rate of return*.

- **Standard 7.A.22.** Beginning January 1, 2011, for fund of funds composites, firms must present the SI-IRR of the underlying investments grouped by vintage year as well as the other measures required by Standard 7.A.23. All measures must be presented gross of the fund of funds investment management fees and for the most recent annual accounting period.

- **Standard 7.A.23.** For each period presented, firms must report:

  a. Since-inception paid-in capital.

  b. Cumulative committed capital.

  c. Since-inception distributions.

  d. Total value to paid-in capital (investment multiple or TVPI).

  e. Cumulative distributions to paid-in capital (realization multiple or DPI).

  f. Paid-in capital to committed capital (PIC multiple).

  g. Residual value to paid-in capital (unrealized multiple or RVPI).

- **Standard 7.A.24.** If a benchmark is shown, the cumulative annualized SI-IRR for the benchmark that reflects the same strategy and vintage year of the composite must be presented for the same periods for which the composite is presented. If no benchmark is shown, the presentation must explain why no benchmark is disclosed.

- **Standard 7.A.25.** For fund of funds composites, if a benchmark is presented, it must be of the same vintage year and investment objective, strategy, or mandate as the underlying investments.

- **Standard 7.A.26.** Beginning January 1, 2011, fund of funds composites must present the percentage of composite assets invested in direct investments.

- **Standard 7.A.27.** Beginning January 1, 2011, primary fund composites must present the percentage of composite assets invested in fund investment vehicles (instead of direct investments) as of the end of each annual period-end.

- **Standard 7.A.28.** Prior to January 1, 2006, firms may present non-GIPS-compliant performance.

LOS 32.p
These GIPS provisions were adopted January 1, 2006, and apply to wrap fee/separately managed accounts (WFSMAs) where a GIPS-compliant investment manager serves as the subadvisor to a sponsor.

These specific WFSMA provisions apply where the underlying investment management firm has discretion to manage the client portfolio and a bundled fee is charged by the sponsor. All of the normal provisions of GIPS still apply with the following being particularly important: (1) the performance results of the end user client must be computed, documented, and verified. The underlying investment manager may choose to rely on the sponsor to do so (with due diligence to verify the sponsor's ability) or maintain her own tracking and shadow accounting of the account's performance. (2) Returns must be calculated after actual trading expenses. If the trading expenses cannot be identified and separated from the bundled wrap fee, the entire bundled fee including the trading expenses must be deducted from the return. (3) Disclose all of the other items included in the bundled fee. (4) Composite results must disclose the percentage of composite assets made up of portfolios with bundled fees.

The additional provisions of this section are the following:

- Include the performance of actual WFSMAs in appropriate composites and then use the composite results for presentations to prospective new WFSMA prospects.
- If the composite presentation includes time periods when WFSMA accounts were not included, the details of when this occurred must be disclosed.
- If any non-GIPS compliant results prior to January 1, 2006, are included, this must be disclosed. After January 1, 2006, (the adoption date of these provisions) non-compliant results cannot be included.
- If an investment management firm manages assets for more than one sponsor for the same investment style, the composite presentation to prospective clients must include the results of all WFSMAs that follow that style (regardless of sponsor). The composite is style specific, not sponsor specific, and results must be after the entire wrap fee.
- In addition a sponsor specific composite may also be produced if desired. In this case, the sponsor's name must be disclosed. For this sponsor-specific composite, the entire wrap fee does not have to be deducted, but if it is not deducted, this must be disclosed and the presentation must be labeled as only for the use of that sponsor (to discourage the sponsor from using it for prospective WFSMA client presentations).

LOS 32.q
GIPS valuation requirements
- If local laws or regulations related to valuation conflict with the GIPS, firms are required to follow the local laws or regulations and disclose the conflict.
- Firms must disclose their portfolio valuation policies and hierarchy.
- For periods beginning on or after January 1, 2011, firms must disclose any subjective valuation if the portfolio is a significant portion of the composite.
- Firms must disclose if the valuation hierarchy used to value composites differs from the GIPS recommended hierarchy.

The GIPS valuation hierarchy is a list of value sources. Starting at the top, if the firm is unable to utilize the source, it should proceed to the next source on the list:
1. Objective, observable, unadjusted market prices for similar investments in active markets.

2. Quoted prices for identical or similar investments in markets that are not active.

3. Market-based inputs other than quoted prices that are observable for the investment.

4. Subjective, unobservable inputs.

Real estate valuation principles
- The GIPS require that real estate investments be valued externally by outside sources following accepted industry and governmental valuation standards.
- The amount of the external valuator's fee must not be based on the resulting value.
- Although appraisal standards allow reporting values in ranges, the GIPS recommend a single value be reported for returns purposes.
- The firm should rotate external valuators every three to five years.

Private equity valuation principles
- The valuation methodology utilized must be "the most appropriate for a particular investment based on the nature, facts, and circumstances of the investment."
- When valuing private enterprises, the process should consider:
  - Reliable appraisal data.
  - Comparable enterprise or transaction data.
  - The enterprise's stage of development.
  - Additional characteristics unique to the enterprise.

The GIPS require *fair representation of values*. This means firms should follow standard industry and governmental valuation guidelines as closely and consistently as possible in an effort to obtain the best possible value estimates.

LOS 32.r
All advertisements that include a claim of compliance with the GIPS Advertising Guidelines must include the following:
1. A description of the firm.

2. How an interested party can obtain a presentation that complies with the requirements of GIPS standards and/or a list and description of all firm composites.

3. The GIPS Advertising Guidelines compliance statement:

   [Insert name of firm] claims compliance with the Global Investment Performance Standards (GIPS®).

4. A description of the composite being advertised.

5. One of the following sets of total returns:

   a. 1-, 3-, and 5-year annualized composite returns through the most recent period.
   b. Period-to-date composite performance results in addition to 1-, 3-, and 5-year cumulative annualized composite returns with the end-of-period date clearly identified (or annualized period since composite inception if inception is greater than one and less than five years). Periods of less than one year are not permitted to be annualized. The annualized returns must be calculated through the same period of time as presented in the corresponding compliant presentation.
   c. Period-to-date composite returns in addition to five years of annual composite returns calculated through the same period of time as presented in the corresponding compliant presentation.

6. Whether performance is shown gross and/or net of investment management fees.

7. The benchmark total return for the same periods for which the composite return is presented and a description of that benchmark. (The appropriate composite benchmark return is the same benchmark total return as presented in the

corresponding GIPS-compliant presentation.) If no benchmark is presented, the advertisement must disclose why no benchmark is presented.

8. The currency used to express returns.

9. The description of the use and extent of leverage and derivatives if leverage or derivatives are used as an active part of the investment strategy (i.e., not merely for efficient portfolio management) of the composite. Where leverage/derivatives do not have a material effect on returns, no disclosure is required.

10. When presenting noncompliant performance information for periods prior to January 1, 2000, in an advertisement, firms must disclose the period(s) and which specific information is not in compliance with the GIPS standards.

The Advertising Guidelines also suggest that firms may present other information, though this supplemental information should be of equal or lesser prominence than the required information described previously.

LOS 32.s

The *primary purpose of verification* is to increase the level of confidence that a firm claiming GIPS compliance did, indeed, adhere to the Standards on a firm-wide basis.

Verification involves the review of an investment management firm's performance-measurement processes and procedures by an *independent third-party verifier*. Upon completion of verification, a verification report is issued that must confirm the following:

- The investment firm has complied with all the composite construction requirements of GIPS on a firm-wide basis.
- The firm's processes and procedures are designed to calculate and present performance results in compliance with the GIPS.

Other noteworthy aspects of GIPS verification include the following:

- A single verification report is issued to the entire firm; *GIPS verification cannot be carried out for a single composite.*
- Verification cannot be partial: it is all or nothing. In other words, verification cannot enable a firm to claim that its performance presentation is in compliance with GIPS "except for ...."
- Verification is not a requirement for GIPS compliance, but it is *strongly encouraged* and may eventually become mandatory.
- The initial minimum period for which verification can be performed is one year of a firm's presented performance. The recommended period over which verification is performed will be that part of the firm's track record for which GIPS compliance is claimed.
- After performing the verification, the verifier may conclude that the firm is not in compliance with the GIPS or that the records of the firm cannot support a complete verification. In such situations, the verifier must issue a statement to the firm clarifying why a verification report was not possible.

LOS 32.t

For periods beginning on or after January 1, 2011, when firms include after-tax return information in a compliant performance presentation, the information must be presented as supplemental information.

The *pre-liquidation* method calculates after-tax returns based on income earned and gains and losses actually recognized over the period through asset sales. This method effectively ignores the effects of future capital gains taxes.

The *mark-to-liquidation* method assumes all gains, whether recognized or not, are taxed each period. It ignores the time value of money benefits of postponing capital gains and the associated taxes.

Client-directed trades: Because we are attempting to measure the after-tax return resulting from the manager's actions, firms must remove the effects of the resulting capital gains taxes by adjusting the ending value of the portfolio (on paper) by adding back the amount of the these non-discretionary taxes before calculating returns.

LOS 32.u

The following are the minimum items that should be present in a performance presentation:

- The correct compliance statement of the firm claiming compliance with the GIPS standards.
- The definition of the firm.
- The composite description.
- The composite creation date and that a complete list of firm composites and performance results are available upon request.
- Policies for valuing portfolios, calculating performance, and preparing compliant presentations are available upon request.
- The currency used.
- A complete description of the benchmark used, and if no benchmark is used, explain why none is suitable.
- Present at least five years of annual returns if available, adding an additional year until ten years are present.
- Present gross-of-fees or net-of-fees.
  1. If gross-of-fees disclose, if any other fees are deducted in addition to trading expenses.
  2. If net-of-fees disclose, if any other fees in addition to trading expenses and management fees are deducted.
- The management fee schedule is available upon request.
- The presentation of the data should contain at least seven columns.
  1. The years.
  2. The composite return, either gross or net of fees for each year.
  3. The corresponding benchmark return for each year.
  4. Number of portfolios in the composite for each year.
  5. An internal measure of dispersion for each year.
  6. The amount of composite assets at the end of each year.
  7. Either total firm assets or composite assets as a percentage of total firm assets at the end of each year.
- Beginning 2011, present for each year an annualized 3-year ex post standard deviation, or some other measure, for both the composite and benchmark.

CONCEPT CHECKERS

1. McGregor Asset Management has prepared the performance presentation displayed in the following table. McGregor is of the opinion that the presentation is in compliance with the Global Investment Performance Standards (GIPS).

McGregor Asset Management, Inc.

Investment Results: Aggressive Growth Equity Composite

January 1, 2011, through December 31, 2015

Year	Total Return (%)	Benchmark Return (%)	Number of Portfolios	Total Assets at End of Period	Percentage of Firm Assets	Total Firm Assets
2011	16.5	13.9	25	130.65	67	195.00
2012	4.2	4.2	31	166.85	71	235.00
2013	18.9	23.0	34	197.82	63	314.00
2014	8.1	7.8	46	286.70	61	470.00
2015	7.5	9.1	47	550.00	58	948.28

McGregor Asset Management has prepared and presented this report in compliance with the Global Investment Performance Standards (GIPS®).

State *five* errors or omissions that invalidate McGregor's belief that its presentation is in compliance with GIPS.

2. Alan Tribon, compliance officer at Frankfurt Investment Management, has scheduled a meeting with one of Frankfurt's portfolio managers, Ashon Guptar, to discuss an investment performance presentation that he recently prepared.

The following are excerpts from the conversation between Tribon and Guptar:

Excerpt 1

Tribon: "I see that the returns in the presentation are reported net of investment management fees. I seem to recall that the GIPS require firms to present performance on a gross of management fees basis."

Guptar: "You are correct, and I will promptly see that the performance results are recalculated and the presentation is changed to reflect gross-of-fees performance."

Excerpt 2

Tribon: "I notice that there is disclosure of total firm assets for each period. I know this has always been a GIPS requirement, but must we disclose the assets that we direct to sub-advisers under client mandate?"

Guptar: "Yes, unfortunately, the GIPS require that the firm include as total assets under management those assets managed by client-appointed sub-advisers if the firm retains discretion of more than 50% of the portfolio from which the assets were drawn."

Excerpt 3

Tribon: "I couldn't help but notice that the only compliance statement in the presentation indicates firmwide compliance with the Global Performance Standards of CFA Institute. Does this also satisfy the statement of compliance requirements under the GIPS?"

Guptar: "Yes, under the GIPS, there is considerable flexibility in the wording of the GIPS compliance statement, but the one we included is recommended."

Using the template provided, **identify** whether each of the statements is correct or incorrect. If incorrect, briefly **explain** why.

Template for Question 2

Comments	Correct or Incorrect (Circle One)	If Incorrect, State Reason
"I seem to recall that the GIPS require firms to present performance on a gross of management fees basis."	Correct Incorrect	
"…the GIPS require that the firm include as total assets under management those assets managed by a client-selected sub-advisers if the firm retains discretion of more than 50% of the portfolio from which the assets were drawn."	Correct Incorrect	
"Yes, under the GIPS, there is considerable flexibility in the wording of the GIPS compliance statement, but the one we included is recommended."	Correct Incorrect	

3. In July 2007, Edith Poloski, Jason Masserelli, and Rajesh Granta formed PMG Investment Management (PMG). Poloski has considerable experience in the area of security analysis, and Masserelli and Granta have expertise in fixed income and equity portfolio management, respectively.

Initially, PMG exclusively managed the portfolios of high-net-worth individuals with a minimum investment requirement of $3 million. However, recently, PMG has decided to broaden its client base by lowering its minimum investment requirement. To attract new clients and improve the information that its current clients receive, PMG has prepared a performance presentation that reflects the results of its major investment styles. Performance results are presented for a fixed income, an equity, and a balanced composite. The following list contains the actions that PMG took when preparing its current performance presentation.

Action 1:   The S&P 500 Index was used as the benchmark for comparison with all three composite styles.

Action 2:   PMG used accrual accounting, and book values are used for computations of fixed-income returns.

Action 3:   For fixed-income return calculations, accrued income is included.

Action 4:   Due to the change in the firm's client base, PMG did not include its fee schedule.

Action 5:   All actual fee-paying discretionary accounts were included in at least one of the three composites.

Action 6:   Asset-weighted composite returns were calculated using end-of-period weightings.

Action 7:   The performance of the equity portion of the balanced accounts, excluding cash, was combined with the equity composite results.

Action 8:   All composites included only assets under management and were not linked with simulated or model portfolio performance.

Action 9:   Equal-weighted rates of return that adjust for cash flows are used for portfolio returns.

Action 10: Performance calculations were made after the deduction of actual trading expenses.

Using the template provided, **cite** *five* actions in the list of actions that PMG took that are not in compliance with the GIPS, and **describe** how the actions you select are not compliant with the GIPS.

Template for Question 3

	Action Number	Explanation of Why Action is Not GIPS Compliant
1.		
2.		
3.		
4.		
5.		

4. Assume that Firm Z is the investment manager for 15 retail clients and has full discretion over the investment of the clients' assets. At the end of each day, any excess cash in the portfolios is swept into a money market fund. Firm Z does not manage the money market fund, so it does not include the cash portion of the portfolio in its total return performance calculation. **Discuss** whether it is an acceptable practice for Firm Z to claim compliance with the GIPS.

5. Consider the total quarterly returns for the growth and income composite of the investment firm ADA: Q1 = 3.00%, Q2 = 4.15%, Q3 = 3.75%, Q4 = 3.15%. **Calculate** the appropriate total annual return under the calculation methodology under the GIPS.

6.   Johnson Investment Management (JIM) removes terminated portfolios from its composites on the first day of the quarter that the firm was notified of the termination. Assuming that JIM uses quarterly valuation, **discuss** when it would be appropriate to remove a portfolio from its composite if the portfolio is terminated on July 15, 2015.

7.   The investment management firm of Rangan, Rollins, and Cramer (RRC) manages portfolios using a long-short strategy. However, RRC does not ever intend to market this strategy and, thus, does not include the performance of these portfolios in any of the firm's composites. **Discuss** whether this practice is acceptable if RRC claims that its performance presentation results are compliant with the GIPS.

8.   The Teletron Investment Management firm (TIM) plans to market an aggressive growth investment strategy using a newly developed proprietary prediction model. To test the model, TIM created an aggressive growth composite and produced years of returns history using hypothetical assets and a back-tested asset allocation strategy. TIM intends to show the model composite results in its performance presentation. **Discuss** whether this practice is acceptable under the GIPS.

9. For promotional purposes, the Jaspre Investment Management firm (JIM) wants to take advantage of the prestige associated with presenting performance results that are in compliance with the GIPS. To save time and expense, JIM decides to create five composites for marketing purposes. These portfolios represent 60% of the firm's fee-paying discretionary portfolios. Recognizing that the firm cannot claim compliance for all of its portfolios, JIM plans to include the following compliance statement with its performance presentation: *"The investment results presented in this report have been prepared and presented in compliance with the Global Investment Performance Standards (GIPS®) for the majority of the assets under management by Jaspre Investment Management, Incorporated."* **Discuss** whether JIM's claim of compliance is acceptable under the GIPS.

10. Kenzo Fund Managers (KFM) manages a fund that has the following cash flows and valuations (in US$ millions) for the month of September:

Date	Value (Before Cash Flow)	Cash Flow	Value (After Cash Flow)
1 September	50.0	N/A	50.0
10 September	51.5	5.0	56.5
20 September	59.0	–2.0	57.0
30 September	55.0	N/A	55.0

(a) Assuming this data is for September 2002, **calculate** an approximate time-weighted rate of return (TWRR) for KFM using the Original Dietz Method.

(b) Now suppose this data is for September 2005. **Calculate** the TWRR for KFM using the Modified Dietz Method.

(c) If this data were for September 2012, **calculate** the accurate TWRR for KFM for the month.

11. It would be *most likely* that since inception (SI-IRR), as well as component returns for private equity and real estate would be required for the GIPS report if:
    A. The account is large.
    B. The account is non-discretionary.
    C. The manager can control the timing of external cash flows into and out of the portfolio.

12. Jeff Gunthorpe, CFA, is presenting recommendations to the team responsible for constructing and presenting composite performance. In his discussion, he mentions that, according to the GIPS, open-ended and evergreen funds must be presented as part of the company's managed private equity holdings. In the template below, **indicate** whether you agree or disagree with Gunthorpe and, if you disagree, **explain** your decision.

Template for Question 12

Statement	Agree or Disagree	Explanation
"Open-ended and evergreen funds must be presented as part of the company's managed private equity holdings."	Agree Disagree	

13. **Indicate** whether *may be included* or *must be excluded* describes the GIPS with respect to the handling of a portfolio with the indicated characteristics. **Circle** the appropriate indicator in the following template and **explain** your decision.

Template for Question 13

Characteristic	May be Included in a Composite Must be Excluded From Composite	Explanation
Client has significant liquidity needs with an accompanying significant cash position.	May be Included Must be Excluded	
Client does not pay fees.	May be Included Must be Excluded	
Client requests strictly following an index.	May be Included Must be Excluded	

14. For a firm currently reporting to be compliant with GIPS real estate reporting requirements, it is *most correct* to say: "Valuation must be done
    A. annually, and only the presentation of total returns are required."
    B. quarterly, and only the presentation of total returns are required."
    C. quarterly, and income and capital appreciation component returns must be presented in addition to total return."

15. Lambert Capital Management (LCM) manages portfolios for wealthy individuals and serves as a sub-adviser to several pension funds and endowments through wrap fee/separately managed accounts. LCM manages money for several sponsors and reports style-specific composite results. One of those sponsors, Quick and Ready Advisors, has requested LCM prepare a GIPS-compliant composite for only the LCM accounts managed for Quick with results gross of the bundled fee. According to GIPS standards, which of the following is acceptable? LCM could use the composite results in presentations:
    A. to prospective accounts where Quick will be the sponsor.
    B. only to Quick.
    C. this is not allowed under GIPS.

16. If a security does not have an observable, quoted market price available from an active market, the next best valuation basis, according to the GIPS valuation hierarchy, is:
    A. subjective, unobservable inputs.
    B. observable market-based inputs other than quoted prices.
    C. quoted prices from an inactive market for the same or a similar security.

17. Regarding the reporting of after-tax performance after January 1, 2011, which of the following is *most likely* correct?
    A. Firms are required to report returns on an after-tax basis.
    B. Firms may report after-tax performance as supplemental information.
    C. Because of the subjective nature of after-tax performance reporting, firms cannot show after-tax performance.

18. Hicks Capital Management manages assets for high-net-worth clients and specializes in managing taxable accounts. The management team implements strategies to reduce dividend and capital gains taxes. To illustrate its superior performance, the management team would like to report performance on an after-tax basis. Which of the following is *least likely* to be a suitable benchmark option for Hicks Capital Management?
    A. An after-tax capital market index.
    B. Mutual funds or exchange-trade funds.
    C. Developing a custom shadow portfolio.

For more questions related to this topic review, log in to your Schweser online account and launch SchweserPro™ QBank; and for video instruction covering each LOS in this topic review, log in to your Schweser online account and launch the OnDemand video lectures, if you have purchased these products.

ANSWERS – CONCEPT CHECKERS

1. Errors and omissions in the McGregor performance presentation:
    1. The proper GIPS compliance statement.
    2. Definition of firm.
    3. Composite description.
    4. Benchmark description.
    5. If gross-of-fees returns, any fees in addition to trading expenses.
    6. If net-of-fees, any fees in addition to management fees and trading expenses that are deducted; if model or actual management fees are deducted; if net of any performance-based fees.
    7. Currency used to express returns.
    8. Internal dispersion and the measure used.
    9. Fee schedule.
    10. Composite creation date.
    11. That a list of composite descriptions is available.
    12. That the policies for valuing portfolios, calculating performance, and preparing compliant statements are available.

    Other omissions or errors:
    - The correct compliance statement for an unverified GIPS-compliant performance presentation should read as follows:

      McGregor Asset Management claims compliance with the Global Investment Performance Standards (GIPS®) and has prepared and presented this report in compliance with the GIPS standards. McGregor Asset Management has not been independently verified.

    - For periods beginning on or after 2011, 3-year ex post standard deviation of monthly returns for composite and benchmark must be presented. Additional measure must be presented if management feels ex post standard deviation is inappropriate.

2. Comment: I seem to recall that the GIPS require firms to present performance on a gross of management fees basis.

    Incorrect. Under the GIPS, firms may present performance net or gross of fees, but gross-of-fees performance is recommended. The GIPS do require firms to disclose whether performance results are calculated gross or net of investment management and other fees paid by clients to the firm or to the firm's affiliates.

    Comment: GIPS require that the firm include as total assets under management those assets managed by client-selected sub-advisers if the firm retains discretion of more than 50% of the portfolio from which the assets were drawn.

    Incorrect. Total firm assets include all discretionary and non-discretionary assets under management within the defined firm. They do not include assets assigned to a sub-adviser unless the firm has discretion over the selection of the sub-adviser.

    Comment: Yes, under the GIPS, there is considerable flexibility in the wording of the GIPS compliance statement, but the one we included is recommended.

Incorrect. Firms that wish to claim non-verified compliance with the GIPS must use the following statement:

McGregor Asset Management claims compliance with the Global Investment Performance Standards (GIPS®) and has prepared and presented this report in compliance with the GIPS standards. McGregor Asset Management has not been independently verified.

3.

	Action Number	Explanation of Why Action is Not GIPS Compliant
1.	1	The total return for the benchmark (or benchmarks) that reflects the investment strategy or mandate represented by the composite must be presented for the same periods for which the composite return is presented. The S&P 500 Index should not be used as a benchmark for the fixed-income and balanced composites.
2.	2	Portfolio valuations must be based on fair values (not cost basis or book values).
3.	4	GIPS requires the disclosure of an appropriate fee schedule.
4.	6	Composites must be asset-weighted using beginning-of-period weightings or another method that reflects both beginning market value and cash flows.
5.	7	For periods beginning on or after January 1, 2010, a carve-out cannot be included as part of a composite unless it is managed separately with its own cash balance.
6.	9	Time-weighted rates of return that adjust for cash flows must be used. Periodic returns must be geometrically linked.

Actions 3, 5, 8, and 10 are in compliance with GIPS.

4. GIPS require the returns from cash and cash equivalents held in portfolios must be included in total-return calculations as long as the portfolio manager has control over the amount of the portfolio allocated to cash. This requirement stands even if the manager does not actually invest the cash, as is the case when it is held in a money market sweep account. This would not be an acceptable practice.

5. GIPS require periodic returns to be geometrically linked. Thus, the annual return is computed as follows:

$$R_{annual} = [(1 + R_{Q1}) \times (1 + R_{Q2}) \times (1 + R_{Q3}) \times (1 + R_{Q4})] - 1 = [(1.0300)(1.0415)(1.0375)(1.0315)] - 1 = 14.8\%$$

6. GIPS require terminated portfolios to be included in the historical record of the appropriate composite(s) through the last full reporting period that the portfolio was under management. This prevents the inclusion of the returns from a terminated portfolio for partial periods in a composite's return. Also, retaining the performance of a terminated portfolio in a composite's historical performance avoids survivorship bias. In the case of JIM, the terminated portfolio should be included in the composite until June 30 (i.e., the end of the month preceding July 15).

7.　　All actual fee-paying discretionary portfolios must be included in at least one composite. This requirement prevents firms from *cherry-picking* their best performing portfolios for presentation purposes. It does not matter if the firm ever plans to market the particular strategy to which a portfolio is being managed; if the portfolio is fee-paying and discretionary, it must be included in a composite.

8.　　TIM cannot include model performance results in its presentation and claim compliance with the GIPS. Composites must include only assets under management and may not link simulated or model portfolios with actual performance. Simulated, back-tested, or model portfolio results do not represent the returns of actual assets under management and, thus, may not be included in the composites' GIPS-compliant performance results. The model results must be presented as simulated rather than real assets.

9.　　JIM may not claim compliance with the GIPS. A firm must be in full compliance with the GIPS in order to claim GIPS compliance. There is no such thing as *partial* compliance under the GIPS.

10. (a)　The original Dietz method assumes that cash flows occur on average halfway through the month. This method is permissible for periods up to January 1, 2005.

$$R_{Dietz} = \frac{EMV - BMV - CF}{BMV + 0.5CF}$$

$$= \frac{55 - 50 - 3}{50 + 0.5 \times 3}$$

$$= 3.88\%$$

(b)　The modified Dietz method gives a weighting to each cash flow but assumes that returns are even during the month. This method may be used for any period up to January 1, 2010.

$$R_{MDietz} = \frac{EMV - BMV - CF}{BMV + \sum_{i=1}^{n} W_i \times CF_i}$$

$$= \frac{55 - 50 - 3}{50 + \left(\frac{20}{30} \times 5\right) + \left(\frac{10}{30} \times (-2)\right)}$$

$$= 3.80\%$$

(c)　The most accurate calculation is the Daily Valuation Method, for which a new subperiod is defined on the date of any cash flows. This method will be necessary for all periods after January 1, 2010.

The month divides into three periods:

period 1 return = (51.5 − 50.0) / 50 = 1.5 / 50 = 3.00%

period 2 return = (59.0 − 56.5) / 56.5 = 2.5 / 56.5 = 4.42%

period 3 return = (55.0 − 57.0) / 57.0 = −2 / 57.0 = −3.51%

geometric linking for the month = (1.0300 × 1.0442 × 0.9649) − 1 = 3.78%

11. **C**   The most relevant and correct statement is that these special provisions apply when the manager controls the timing of ECFs. Normally time weighted returns must be used and IRR cannot be used because the client's decisions of when to add or withdraw funds from the account affect the IRR. A special case often applies to RE and PE because they are infrequently priced and generally lack liquidity. Therefore, the manager decides when the client can add or remove funds and SI-IRR is required.

The requirement to separately disclose income and pricing based return components is due to the general lack of objective market prices for these assets and it is not relevant to the question asked. It is true that small account results may be excluded from the GIPS report if the cutoff size is disclosed but that is unrelated to RE and PE issues, making it a very poor answer choice. Non-discretionary accounts can never be included in GIPS results (though they are included in the firm's total assets).

12.

Statement	Agree or Disagree	Explanation*
"Open-ended and evergreen funds must be presented as part of the company's managed private equity holdings."	Disagree	*Open-ended and evergreen funds are covered by the general provisions of the GIPS.* This is because redemptions and subscriptions may be made after the funds' inceptions; therefore, open-ended and evergreen funds do not have fixed levels of capital with a set number of investors.

* Italics indicate an answer that would be sufficient for the exam.

13.

Characteristic	May be Included in a Composite Must be Excluded From Composite	Explanation*
Client has significant liquidity needs with an accompanying significant cash position.	<u>Must</u> be Excluded	With both a significant liquidity requirement and cash position, *the manager's actions are limited to the point that the portfolio would probably not qualify as discretionary and thus should not be included.*
Client does not pay fees.	<u>May</u> be Included	Fee-paying portfolios are required to be in a composite. *Non-fee-paying portfolios that are discretionary may be included.*
Client requests strictly following an index.	<u>Must</u> be Excluded	If the portfolio has minimal tracking limits from an index portfolio, then *the description of discretionary is no longer appropriate.*

* Italics indicate an answer that would be sufficient for the exam.

14. **C** For periods beginning January 1, 2008, real estate investments must be valued at least quarterly. External valuation must be done at least every 36 months by an outside, independent party certified to perform such valuations. For periods beginning on or after January 1, 2012, this must be done at least every 12 months. The income and capital appreciation component returns must be presented in addition to the total return.

15. **B** A sponsor-specific composite is additional reporting the investment manager can make if desired. The primary requirement is for style-specific composites, regardless of who is the sponsor. Sponsor-specific composites must still group accounts by comparable style/objective and are then to be used only for reporting to that sponsor. These special purpose sponsor-specific composites are reported before deduction of wrap fees and are to be labeled as only for the use of that sponsor to discourage the sponsor from using the results for client presentations. Certainly, LCM cannot use it for any purpose other than presentation to the sponsor, Quick.

16. **C** The GIPS valuation hierarchy is as follows:

    1. Quoted prices from an active market for the same or a similar security.
    2. Quoted prices from an inactive market for the same or a similar security.
    3. Observable market-based inputs other than quoted prices.
    4. Subjective, unobservable inputs.

    Based on this hierarchy, if observed market prices from an active market are not available, the next best valuation basis is to use quoted prices from an inactive market.

17. **B** Prior to January 1, 2011, after-tax performance reporting was encouraged. Effective January 1, 2011, after-tax performance reporting is considered supplemental information.

18. **A** One of the major difficulties with after-tax performance reporting is finding an appropriate benchmark. There are no after-tax capital market indices available that account for capital gains taxes, so an after-tax capital market index would not be a suitable benchmark.

You have now finished the GIPS topic section. To get immediate feedback on how effective your study has been for this material, log in to your Schweser online account and take the self-test for this topic area. Questions are more exam-like than typical Concept Checkers or QBank questions; a score of less than 70% indicates that your study likely needs improvement. These tests are timed and allow three minutes per question.

Formulas

CPPI strategies: $ in stock $= m (TA - F)$

cash flow at the *beginning* of the evaluation period:

$$r_t = \frac{MV_1 - (MV_0 + CF)}{MV_0 + CF}$$

cash flow at the *end* of the evaluation period:

$$r_t = \frac{(MV_1 - CF) - MV_0}{MV_0}$$

MWRR is the rate, R, that solves the following:

$$MV_1 = MV_0(1+R)^m + \sum_{i=1}^{n} CF_i(1+R)^{L(i)}$$

$P = M + S + A$

Sharpe ratio:

$$S_P = \frac{\overline{R}_P - \overline{R}_F}{\sigma_P}$$

incremental return to the asset category level:

$$R_{AC} = \sum_{i=1}^{A}(w_i)(R_i - R_F)$$

incremental return at the benchmark level:

$$R_B = \sum_{i=1}^{A}\sum_{j=1}^{M}(w_i)(w_{i,j})(R_{B,i,j} - R_i)$$

return to the *investment managers* level:

$$R_{IM} = \sum_{i=1}^{A}\sum_{j=1}^{M}(w_i)(w_{i,j})(R_{A,i,j} - R_{B,i,j})$$

micro performance attribution:

$$R_V = \underbrace{\sum_{j=1}^{S}\left(w_{Pj}-w_{Bj}\right)\left(R_{Bj}-R_B\right)}_{\text{pure sector allocation}} + \underbrace{\sum_{j=1}^{S}\left(w_{Pj}-w_{Bj}\right)\left(R_{Pj}-R_{Bj}\right)}_{\text{allocation/selection interaction}} + \underbrace{\sum_{j=1}^{S}w_{Bj}\left(R_{Pj}-R_{Bj}\right)}_{\text{within-sector selection}}$$

SML: $\hat{R}_A = R_F + \beta_A\left(\hat{R}_M - R_F\right)$

ex post alpha: $\alpha_A = R_{At} - \hat{R}_A$

information ratio: $IR_P = \dfrac{\text{active return}}{\text{active risk}} = \dfrac{R_P - R_B}{\sigma_{(R_P - R_B)}}$

Treynor measure: $T_A = \dfrac{\overline{R}_A - \overline{R}_F}{\beta_A}$

Sharpe ratio: $S_A = \dfrac{\overline{R}_A - \overline{R}_F}{\sigma_A}$

M^2 measure: $M_P^2 = \overline{R}_F + \left(\dfrac{\overline{R}_P - \overline{R}_F}{\sigma_P}\right)\sigma_M$

INDEX

Notes

Notes

Notes